Renée Richards, MD

with Ray Dyson

1999

An
Eye-Opening
Medical Memoir

HALLARD PRESS

Cover Design, Page Design, Typography & Production by Hallard Press LLC/ John W Prince   / Cover Photo by Bianca Tranquillo / Model: Aden Tranquillo
www.HallardPress.com   Info@HallardPress.com

Bulk copies of this book can be ordered at Info@HallardPress.com

Hallard Press LLC gratefully acknowledges the generous support of the Strabismus Research Foundation toward the publication of this book.

The names and identifying details of certain individuals have been changed to protect their privacy.

Printed in the United States of America

Publisher's Cataloging-in-Publication data

Names: Richards, Renée, author. | Dyson, Ray, author.
Title: 1999 : an eye-opening medical memoir / Renée Richards, MD ; with Ray Dyson.
Description: The Villages, FL: Hallard Press LLC, 2021.
Identifiers: LCCN: 2021916799 | ISBN: 978-1-951188-32-0 (paperback) | 978-1-951188-33-7 (ebook)
Subjects: LCSH Richards, Renée. | Ophthalmologists--United States--Biography. | Surgeons--Biography. | Physicians--United States--Biography. | Ophthalmology--Practice--United States. | Transsexuals--United States--Biography. | Managed care plans (Medical care)--United States. | Manhattan Eye, Ear, and Throat Hospital. | Strabismus. | BISAC BIOGRAPHY & AUTOBIOGRAPHY / Medical | BIOGRAPHY & AUTOBIOGRAPHY / Women | BIOGRAPHY & AUTOBIOGRAPHY / LGBTQ+
Classification: LCC RE36 .R53 2021 | DDC 617.7092--dc23

ISBN Print 978-1-951188-32-0
ISBN Ebook 978-1-951188-33-7

Renée Richards, MD

Dedication

To my patients—
for their loyalty
and their trust.

A Remarkable Impact

A few years ago, I had the distinct pleasure of being asked to edit Renée's third autobiography, *Spy Night and Other Memories*, which came on the heels of *Second Serve* and *No Way Renée*. When Renée requested my help on this project—the fourth installment of her inspiring saga—I was delighted to say yes.

This is a diary of Renée Richards' private practice of ophthalmology for the year 1999. It was a very quiet start. It didn't stay quiet for long. It was a year of upheaval, a year of marked changes and varied troubles. I think Renée would agree it was a watershed year in her career and life.

Renée had a remarkable impact in two professions. She was one of the world's best tennis players. She remains one of the top ophthalmologists. This journal will give readers an appreciation of the skill and dedication she has brought to both professions and provide insight as to why she has such a long list of friends. I hope, in some small way, I am one of them.

To Renée, my sincerest thanks,

Ray Dyson

Table of Contents

Foreword–and Forewarned

This book is not for other MDs. It is not a collection of case reports. There are no scientific data, no research, no clinical trials, nor discussion of treatment outcomes. It is not written for other MDs, although it may well be of interest to some. I have written many professional articles, some chapters in medical books, and a textbook and atlas (of eye muscle surgery), and this book is none of the above.

What it is can be called a diary—a diary of my life for the year 1999. It does contain some personal recounting—mostly of weekends away from my medical practice. But it is primarily a diary of my medical practice for the year—a brief description of the roster of patients every day. Its primary purpose is to describe what a private practice, albeit what some of my colleagues would call a boutique practice (in terms of size), looked like in 1999.

It also contains contributions from close colleagues of mine in ophthalmology, concentrating on their frustrations with dealing with the increasing takeover by insurance companies, mainly of private medical practice, at the end of the century. Predictions for healthcare in this century are included by some.

Most private practice physicians, eye surgeons included, have had a similar experience to mine during the years both before and after the turn of the century. Many would have similar stories to mine. I was simply compulsive enough to write it all down; so be it.

Introduction

In 2005, I was asked to write a personal essay for a slightly private book published by Yale University for the members of the Class of 1955 called 55... Then and Now, Yale 1955 50th Reunion. *My subject was "Scaling the Barriers." This is what I wrote:*

I remember my first day at Yale, Indian summer glory of New England. My father helped me haul my stuff up to the fourth-floor suite in Vanderbilt Hall that was to be my freshman home. When we said goodbye, I asked him how I was to get from my dorm to the tennis courts every day. He replied, without a pause, "You take the trolley, same way I did." When he was my age, in 1917, there was a trolley. The tracks were torn up long before the class of '55 arrived in New Haven. There have been many changes since his time and ours, some of them seemingly impossible, now part of our ordinary life. Yet... the principles of medicine, for example, the way he practiced it and the way I did, remain the same.

In medicine, advances are occurring at breakneck speed. The body of knowledge a graduating student must learn now is staggering. We have mapped the genome. We have effected in-vitro fertilization. We have separated conjoined twins. We have devised imaging techniques, and we wend catheter tubes into every organ of the body. We do surgery through minute openings, and not always with a knife. When I learned to do a cataract operation, the procedure consisted of an incision around half the circumference of the eye followed by extraction of the entire cloudy lens, suturing of the incision, bed rest, and prescription of thick glasses or contact lenses. Now, a 3 mm incision, vacusonic (ultrasound) emulsification of the lens, insertion of a foldable lens replacement of any power desired. No sutures, and up and about immediately.

When I left my practice of ophthalmology in 1976 to play and coach on the women's professional tennis tour, the technology in my field took off. When I returned in 1982, we had the new cataract technique; we had lasers (light amplification by stimulated emission of radiation) to treat retinal detachments as well as glaucoma. And we had the beginning of refractive surgery to reshape the cornea to treat myopia and astigmatism, also without a knife.

In the early '80s, I experimented with implanting an electronic stimulator into primates to power paralyzed eye muscles. Now computer chips are used, not only for heart pacemaker defibrillators but also to provide an electronic signal in blind eyes to stimulate the visual cortex in the brain. Cochlear implants in the ear give hearing to the deaf.

And yet we have diseases still baffling, still blinding. Leber's congenital amaurosis, the worst blinding disease of early childhood, is still a mystery. But, early in this century, six genes have been discovered that cause Leber's. There is hope gene therapy will be a reality in the near future. Will the impossible be achieved—sight for eyes with retinas and optic nerves previously nonfunctioning?

When I was a resident in 1961 at Manhattan Eye and Ear Hospital, I performed open-heart massage on a young woman whose heart arrested on the operating room table. Later that year, external cardiac massage was performed for the first time, ending the use forever of the emergency scalpel on the anesthetist's table in the operating room. In 1967, Christiaan Barnard transplanted a whole heart, and in 1982 William DeVries implanted an artificial heart. Yet people still smoke, even after angioplasty, and die from heart and lung disease.

Yes, we have eradicated polio and smallpox completely, and early detection and treatment for prostate and colon cancer now give hope for eradication of those two killers. However, although smallpox has been eradicated from the world, it might still be a threat for terrorists' use. AIDS in Africa is still killing millions of people. And children die from starvation. I am reminded of the saga of syphilis. In the early part of the last century it was a terrible affliction—hard to diagnose, hard to treat. Then along came Wasserman and a blood test by his name—Wasserman positive or negative—and we could diagnose syphilis but not treat it. Then Fleming discovered penicillin and we could treat it. But we soon learned there could be false positives and false negatives, and it was then hard to diagnose, but easy to treat. Resistant strains of the spirochete defied penicillin, and once more syphilis was hard to diagnose and hard to treat.

And mental disease: Thorazine and its derivative closed many of the dismal state mental hospitals that housed schizophrenics, and Prozac gave hope for depression. But we still have suicides.

A final medical note: For the past 20 years, I have taken care of a young man, from infancy, born with excessive farsightedness that made his eyes cross. I treated him over the years, controlling his crossing with glasses. When he was in grade school, he told me he wanted to be a pilot and fly for the Navy. I did not encourage him because I remembered my days as an ophthalmologist in charge at the naval hospital at St. Albans where I had to examine the naval cadets and that farsightedness of more than a few units was disqualifying. How many brilliant scientists and pilots did we keep out? But when he was ready for college, I wrote the appropriate supporting letters for him to the academy. He got in. Three years later he was examined at Annapolis and told his farsightedness was over the limit by a fraction. His father called me for advice, distraught they were going to put his son in a submarine. All he ever wanted was to fly for the Navy. He had been doing it for three years. He was at the top of his class. If he allowed them to do PRK (a refractive laser procedure) on his eyes he could fly. They would do it at Bethesda.

"Go for it," I blurted.

Shifting to sports, 1973 was the year of the Billie Jean King-Bobby Riggs tennis match, which did so much to help women's tennis. That was quite a leap from 1946, when the then women's champion, Pauline Betz, was censured for trying to organize a professional women's tour. I owe Billie Jean King much. She gave the crucial affidavit in my landmark victory in court to be allowed to play on the women's tour in 1976. And Billie Jean backed up her support of me by playing as my partner in professional doubles events. She was instrumental in getting the women's pro tour going, and was the most important figure in women's sports, perhaps women's rights, of her time. Truly courageous, she and my student Martina Navratilova further fought for the rights of women, and Martina in particular for the rights of others disenfranchised.

Speaking of records: consider Martina with nine Wimbledon singles wins, and she and Billie Jean each with 20 Wimbledon titles overall. Some records might stand the test of time. But, if they do fall, it will be in part due to the training methods first employed by athletes like them. When I worked with Martina, the easiest time of the year was during the actual matches. The training sessions, the running, weight lifting, stretching, were the real work, day after day and week after week. They broke barriers for women to enable them to feel right about physical training, true progress from the days when people would murmur secretly about the great Australian champ Margaret Smith Court that "she lifts weights in a gym." The rules have changed. What was acceptable is now encouraged. Did we even know what a soccer mom was in our youth? Who knows where it will go? Michelle Wie, an early teenager from Hawaii, is playing golf on the PGA men's tour.

Some barriers are hard to scale. Althea Gibson was too early for her times. She won Wimbledon and the U.S. Nationals in 1956—a black woman years before Arthur Ashe won the U.S. Open in 1968 and then Wimbledon in 1975. A quiet, gentle person—as was Arthur—she broke ground without any fanfare and was virtually forgotten until the arrival of Serena and Venus Williams, who made us remember Althea. No stadium is named for her at Flushing Meadows, however; the main stadium there is the Ashe Stadium. And although Martina has been open about her sexuality, with financial-endorsement consequences, it is still not accepted for a gay football player or gay baseball player to be open in that area. And maybe never?

In my own life experience, acceptance was a baffling issue. As a child, adolescent, and young man, I never had to face barriers, but later, when my former identity as Richard Raskind was discovered at that infamous tournament in La Jolla, California, I was told: "No, you cannot play tournament tennis as a woman." I was told by the world what I could and could not do. "No, you cannot go back to practice medicine at your old hospital in New York City. (I was able to continue to practice in California in my new persona.) Doors were closed, a new experience for a hard-working young doctor who had never been kept out of anywhere, ever. In my family, my mother and sister (both practicing physicians and very independent women) were emancipated and equal long before women's issues became a subject.

Was I in for a surprise when the world media descended on me and I dared to stand up and demand to be treated as I had been treated as a man! Of course, trying to play on the women's tour might have been asking too much, but I thought otherwise. What happened soon after was, I became part of the sexual revolution in America, totally unwittingly on my part. I became the poster child for the disenfranchised, for gays, for blacks, for a new category of people I had never heard of, the transgendered. It was ironic: conventional, conservative father, husband, amateur athlete now the pariah, the freak to some, the evil embodiment of the fringe, the small and weak minorities I hardly knew at all. I came along at just that moment in time when women were asserting their rights along with the others in the civil rights movement.

One of my best friends, wife of another ancient Yale tennis captain, even scolded me. "Renée, we [genetic women] have worked so hard in the '70s to get our rights, and you just sail into womanhood now after we did all the work." Not so fast, Sue. I paid my dues, too. I became the groundbreaker for acceptance of those with gender dysphoria, what is now called the transgendered, besides standing up for the other not-gender-connected minorities. Societal barriers broke down. It was a revolutionary time: women's lib, a term I personally dislike, shifting roles for men and women, the glass ceiling getting shattered, moving from the old world to the Age of Aquarius.

Amazingly, the impossible took place in my instance. I played on the tour for four years. I became accepted. I made friends. I allayed fears. There was no takeover of professional sports by transsexual athletes. Genetic women (Serena and Venus) came along who were bigger and more powerful than I was on the court. I came back to my old hospital. I resumed my career in medicine. Old patients came back. New ones only knew Dr. Richards. Doors gradually opened. I was living in a new age. I was able to keep my old values, even some of my old prejudices.

I was invited to dinner at one of the secret societies in New

Haven. The subject for discussion at that time was the question of admitting women to the society. I hope I helped with the decision. I think I surprised them—an unconventional life, some conventional views. A young woman who had been a patient of mine since infancy and whom I watched grow up as a student at my alma mater, the Horace Mann School for Boys (not anymore), and then as a pre-med at Yale, asked me if I would do a master's tea in her college, Saybrook. Saybrook was my college some years ago. I reflected, "A master's tea at Saybrook. What would my master then, Basil Duke Henning, say?" The present master is a woman, by the way.

Another patient came in, only a few years ago, new to me, with double vision. He told me he had been a swimmer at Yale in the 1940s. He looked as true an "old Blue" as one could, so I don't know why I said it, but I volunteered that I had been on the tennis team not long after he was at school. When he asked where, I smiled and said, "New Haven." He barked, "That's impossible. Yale didn't admit women until the Seventies." I replied softly, "I was a special case." He thought for a moment and said, "Oh, I get it."

Attitude may change a little, acceptance a lot. Here was an "old Blue" in the 21st century. How wonderful, I thought: the more things change, the more they stay the same. We are living in an old new world.

Why 1999?

I have to think back to 1999 to understand why I decided to write a diary of every day—especially every working day—of that particular year. I have been practicing ophthalmology for 55 years—with one five-year sabbatical in the late 1970s—so why pick out 1999 for special attention? I often don't recall what happens in the present from one day to the next, so my memory of my thought processes on January 1, 1999, might be a little cloudy. This I remember:

Nineteen ninety-nine was the end of the decade, the end of the century, and the end of the millennium. That alone marks it special. But it was special for me personally. My private practice of ophthalmology, which had been reestablished in 1982 with my return to NYC to a new private office, and to Manhattan Eye, Ear and Throat Hospital—where I operated and taught the residents and post-graduate Fellows—had flourished. My reputation as an eye surgeon was back to where it had been in the years before the five-year hiatus. I had a good name in my subspecialty (strabismus—disorders of the eye muscles)—and financially I had mostly paid off the debts I had accrued during the five years I was not practicing medicine.

However, by 1999, changes in the business of delivery of healthcare meant the old ways—for individual or small group private practices like mine—were on the way out. That meant the something above $500,000 dollar income I and several of my colleagues earned a year would soon be cut in half by what is now known as managed care—the rise of insurance companies involved in the delivery of healthcare.

In 1999, I was beginning to understand that a solo private practice like mine would likely become obsolete in the new century. I wanted to document that.

In addition, my hospital—Manhattan Eye, Ear and Throat Hospital, first chartered in 1869 specifically and only for the care of eyes and ears—was on the brink of being dissolved by its board of directors and sold for real estate and for investment other than in the care of eyes and ears. It took the New York State Supreme Court to save the hospital at the end of 1999.

If the hospital's survival and my own practice's survival were not enough to mark the year 1999, I had other, more personal reasons, to punctuate it. My father was turning 100 in January. My assistant (and personal manager) Arleen Larzelere and I were in charge of his care—sometimes with him living in his house in Forest Hills, Queens, sometimes in our apartment above the office on Park Avenue. My son Nicholas was sometimes living in those years in the house in Forest Hills, and then later he too was in the apartment in NYC, struggling in his real estate business and sometimes living with his fiancée at that time, Oxana. In

1999, they were living with Nick's grandpa in Forest Hills. Arleen and I would drive from the office on Park Avenue in NYC to pick up my father in Forest Hills on Thursdays and drive up to the country house in Putnam County for the weekend, where I would see patients in the country office nearby on Fridays, then drive my father back to Forest Hills on Monday mornings, and then drive to NYC to the Park Avenue office to start the work week. In 1999, we realized the income from both practices—city and country—was no longer enough to maintain the country house we had built in 1985 and was my dream home on the lake in Carmel, NY, and we were forced to sell it. The taxes on the house alone were huge. I started to think of closing the Park Avenue office and joining another practice close by, my income having started to shrink with each year of managed care. I realized the income from the country office was very small and a new plan would become necessary there too.

The end of the millennium, a significant year in the practice of medicine in the USA, at Manhattan Eye and Ear and in my own private life may all have combined to make me decide to document 1999 in such detail. Perhaps just a look at the way one doctor took care of patients as the century closed is the most important reason. Here it is.

My Diary: 1999

January

Friday, January 1

I am at home in the country and not at work because of the holiday. Ordinarily, on Friday mornings I see children with eye problems in my country office in Brewster, New York. I live 60 miles north of New York City, in Carmel, the adjoining town to Brewster. Every Friday, I spend the morning in the office of a colleague who has a large general practice of ophthalmology in Brewster. Usually, 20 children are scheduled for me to see between 8:30 am and 12:30 pm. Because there are no patients today, I take the opportunity to describe what this diary is meant to be.

The changes in medical care in recent years lead me to believe solo private practice of medicine, including its specialties like ophthalmology, is dwindling down. A solo private practitioner—and that is me—is a dinosaur. I do not believe solo practice will be the way medical care is delivered in the next century. Because

1999 will be the last year of the century and the last year of the millennium—and will mark my 40th year in medicine—I thought it appropriate to chronicle this particular year of my private practice in ophthalmology.

My mother and father were both physicians, as is my only sister, and we never knew anything other than medical practice in our family. Certainly, the way my mother and father conducted their practices in the late 1920s differs from the way I practice medicine toward the end of the century. However, the differences between their delivery of medical care and mine are probably not as great as the differences between the way I practice and the way it will be done in the early 2000s. The cost of delivering medical care has become so prohibitive that new forms of healthcare delivery are being created almost daily in the effort to find a system both affordable and adequate.

I am considered a dinosaur because I am one of the last of a breed of solo practitioners. Many of my friends and colleagues are already in large groups, some employed by organizations that deliver medical care to thousands of constituents. Many colleagues of my age have retired, some of them prematurely because of the changes in the healthcare system.

One friend who has kept up with the times said to me not too long ago, "Renée, you don't have a practice, you have a boutique."

Another asked, "Are you still hanging on, too? How much longer do you think you will do it?"

My answer is, I don't know. As long as I can still contribute and as long as I enjoy it, I'll keep going. Maybe the financial circumstances of medicine will force me out before I might otherwise be ready. More than likely, however, I will simply see a dwindling down of my practice as more and more patients become members of larger and larger groups whose medical care has been assigned by their employers or by the government.

This diary is going to be a daily chronicle of my life in ophthalmology in the year 1999. By no means is my practice a typical one, nor is it very different from the mainstream of ophthalmologic practice.

An ophthalmologist is a physician who takes care of diseases of the eye. The eye is a very small organ, but a very complex organ, and diseases of the eye run the spectrum from the "itchy-burnies," commonly called pink eye, to the more severe afflictions such as glaucoma and neuro-retinal disease. We have several subspecialties in ophthalmology, including external diseases, glaucoma, retina, cornea, neuro-ophthalmology, pediatric ophthalmology, and strabismus and oculoplastic surgery. Some of us are general ophthalmologists who take care of all diseases of the eyes. Some of us have become sub-specialists only. My practice is slightly different because I was trained as a general ophthalmologist with a sub-specialization in strabismus. I still take care of some patients with general ophthalmologic problems, although the majority of my work is with children and adults who have strabismus.

Strabismus simply means the two eyes do not work together and are misaligned—either cross-eyed, wall-eyed, one eye up, or one eye down. Problems of double vision and lazy eye or amblyopia are associated with strabismus. Because so many of the problems of strabismus occur in children, those of us who are strabismus specialists have become also children specialists in a subspecialty called pediatric ophthalmology and strabismus. So, I am known as a pediatric ophthalmologist, as a strabismus specialist, and also as a general ophthalmologist.

I see children only in my country office in Brewster on Friday mornings. Most of them live in the little county of Putnam (Brewster is in the southeast part of the county). In my New York City office on Park Avenue, I see mostly children with strabismus, but I also see many adults with strabismus, and I still have a small practice of general ophthalmology, although I don't do cataract surgery on them anymore. An associate in my New York City office is an expert in cataract surgery who devised the safest form of anesthesia for cataract surgery. His name is Scott Greenbaum, and he was a resident with us at Manhattan Eye, Ear and Throat Hospital some years ago. I have watched him develop into an outstanding cataract surgeon. He has his own private practice in Forest Hills in Queens two days a week, and he sees his own patients, as well as some of mine, in our New York office two days a week. We are not partners, but we are associates, and we each maintain our own private practice.

My practice is somewhat unique because hardly any other pediatric or strabismus specialist sees any general ophthalmology patients. A few of us do. At this point in my career, the only surgery I perform is on patients with eye muscle problems that cause them to be cross-eyed, wall-eyed, or have one eye up or one eye down, forcing them to put their heads into unusual positions to get the eyes lined up at the same time so they do not see double. If I continue to do cataract surgery, I will have to learn radically new techniques that have changed many times during the past 10 years. Even now, cataract surgery is evolving. The use of the operating microscope, the use of no-stitch incisions, the development of phakoemulsification of the cataractous lens with insertion of a foldable intraocular lens, and the use of the YAG laser to make openings in the posterior capsule of the cataract are all recent advances. Interestingly, in my particular specialty of eye muscle surgery, although there have been refinements of technique, some of them by me (among others), the basic surgical maneuver has changed little over many, many years. In fact, in my particular subspecialty, the more experience I gain and the better my judgment on what and how much to do at surgery, the better surgeon I become.

With cataract surgery and some of the new laser keratorefractive procedures, the younger and more recently trained surgeons have a great advantage over their older colleague. Fortunately, in my subspecialty, older is better, as long as I stay focused and have a steady hand. I have been at it for 40 years. I have probably straightened more kids' eyes than anyone else in New York City (save one or two other ancients), nearly 10,000 as a rough estimate.

I operated on three children two days ago. I drove back to my New York City office to see them yesterday. I had done the identical operation on the mother of one of those three children 30 years ago.

When I saw the child yesterday for the first post-op check, she came with her mother and her grandmother. "Does this scene look familiar to you?" I asked her grandmother.

"It seems like it was yesterday," she said.

I agreed. Twenty years later, 1999 does feel like yesterday...

A reflection from 2021:

Students go to medical school for various reasons. I went of course because my father, mother, and sister went before me. There was no choice, as my friends at Yale College would often tell me as they were considering all their opportunities. They knew I would become a doctor—they said I couldn't do anything else. I went. I had no idea what I wanted to do after. It was only when I assisted an eye surgeon with a cataract extraction at Lenox Hill Hospital where I was an intern that I said, "Aha, that's why I went to medical school." Of course, all this is well described in my two autobiographies, so no more here. I mention it as a prelude to describing the numerous paths a graduate of medical school can take. First of all, how hard it is to be admitted to medical school, back in my day in the 1950s, and now! In my day many a future great physician had to study medicine in Geneva, or Edinburgh or Bologna, and even now some students who get their MD from foreign medical schools are not admitted in the USA.

There are many careers in medicine besides the choice of specialty or general practice, among them private solo practice,

practice with partners, or in a private group, sometimes only a few MDs. Nowadays some groups are conglomerates and employ many, many physicians, even employment by a large organization on a salary-based income, like the original and still operating Kaiser Permanente Group in California.

An MD can practice medicine, or teach it, or do research or a combination of all three. One can be on the fulltime salaried faculty of a medical school or hospital. One can be on the faculty of a medical school but still be in private practice too. One can be a fulltime researcher, or be on the fulltime teaching faculty, usually doing some research.

In my case, I was mostly in private practice, with associates in my office, on the faculty of the medical school—first at Cornell-NY Hospital, later at NYU Medical School-Bellevue Hospital and on the voluntary teaching staff of Manhattan Eye and Ear (MEETH) and later the NY Eye and Ear Infirmary and on the medical staff (non-teaching) at Putnam Hospital near where I live.

I taught the residents at MEETH, first as the resident instructor (the only one—in 1967), then as attending in the clinic, then as director of the Eye Muscle Clinic, and I taught the post-graduate Fellows in pediatric ophthalmology and strabismus. I did all of this teaching gratis—no financial compensation. Clinic, lectures, assisting at surgery—these activities occupied probably one full day each work week. I gave a lecture course in strabismus at MEETH, where the residents from many hospitals in NYC attended.

Colleagues of mine had similar schedules, except for those

who were fulltime at the medical schools, and on a salaried status. They too saw private patients. Most of the fees for their service went to the institution, and the doctors received their share. I was never fulltime at the teaching hospital. I always had a private office separate from the hospital. Those on the fulltime staff at the medical school hospitals (Columbia and Cornell, for example) had their offices in the hospital, their secretaries and other staff employees of the hospital.

In the present day, more physicians are employed by conglomerate groups—some of which have taken control even of the large hospitals and the medical schools. For example, Northwell Health has physicians on its staff and is in control of some of the medical schools and hospitals in NYC.

Research in medicine can be basic science or clinical. Most basic science research is done in laboratories at university medical schools or in the private sphere. Clinical research is done by actual clinicians, like me. Now, it seems fewer physicians are doing clinical research.

In my career, I did clinical research, which I have described in the autobiographies—mostly on refining surgical techniques on the eye muscles. The most interesting of course was my work on developing an electrical innervation for paralyzed eye muscles, work I did on implanting a stimulator in chimps at the Primate Center—of NYU (LEMSIP)—which closed when animal rights activists objected to animal experimentation in the late 1980s. My research associate, Yu Quan Chen, on loan to me from Case Western Reserve in Cleveland, went back to Hang Chow, China, his hometown, and the research ended. We did have one publication about it in the *Proceedings of the Electrical Engineering Society.* My other interesting research was done on rabbits at Ethicon Labs in New Jersey. I worked on using superglue (cyanoacrylate) instead of sutures to reattach eye muscles to the eye.

Nobody knows I did much research. But Dr. Virginia Lubkin, probably the first woman ophthalmologist in NYC, who was instrumental in my taking over John Herman's practice when I came back to medicine in 1982, always would ask me when she would see me, "Renée, what are you working on now?" Everyone only knows Dr. Richards as a tennis player and coach, eye muscle surgeon, teacher of ophthalmology. No one knows I ever did any research. Most private practice specialists don't, but some do.

Private practice. How does one start?

The easiest way was—and still is—to join an experienced physician already with a private office and practice. To start alone is difficult. Where are the patients to come from? If the physician is the first heart surgeon in Alaska, like my sister's brother-in-law was years ago, it's fairly easy. Arrive, rent an office and mail out cards announcing your arrival. In my father's day—1920s—physicians, in any specialty, did just that. The engraved card would read, "Dr.----- is pleased to announce the opening of his [usually 'his'] office at ------ for the practice of -----[specialty]." And then wait for patients, usually after some phone calls to other doctors in the area, along with securing an appointment at the community hospital close by. A physician would set out a shingle on the lawn in front of the house. If the office was in an apartment building, and hopefully on the ground floor with a separated entrance, a brass sign would be affixed to the outside wall. I have two such shingles in my possession here at home. One is a brass sign that stood for fifty years in front of my father's office at 5 Court Square in Long Island City, Queens, NY—"David M. Raskind MD." The other is my sign from 40 Park Avenue, NYC—"Renée Richards, MD FACS" (Fellow of the American College of Surgeons).

When I first started private practice in 1967 I saw patients at the Park Avenue Office of one of our senior staff and member of the board of surgeon directors, Dr. Arnold Turtz—no rent paid; he just took me in and helped get me started with some private patients. I had just returned from my Fellowship in Iowa—I was the newly-appointed resident instructor (the only one) at MEETH. I was about to reorganize the residency training program there along the lines of the academic model. I had just spent the winter in Iowa—where graduates in medicine came from all over the world to be post-graduate Fellows studying not just in ophthalmology but in several specialties. As my reputation grew, so did my private practice, and by the time I left medicine to play professional tennis for five years, my practice had grown. I turned it over to my own young associate, Richard Muchnick, who had been a resident just graduated from Cornell-NY Hospital, where I was also director of the eye muscle department at the time. I thought I had left the practice for good, never expecting I would someday return to NYC, to MEETH, to the practice of ophthalmology.

My return to medicine and NYC is all well documented in *No Way Renée*. A few points relate mostly to the discussion of how one starts a practice. In 1982, I had none. After my educational brush-ups and spending several months at the kind invitation of Dr. Charles Titone to see patients—his overflow—in his private office in Jackson Heights, Queens, I was ready for my own office—in Manhattan.

I was still coaching tennis champion Martina Navratilova in the spring of 1982 when Dr. John Herman died suddenly. Dr. Herman was essentially my counterpart. He was at the NY Eye and Infirmary what I had been at MEETH before my sabbatical—the strabismus expert, and director of its strabismus service. He died in June at an orthoptic meeting in Cape Cod. (Orthoptists, the technicians who assist strabismus specialists with measurements and both objective and subjective tests of binocular function and who administer the exercises and amblyopia therapy to patients, have their own association—and with it their own meetings. Strabismus surgeons often attend their meetings.) His widow, Jane Herman, entertained visits from several ophthalmologists in Manhattan interested in buying the charts and essentially buying his practice. It was worth a great deal of money to a strabismus surgeon. Jane Herman was a savvy business person— in her own career the president of the American Ballet Theatre at the Metropolitan Opera House. She dealt with Baryshnikov, all the prima donnas, so a few eager eye surgeons were no problem for her. She was not inclined to sell the practice to just anyone, and she consulted Virginia Lubkin, whose office happened to be across Park Avenue from Dr. Herman's at 41 Park Avenue. She asked Virginia who should take over her husband's practice, see his patients, and operate on them. Dr. Lubkin told her there was really only one appropriate surgeon but Jane wouldn't be able to talk to her.

Annoyed, Mrs. Herman asked, "And why not?" After all, the prima donnas of the American Ballet Theatre were never a problem for her.

Virginia said, "Because it's Renée Richards and she is in London coaching Martina Navratilova at Wimbledon."

Mrs. Herman replied, "I will wait until she gets back."

My father suggested I buy the practice; so did everyone else I knew on the staff at MEETH. So I did just that, and it should be noted my father did not come up with the $50,000 to buy the records. Martina did.

I started seeing Dr. Herman's patients that summer. Fifteen were scheduled for surgery that summer and I operated on all of them. I know I lost a few patients from the practice who did not want to make this switch to come to me, but not very many. I still see a few of his old patients to this day, some 40 years later.

I stayed at 40 Park Avenue until 2003, when I moved it over to Madison Avenue and 37th to join Harvey Rosenblum. My first young associate at 40 Park was Dr. Scott Greenbaum, who wrote a textbook on anesthesia for eye surgery (in which I have a chapter on anesthesia for eye muscle surgery). His office is still in the same building, but around the corner on 36th. My second associate was Paul Finger, who helped me with the research surgery on the chimps. He is now one of the very few experts in the world on treatment for cancer of the eye—specifically melanomas. Both had been residents under my tutelage at MEETH.

Where did my patients come from beyond those whose records had been in John Herman's practice? Where did new surgical patients come from? How does an MD build a private practice? More than 1,000 ophthalmologists live and work in NYC.

If an MD is on the faculty of one of the teaching hospitals like Mt. Sinai, Columbia, Cornell, NYU referrals are made from physicians on those staffs—internists, pediatricians, general surgeons, etc. But if an MD is on the staff only at a specialty hospital, referrals from there come just from other ophthalmologists, or ENT specialists. How does an MD build a practice? In my case referrals came from other ophthalmologists, yes, on our staff—I was the strabismus expert for many of them. Referrals also came from a number of pediatricians, mostly downtown near my office. And then referrals came from other patients. Building a practice does not occur overnight.

Oh well, back to my diary...

Monday, January 4

Scheduled surgery at Putnam Hospital in the country was canceled this morning, and, because of the New Year's holiday, no patients are in the office this afternoon. I find myself with a free day, which is very unusual. Tomorrow at 8:00 am will start our regular schedule. In the meantime, let me take this opportunity to organize this diary. I'll start by describing my main office in New York City at 40 Park Avenue. I am writing this upstairs in my apartment in the same building.

Many offices in New York City are on the ground floor of apartment buildings, especially those on Park Avenue. Some of us are lucky enough to have an entrance directly from the street to our offices, and patients do not have to go through the lobby of the apartment building to get to the office. The entrance to my office is separate, just to the side of the apartment lobby entrance. Arleen and I have an apartment in the same building, which is wonderful because it means that, except for my trips back and forth to the hospital on 64th Street, I have a very small commute—actually, out the lobby door, 15 feet to the left and then into my office.

The office is built in the shape of an upside-down U with the waiting room in the center, my examination room on the right, my orthoptic technician's examining room on the left of the waiting room, and a hallway around the back of the office to the adjacent rooms that form the upper limbs of the U.

The first room is the waiting area, brightly painted yellow with mostly built-in chairs. I set up a few moveable chairs and a few little chairs for children. As is consistent with my practice, the waiting room has to be both for adults and for children, so a few small tables hold an Etch-a-Sketch and crayons and other toys for children. Adults can pass the time with the usual medical practice magazines, including *People* and *Time* and *Tennis Week* and *Golf Digest*. The best thing about the waiting room is the peg board along one entire wall, with hundreds of pictures of the little kids who come to the office. It is updated periodically, and the more recent children's pictures supplant the older ones. Whenever a little child walks in, immediately he or she runs over to the peg board to find his or her picture. Kids also love to look at themselves in the gigantic mirror that stretches from the floor almost to the ceiling.

It is not generally known, but I have always been a germophobe, maybe not like Howard Hughes, but I did inherit from my mother a healthy respect for germs. I have never been a hand-shaker. I had prominently displayed in the office waiting room a sign that read: EYES FIRST AND MOST, HANDS NEXT AND LEAST. I borrowed that slogan from an old British TV series about a famous MD professor in Britain who would exclaim to the interns and residents following him as he made his rounds at the bedside, "First rule of physical diagnosis: eyes first and most, hands next and least."

When Amy Adachi, a few years before 1999, came to work for us, she saw it and asked, "What is this?" (I am sure Amy remembers that even today as she works hard protecting patients at NYU Langone Hospital and NYU Medical School in NYC.)

At the end of the waiting room is the front office. It is really part of the waiting room but is separated by a counter desk. Amy, the front office manager and the surgical coordinator, greets the patients. Amy was personally trained by Arleen, her predecessor, who has now been kicked upstairs to be overall business manager and my personal manager.

Arleen lives with me and she also takes care of my father's needs and sometimes my son's needs and all of our animals' needs—she keeps slightly busy 24 hours a day. She trained Amy and transformed her. More about Amy later.

My office consultation room is to the right of the waiting room and can be entered either through a separate door communicating the two or through a hallway behind where Amy sits at the end of the waiting room. My office is painted a color that I am not sure I know how to label. It's something I want to call mauve, but maybe rose would be more appropriate. My consultation room doubles as an examination area. My desk is adjacent to the area where I examine patients with the various machinery of ophthalmology. This includes a slit lamp microscope to examine the front portions of the eye, the indirect ophthalmoscope to examine the retina and the optic nerve, and all of the various instruments I use to examine the way the two eyes work together for problems of strabismus: prisms, the various lenses, the occluders (the paddle-shaped flat disks to cover one eye while testing the other), the red glass, and all the different trial lenses I use to determine the state of the nearsighted, farsighted, or astigmatic component of a child's refraction.

My retinoscope, my ophthalmoscope, and my muscle light are on the stand, along with a phoropter—an instrument with thousands of lenses rotating inside it. The phoropter is used mostly by optometrists, but also by ophthalmologists, to place different lenses in front of a patient. The days of the eye chart with the big E have been supplanted by a computer operated by a remote controller next to my swiveling, rolling examining stool. The patient sits on an examination chair that can be moved in various directions by a foot switch. The lights are usually dim in the area where the patient is being examined because of the need for contrast, but the room is better lighted near my desk, only 10 feet away.

Some doctors have a consultation room separate from their examining area. I prefer to do everything in the same place.

Well, mostly everything, because I do less-common activities in other rooms. For example, just beyond my consultation/examining room is a small room for minor surgical procedures in which I have an operating microscope and an examining chair that looks like an old barber chair that can be rotated flat or semi-reclined. In this room, minor procedures are done that do not require significant anesthesia other than a local injection at the operative site.

Behind the operating room, another small office contains a desk. At the top of the U is another examining room with equipment for ultrasound and other specialized examinations of the eye, such as the keratometer for measuring the curvature of the cornea. Around back to the left at the bottom of the U is a filing room and Arleen's business office. To the left of the waiting room at the bottom of the U is the orthoptic technician's room, the same size as my examining/consultation room. Here, Barbara Schneekloth does orthoptic examinations of the children and adults with eye muscle problems. The equipment in her room is similar to that in mine.

An orthoptic technician is a specialist for problems of strabismus, including lazy eye and prism work and exercises to make the eyes work better together. An orthoptist is also a dinosaur, as I am, and it is a dying field because it is so super-specialized. Only a strabismus specialist employs an orthoptist and nowadays orthoptists are doing much more than straight orthoptic work—strabismus and amblyopia—and they do technician's work for ophthalmologists of many different types. I'll have more to say about the orthoptists later.

Tuesday, January 5

I saw 20 patients in the New York City office starting at 8:00 am and finishing at 2:00 pm when I had my cheeseburger and fries reheated so I could eat lunch before going to the hospital to clinic and to grand rounds. Grand rounds are the once-a-week meeting of the ophthalmology staff for presentation of cases and discussion.

The day started relatively quietly with evaluation of Cedric Winkleman, whose father had glaucoma and who is always concerned he might develop it as well. So far, so good—his pressure and his visual fields are normal.

Robin Oscher trades stocks and is 40 years old. Sometimes she sees double and sometimes blurry, but she doesn't have the eye muscle problem she had in childhood, and, except for some swelling in her finger joints, she is relatively healthy. She only needed some glasses and not even any prisms to do her computer work.

Jay Tsai is a four-year-old boy doing a good job with his patching of his better eye so that his amblyopic left eye can improve. If he doesn't patch now at the age of four, it will be too late when he is older, and his vision won't be improvable. Fortunately, co-operation between his mother and me has seen him improve to 20/40 in his amblyopic eye. He is going to continue to wear his patch on the good eye two hours a day.

The first problem of the day was Aubrey Lambright. Aubrey was a new patient with a history of previous examinations by another ophthalmologist who had concerns about glaucoma and possibly a tracking problem that might indicate a brain tumor. His history was further complicated by childhood psychological trauma from the broken marriage of his parents. He came with his father, and both were slightly agitated—certainly not without reason—concerning suspicions raised about glaucoma and perhaps a problem needing an MRI.

When I evaluated him, his intraocular pressure was at the high end of the normal range, his optic nerves showed a slight degree of the change sometimes seen in glaucoma but not diagnostic for glaucoma; in other words, he shows soft signs that could be suspicious for an early glaucoma, as unlikely as that might be in an 11-year-old, and his optic nerves also showed a slightly less pink color than normal, which might represent a neurologic disease process.

At the end of the examination, it was my job to decide whether the diagnosis of glaucoma should be vigorously pursued and whether an MRI for a possible brain tumor should be ordered. It is a simple thing for the ophthalmologist to order an MRI to dispel suspicion about the so-called suspected brain tumor, but without true indication for the MRI, it should not be ordered. In addition, if the intraocular pressure is not into the so-called abnormal range and the optic nerves look reasonably healthy, one should think twice about doing all kinds of sophisticated disc analysis testing for a glaucoma that is probably not present in a normal adolescent.

This is where experience is important and the memory of evaluating many, many optic nerves helps to determine what the appropriate course of action should be. I decided to do no invasive tests, and I am going to look at Aubrey again in several months to repeat his intraocular pressure and re-evaluate his optic nerves. In short, I took upon myself the burden of responsibility for his eyes and, in particular, the suspicions that have been aroused.

Mary Beth Holm, at 79, has to contend with fibromyalgia, with tingling in her legs and pain in her back and neck, on top of taking care of a husband with Alzheimer's disease. Fortunately, she showed no new hemorrhages on her optic nerves, and her cataracts were no worse than on her examination six months ago.

Robert Balter had not been here for years. He said he had a brain tumor removed since I last saw him, an acoustic neuroma of the VIIIth cranial nerve on the left side. That nerve transmits sound and balance information from the inner ear to the brain. Fortunately, he has no double vision, and his examination was relatively unremarkable.

Darren Ege is a special case. Darren is now 22 months old, and I have followed him since he was 10 months old. He is one of four quadruplets born prematurely and, because he had been given a lot of oxygen therapy to keep him alive during the first few weeks after birth, he developed retinopathy of prematurity, a devastating retinal condition that sometimes leads to blindness when the retinas become detached. Darren had cryo surgery on his retinas a few weeks after birth, and I have been watching him carefully to see if his retinas have remained healthy.

Darren wears glasses for astigmatism and farsightedness, and he patches his left eye to force him to use his right eye, which is convergent and turns toward his nose unless he is forced to use it with the left eye covered. Today, he came in actually preferring to use his right eye, and I was concerned he was doing that because of a weakness of the retina of his left eye and not because he was wearing his patch too much on the left eye.

A dilated retinal examination revealed the retina to be intact in each eye, and I was happy to reassure his father that Darren's retina appeared normal on both sides. We are going to stop the patching for a while and see if he needs it again in the future if he starts using one eye in preference to the other.

It is difficult to do a retinal examination on a 22-month-old child because the periphery of the retina must be examined in all four quadrants and it takes a very detailed evaluation to be sure no breaks or areas of detachment occur anywhere in the 360-degree attachment line of the retina. So far, so good; his retinas are holding.

Then I saw 11-month-old William Keenan for the first time. William has tilted his head toward the right shoulder since infancy. Head tilts are frequently caused by vertical eye muscle problems, and it is the pediatric ophthalmologist's job to rule out or rule in any vertical eye muscle problems in any child who has a head tilt. As hard as I could try, I could not demonstrate a vertical eye muscle problem in little William. Even though most head tilts are caused by eye muscle problems rather than by neck problems, I could not determine that in William's case. He is going to continue with his physiotherapy to loosen his tight neck, and I am going to watch him closely during the next few years to see if he shows any eye muscle problems I might have missed today.

Gail Poster is the ex-wife of my closest friend, John. I took care of Gail's mother for glaucoma before her death many years ago. Gail is under suspicion for glaucoma, of course, because of her mother's history, and she also happens to have an eye muscle problem where one eye drifts out whenever she is at inattention. I could have operated on her for that many, many years ago, but I never got around to it, and she still has it and doesn't seem to be too bothered by her drifting eye. I did give her a prescription for some prism glasses today, however, for reading so that she doesn't have the full burden of pulling her eyes together to try to see single at close range.

By noon, I was getting a little worn out but managed to keep going fairly well without lunch until Brenda Bass came in. She was the one who put me under today.

Frequently, on a busy day, I can get through the whole schedule and be reasonably okay to go to the clinic and to grand rounds. Sometimes, the last hour or two can be difficult and exhaust me, and today was that day. Brenda had not been here for several years. I had operated on her eye for thyroid myopathy long ago. Because of her thyroid condition, she developed eye muscles so stiff she could not raise her eyes above the midline. I operated on her inferior rectus muscles many, many years ago to free them from the restriction.

That is not the whole story with Brenda. She has mixed connective tissue disease that involves not only her thyroid but many organs of her body. She is on cortisone, as well as immunosuppressive agents. It takes a long time to examine a patient with her complicated set of problems and an even longer time to get the interim history from her of her cortisone and immunosuppressant therapy and their side effects on her overall physical and mental well-being. Her face—totally red, slightly swollen, and irregular in surface—looks like she has just suffered severe second-degree burns. Her eyelids are swollen, and her lower eyelids leave a space of white between her eyelid margins and the lower edge of her eyeball.

I tried to dope out her complex history as best I could and evaluate the various complaints she had, including bruising of her eyelids, bumps on her eyes, tightness of her eyes, difficulty in moving them, and self-medication of cortisone drops when her eyes felt tight. The possible risk of elevating the intraocular pressure in her eyes has been monitored by another ophthalmologist these past several years. Along the way, she had cataract surgery on both eyes. I could not do much on this examination except tell her to try to stop using the cortisone drops in her eyes of her own volition. I ordered a visual field test to evaluate her optic nerve function, and I spent 20 minutes dictating letters to her endocrinologist and to her rheumatologist to try to come together on some overall treatment plan for her.

I finished her exam exhausted. How do some of my colleagues see 80 to 90 patients a day?

But that was not the end of the morning. Immediately after Brenda, I saw the three little children I operated on last Wednesday. Danielle Levine looked wonderful, with straight eyes and minimal inflammation. Gloria Sit revealed no more turning of her face, and she used both eyes together with her head perfectly straight. Michael McCarthy, five, with a vertical and a horizontal misalignment, looked straight and was unaware one of his superficial dissolving sutures was loose and almost ready to be washed away. All three children can now resume fairly normal activities and even start careful baths. Running and jumping were now permitted.

I saw one final patient as an emergency. Joseph Levy, 11 months, is the grand-nephew of one of my dearest friends, Steve Levy. Even though he is under the care of another ophthalmologist I saw him as an emergency case because of my friendship with Steve. Joseph fell down a flight of stairs at home, lacerating his eye on a piece of wood extending from a radiator—a disastrous injury of a penetrating laceration of his cornea into the interior of his eye. The corneal laceration was sutured in Brooklyn by the ophthalmologist whom they brought him to as an emergency, and the parents were told he might need further repair. It was very difficult to examine the little boy's eye because of crying, and I did not want him to squeeze his eye during crying and risk the opening up of the tiny sutures holding his eye closed with the corneal laceration having penetrated the interior of his eye. I did the best I could in the office setting, but I knew he would need further evaluation under anesthesia so the interior of the eye could be better examined.

Damage to the retina, damage to the intraocular lens, damage to the cornea, intraocular hemorrhage—all severe complications of a penetrating injury that have to be attended to in the future. But first things first. We must evaluate his retina to see if it is detached and if the interior of the eye is clear enough to do retinal surgery. Not a good situation. I spent a long time with his parents explaining all possible problems this little boy might face—and probably will—during the next several months. I called a friend of mine, Ken Wald, an expert pediatric retinal specialist, and he is going to see him this afternoon.

At 2:00 pm, I was finished, and I could get ready to go to the hospital after lunch at my desk. Before I left, I had to reassure Angela Dillon, scheduled for surgery tomorrow, that she would not need a transfusion at the time of her eye muscle surgery. She was adamant about getting her own blood taken to be used in such an event. With difficulty, I convinced her she was not going to need a transfusion. In these days of the HIV virus, patients are terrified they will be given transfusions contaminated with the virus. All I could say to her was that, in 40 years of surgery, I have never had to give a transfusion for an eye muscle operation.

I am still upset about Joseph Levy, the baby who fell down and had a ruptured globe. His grand-uncle, Steve, is a good and dear friend. Steve is a Syrian Jew and the community of Syrian Jews in the New York area is very, very close. They all have only a few names, like Steve, Joe, Morris, Adele and Rachel. The father is a young man working in a yeshiva and comes in with his black hat and his black coat and his young wife in her red velvet dress, and they had five kids before little

Joe. Most of the Syrian Jews live in Borough Park in Brooklyn. A few, like my friend Steve, live in Kings Point, Long Island, and the rest of them live out on the Jersey Shore in Deal. To have a ruptured globe is terrible, and to have it happen when you're only 11 months old is a catastrophe. I hope the retina is still in place, and I hope the lens has not been disrupted or lost. If the retina is in place, some hope exists for the eye because the problem with the lens can be taken care of with further surgery. After I speak to Ken, the retinal specialist, I'll know better about the prognosis for this eye. Needless to say, the young parents are very, very upset and, of course, they feel guilty that little Joe fell down the stairs.

Who would have known that a sharp wooden edge that projected from the radiator at the foot of the stairs would be caught by the little boy's eye?

A reflection on eye muscle research:

Medicine has so many possible careers—patient care (both medical and surgical), teaching, research, administration, etc. Most doctors concentrate on one, maybe two. In my case, I did most of my work in patient care and teaching, but I also did a little research—on my own time, as they say, because I was not fulltime at the medical school and did not receive financial grants for formal research (for example, from the National Institutes of Health). I was always dabbling in one project or another related to strabismus mostly. Dr. Virginia Lubkin, who well might have been the first woman ophthalmologist in New York City, would always greet me with, "So Renée, what are you working on now?" because she knew my interest in research.

I was always trying to improve surgical procedures on the superior oblique muscle of the eye, the most complicated of the eye muscles. Such research would be defined as clinical. More basic research was when I was working on cyanoacrylate (superglue) to attach muscles back to the eye after doing procedures on them. I did that work on rabbits at Ethicon Labs, in New Jersey. Rabbits do have a muscle that moves their eyes—a superior rectus muscle. The bond was good between muscle and eye with the cyanoacrylate and its use would avoid the potentially disastrous complication of perforation of an eye when reattaching the muscle to the eye with needle and suture. Nevertheless, permission was never given for using it because a few rare cases of cancer in mice kidneys had been described after using cyanoacrylate for another medical condition. That ended the superglue project. I also worked with one of my residents on using laser energy to reattach the muscles to the eye. I always had one of the residents interested in my projects, and he or she would do the research with me. The laser bond of muscle to eye that we created in the laboratory at NYU Medical School was satisfactory, but by the time we did that work adjustable sutures were becoming popular and neither laser nor superglue would be appropriate for the adjustable technique, which required sutures.

Apart from my clinical research on muscles other than the superior oblique, my most interesting work was on the development of an electrical stimulator for eye muscles. I had heard of a number of projects relating to stimulation of paralyzed muscles elsewhere in the body—spinal cord paralysis, upper limb paralysis, etc.—but no one was working on stimulating paralyzed eye muscles. I decided to work on the development of an electrical stimulator.

I researched the top electrical engineers and discovered that Professor Wen Ko at Case Western Reserve University in Cleveland was one of the best. I flew out to Cleveland and told him of my ideas. Fortunately for me, he became interested and assigned a postgraduate Fellow, Yuquon Chen, from the People's Republic of China, who was on a research Fellowship with Dr. Ko, to come to New York City and work with me for the final six months of his Fellowship before returning to his hometown of Hang Chow. (As the Chinese say, "Hang Chow Soochow." Not sure exactly what that means, but communicating with Yuquon Chen was never easy.) Anyway, Yuquon Chen showed up at my door for six months to work on an electrical stimulator for eye muscles. He was quartered at the Chinese Embassy on the west side of Manhattan, near the Hudson River where the aircraft carrier *Intrepid* was docked. When I first took him there, he gave me directions because the Chinese kept the location of the embassy a secret, and I had some trouble deciphering his words—"by the fi ship, by the fi ship." What he meant was that the embassy was by the fight ship *Intrepid*. Always difficult but manageable with Chen. When I would drop him off there after our work during the day, there was no sign on the door; a little slit would open, two eyes would see Chen standing there and open up. I also remember he could not eat out. If I wanted to take him to Chinatown for dinner, unless he had cleared it beforehand with the embassy, they always had his dinner ready for him.

Language notwithstanding, our larger problem was in finding a laboratory for our research. We needed primates—animals like us humans, with two eyes focused together, tracking, converging, synchronously. Rabbit eye muscles are not feasible for this work. And to find primates is not an easy task. There were less than a dozen primate centers in the USA at that time where research could be done by animal experimentation (the mid-1980s), and even then animal rights groups were protesting their existence. Fortunately for us, I had a connection at LEMSIP (Laboratory for Experimental Medicine and Surgery in Primates), and we were given permission to implant an electronic stimulator that Chen was to design in one of the chimpanzees (not quite sure whether he was a chimp or a gorilla, but he was large). In return for this, I agreed to be the ophthalmic consultant to the veterinarians caring for the chimps for that year.

Chen worked on a stimulator for implantation on an eye muscle. I won't go into details here, but it was an ingenious design for a bipolar current device that wrapped around an eye muscle near the neuromuscular junction like a sandwich. It could be turned on and off, and it received its signal from a small plaque made of *gutta percha* (like rubber) about the size of a penny implanted on the floor of the orbit. When he finished the stimulator and its source, it was time to do the surgery.

Our team consisted of Chen, me, my assistant Arleen, and my resident in training at the Manhattan Eye and Ear, Dr. Paul Finger. We assembled our equipment, the big suitcase in Chen's hand containing the electronics and the implantable devices, and headed for LEMSIP, about forty miles north of NYC in

Tuxedo Park, hidden away from the animal rights advocates in the woods down a long dirt road, with no sign in front, no sign on the concrete block building that made up the Primate Center. Greeted by the head veterinarian, we were first given some information about the lab. LEMSIP was used primarily for experimentation with the use of drugs for the worst infectious diseases imaginable (HIV-AIDS, other blood-born killer viruses, names I never heard of). The chimps were all infected with one or another of these deadly viruses. When we walked past some of the cages, I remember Howie, the biggest gorilla, who was always angry (who wouldn't be), throwing feces, and spitting at us as we passed. And it was also Howie who developed a corneal ulcer from being scratched in the eye by another chimp, and I, as consultant ophthalmologist, cauterized the ulcer with silver nitrate to save the eye.

I remember that first day vividly. We were instructed and helped into our protective gear—like the astronauts would do before going into space, like what is necessary now during the COVID crisis in the hospitals (PPE—personal protective equipment). Space suits, double gloves, double boots, helmet, shield, every body part doubly covered. We were a little startled. We had not realized what we had bargained for.

When it was time for surgery, Paul Finger and I operated, and Chen stood by with his black box and the electrical apparatus. Under general anesthesia, we exposed the external (lateral) rectus of one eye of the chimp and wrapped the sandwich-like stimulator around the muscle, threading it back toward the neuromuscular junction under electronic control. No electrical engineer was I, but I knew my way around the nerves to an eye muscle. I had started the first electromyography clinic at MEETH some years before after I returned from Iowa and my studies with Fred Blodi on EMG (electromyography). Then we implanted the little *gutta percha* disk on the floor of the orbit with wire connecting it to the stimulator on the eye muscle.

Chen at the control gave the electronic signal to stimulate the lateral rectus and the eye turned out to the side. He turned off the signal and it returned to straight ahead. Each time he did it the eye responded. We closed the conjunctiva, and the chimp was allowed to wake up. Maybe the first electronic stimulation of an eye muscle. I don't know.

We took off our protective gear, the double face masks, the double body covering, the double boots, and drove back to New York City. We left the electronic stimulator in our chimp for two months and then returned to examine the stimulator and do another trial. We wanted to evaluate the effect on the eye and the orbit of the little rubbery implant and to see if it still worked. When we came back, we were confronted by protestors walking back and forth outside the research buildings. The animal rights activists had found the location of LEMSIP. We knew it would not be long before the few remaining primate centers in the U.S. would be closed.

We did the usual routine of prep, again quite similar to the garb in the ICUs in 2020 for hospitalized COVID patients. We understood the virulence of some of the viruses with which the chimps at LEMSIP had been infected. When our chimp had been put under anesthesia, Paul Finger and I examined the implanted *gutta percha* stimulator and its wire to the lateral rectus muscle near the neuromuscular junction. Everything seemed intact as it had been when we had implanted them. Yuquon Chen turned on the current, and the eye turned laterally (to the side). Several stimulations, with identical responses each time. We expected that it would—no reason not to. Then we removed the cuff of the stimulator from the muscle and its wire to the *gutta percha* stimulator and removed them from the orbit. Our chimp woke up, his eye movements normal as before.

We had made a very simple experiment, external electronic stimulation of an eye muscle. Research in the future may develop implantable devices to innervate paralyzed eye muscles, as has been done to paralyzed limbs and other body parts innervated by voluntary and involuntary nerves. A daunting task for sure to make the two eyes work together for binocular single vision and no double vision. Every muscle in each eye (six in each eye) is innervated properly for every position of gaze. We know this from Hering's Law, "equal and simultaneous innervation to all the muscles of the eye."

It was a simple experiment. It only demonstrated that an eye muscle could be electronically stimulated from an external source. However, one should remember, this was done before the age of computer microchips. One can only imagine what a young computer engineer could do in 2020 and beyond.

We would have wished to continue the research, but LEMSIP was not to be available for much longer, nor was Yuquon Chen, whose Fellowship at Case Western Reserve was soon to end and he would return to his hometown, as he called Hang Chow in the

People's Republic of China.

I returned, with my assistant Arleen, a few more times to LEMSIP to check on some eye problems in a few chimps, as I had promised before we did our research. Howie, the giant gorilla with the corneal ulcer I had treated, was fine, although still angry, and throwing feces and spitting through the bars of his cage at anyone walking by. Unfortunately, the little six-month-old chimp, who tightly held Arleen's hand while I looked at his swollen optic nerves with my ophthalmoscope, would not make it. Meningitis, I told his vet, would be the cause of his death, the etiology of which I do not know.

The closing of the primate centers meant the end of primate research into binocular problems. Only primates have simultaneous binocular vision like humans. My clinical research after that time was mostly on devising modifications on surgical procedures on eye muscles. For my young associate Paul Finger, his experience in research was just beginning. He became one of the leading experts in the world on treating eye cancers. He runs the Eye Cancer Center at NYU. One of his most important contributions is the development of the radioactive disks—about one inch in diameter or smaller—that are implanted on the sclera overlying the cancerous growth beneath it. Did he get the idea for those disks from the small rubbery *gutta percha* electronic implant we sewed into the chimp's orbit at LEMSIP in the 1980s? Maybe.

Oh well, back to my diary...

Wednesday, January 6

Surgery day. After breakfast—cereal and an English muffin with decaffeinated coffee—at the apartment, I went to the garage below the apartment building and took my truck to Manhattan Eye, Ear and Throat Hospital, where I do my surgery. I put the truck in the garage a few doors from the hospital. We used to have a hospital parking lot when I first came to Manhattan Eye and Ear, but now the parking lot space is occupied by the building in which I do my surgery.

I changed into my green scrub suit. Because so many scrub suits have been stolen, mostly by orderlies or other hospital personnel, each surgeon picks up fresh scrubs on arrival near the operating room. I put on my scrubs and went one flight down to the operating floor to see my first surgical patient. The holding area has a large desk in the center, and along either wall patients are lined up in reclining chairs because most of the surgery is done ambulatory, with same-day admission and discharge from surgery. My patient was sitting in one of the ambulatory chairs being checked in by the operating room nurses. Her name plate, her chart—a detailed history of possible previous or future anesthetic problems or surgical problems was elicited three and four times over, and the anesthetist, Sue Albano, started an IV to get ready for the trip down the hall to the operating room.

The patient was Angela Dillon, a 40-year-old woman who is so nearsighted that, without her thick myopic lenses, she can only see clearly out to four inches in front of her face. She was sitting there, of course, without her glasses, because she was about to have surgery. When I got about five feet away from her, she recognized me because I'm hard to miss, standing six feet tall and, even in my scrubs, with my stocking feet and no shoes, only the shoe covers for the operating room, I'm still hard to miss.

I took a quick look at her eyes, made sure I remembered which eye I was going to operate on, and then checked her consent form, to see that the wrong eye was marked on the consent form. I promptly crossed it out, put in the right eye, and initialed it with the date. I then reassured her again that she was not going to have any transfusions, at which point my associate, Dr. Dovelet Shashou, arrived. Dr. Shashou, an ex-Iraqi Jewish woman, is a brilliant pediatric ophthalmologist. She escaped Iraq at age nine, walking with her sister partway across the Middle East to reach Israel. She finally made it to New York City—Queens College in New York City, Yale Medical School, postgraduate Fellowship with me at Manhattan Eye and Ear. A mother of two, she now works in three different city clinics for children. This day she helped me not make any mistakes in the operating room.

As tall as I am, that is how little Dovelet Shashou is. She stands all of five feet tall in heels. We look like Mutt and Jeff in the operating room. She comes to help me operate on alternate Wednesdays and the pediatric Fellow, Dr. Michelle McLeod, helps me on the other Wednesdays. Dr. McLeod showed up too. It was not her day to help me, but she came just to observe, as did Dr. Gupta, our second-year resident in ophthalmology. He wanted to watch some eye muscle cases before he begins his own surgical training. So, we had a full house in the operating room: Angela, the patient who came in from Staten Island at six in the morning, myself, Dr. Shashou, Dr. McLeod, Gupta, the anesthetist, Sue Albano (who works with the anesthesiologist, Dr. Barry Karaker, another ex-Yalie). Sometimes that happens; so we had in the operating room today three ex-Yalies. As a purist, though, I don't really consider the anesthesiologist, Dr. Karaker, and my associate, Dr. Shashou, to be Yalies because they only went to the medical school. They weren't graduates of Yale College the way I was.

Angela had a convergent strabismus, which meant she looked at people with her left eye and with her right eye turned in. We had to straighten her right eye by detaching the internal rectus muscle and moving it back just the right amount so it would not pull the eye in so hard. However, we had to move it back enough to make the eye straight, but not so much the muscle became weak and the eye drifted out in the opposite direction toward her ear. That's where the skill and the judgment of doing eye muscle surgery come in. The numbers are not etched in stone for how much you move the muscle for how many degrees of turn of the eye you've measured. Many things come into account: whether it's a large myopic eye or a very small child's eye; whether there has been previous surgery; what the condition of the muscle is when we expose it and look at it—many, many possibilities for variation in the result from a predicted amount of surgery.

Ms. Barnes, my trusted scrub nurse, waited for me with

my instruments sterilized and ready to go along with all the things I need without my ever telling her anything. About the only thing she asks me when I come in every morning is, "how many muscles," "how many eyes," because that tells her how many sets of sutures to get ready.

Angela was placed under general anesthesia with a tube through her larynx into her trachea. The circulating nurse put a drop of aqueous iodine in the eye to be operated on, and we were ready to go to work.

I prepped the eye with Phisohex soap and then irrigation with saline and painting of the skin with iodine to be wiped off with alcohol. I am probably the only surgeon in the hospital who does her own surgical prep, but I just do it that way. Most other surgeons have one of the OR techs or the circulating nurse or a resident prep the cases for them. It's just one of my idiosyncrasies; I insist on doing my own prep. The surgery was easy. There was very little blood, as expected since this was not a re-operation, and a half hour later a patch was on the eye. Dr. Shashou stood by and watched the anesthesia team bring the patient out of anesthesia, remove the endotracheal tube, and take the patient down the hall to the recovery room. Once we were sure she was waking up with no anesthetic complications in the immediate post-op period, we took the elevator to the sixth floor to let the family know the patient was okay.

As soon as I saw the patient's mother, the first thing I said was, "She's fine." That's what I always say. Before I say anything else, I say "she's fine," and then I tell the family what the surgery entailed and what surprises occurred. In this case there were none—no anesthetic problems, and no surgical problems. We gave them a few instructions, to keep the patch on until I see her in the office tomorrow, and we gave them a prescription for some drops to get in the hospital pharmacy to be used staring tomorrow. We then returned to the second floor holding area to see our second patent and to check her in the same way as the first.

The second patient, Sally Switzer, is 50 years old and has had an eye drifting out most of her life despite two previous operations in childhood. If you look at her at one moment, she can pull her eye straight and, when she relaxes the next moment, one eye is pointing out while the other is straight, and she looks quite wall-eyed, measuring approximately 20 degrees of drift. I knew she would be a difficult case because she had had two previous operations, and that makes the numbers not too accurate for how much is done for how many degrees of misalignment. It makes judgment very, very important because changes in the amount of surgery have to be made on the spot, depending on where and in what condition the muscles of the eye are found.

Once she was asleep, I exposed the muscles of the left eye. As expected, I saw they had been previously operated on and the external rectus muscle had already been moved into a weaker position and was surrounded by scar tissue. After dissecting out all the scar tissue, I measured exactly where the muscle was found and then computed in my head how much further I would have to put that muscle back in order to obtain the desired amount of weakening on the external rectus muscle that pulled the eye out. I did what I thought was the appropriate amount, and then I exposed the internal rectus muscle to be strengthened, and I saw it had been placed in a slightly weakened position. I shortened it, and I advanced it toward the front of the eye to put it in a mechanically better position in order to strengthen it. I loosened the outer muscle, and I strengthened the inner muscle, and I hope I did the right amount. I hope I did enough to get her straight, but not too much to make her cross-eyed and have her see double.

I don't always get it exactly right, and I don't always get it reasonably close to right, but I do most of the time, and the more I do it, the better at it I become. There is no substitute for experience in this kind of surgery, and the more I see the way eyes behave from all the different operations that have been performed on them, the better feel I have for how much surgery to do in each new individual case.

We went upstairs to speak to the mother and father, only to find a husband instead. We assured him Sally was doing well and gave him his instructions for the drops and the visit tomorrow.

I changed out of my scrubs and went down to the hospital cafeteria to have lunch because surgery was over. We had scheduled a third operation, but the problems of modern-day insurance caused the case to be canceled. The patient's insurance company asked for a mandatory second opinion, and nobody seemed to know that was necessary until this week, which was too late to get the necessary clearance. The case will be rescheduled.

Insurance companies sometimes ask for a second opinion to make sure unnecessary surgery isn't done. It's probably a good idea in some cases, but whose opinion, in my mind, as to the necessity of eye muscle surgery is more valid than mine? Anyway, no third case today, and I left the hospital in my truck to go hit a few golf balls. When I got back to the office, no patients were scheduled on my operating day, so I did some dictation and answered some phone calls and otherwise took care of some business concerns. Fortunately, I had a hopeful message from Dr. Wald, the pediatric retinal specialist, concerning little Joseph Levy. When I called Ken, he said the ultrasound examination looked like the retina was intact in the boy's eye. He couldn't be too sure about the lens, but the most important structure is the retina. That was indeed encouraging news.

Tonight at six, after my day of surgery, I attended a memorial service for Dr. Marsha Storch at the New School down in the Village. Marsha was a wonderful woman, a very strong, warm, witty, powerful gynecologist I first met at the Women's Forum, a women's leadership organization we both had been invited to attend in 1976, soon after I had become very notorious. Marsha had become very famous for her role as the leader of the women's movement in the early '70s— especially the women's medical movement and, especially, the movement to liberate women and allow them to gain control over their bodies. Marsha died of ovarian cancer. She had become a patient of mine during her later years, and I think she helped save my life by getting me to stop smoking.

She said a time bomb was ticking in my head because I kept getting migraine headaches. I was on estrogen therapy and I was still smoking, so I quit. And that was 15 years ago. I was going to get up and speak at the memorial for her. A lot of people got up and spoke, but I didn't because I just didn't want to call attention to myself. I listened to the other people say some wonderful things about Marsha, which I knew too.

A reflection from 2021:

In my sixty-seventh year, old for a man or woman, and certainly for a surgeon—an occupation that requires steady hands, good eyes, patience, nerve, judgment, energy, and who knows what other intangibles to be safe and successful—I found myself still doing complicated eye muscle operations at Manhattan Eye and Ear. Not the five difficult cases a day I used to do, but two a day still calling up my concentration and attention for a full morning's work. One of my mentors continued to operate into his late seventies—Marshall Parks. Another, Gunter Von Noorden, stopped at 68 when he underwent coronary by-pass surgery. And Phil Knapp retired in his seventies when he got ill. Eye surgeons seem to have good longevity in the operating room. I knew of one—Fred Verhoef—who did cataract surgery until he was ninety at Massachusetts Eye and Ear Infirmary.

My operating day for years was Wednesday. Senior surgeons have their own day reserved for them. One morning in early July 2002, I was doing two fairly complicated re-ops, procedures on eyes previously operated on, with scarring to deal with and an operative field made more difficult by the previous operations. In addition, one of the patients was a -23 diopter myope, meaning her eyes were extremely nearsighted (any refraction over 8 is called pathologic myopia) and thin-walled. It is easy to perforate the thin scleral wall with the fine needles used to reattach the muscles to the eye. I was assisted by my associate for surgery, Dr. Shashou.

Also assisting was Dr. Ilana Sternfield, the just-starting post-graduate Fellow in pediatric ophthalmology, who left the then Soviet Russia (Odessa in the Ukraine, where my grandparents came from) at the age of nine to attend eventually Columbia College and New York Medical School and had already had two years of private practice in general ophthalmology before deciding to take the Fellowship with us. Observing the surgery was Carolyn Wu, third-year resident originally from mainland China, and Linda Kleinman, second-year resident, a New Yorker who thought she might be interested in "peds," as we say. The anesthetist was Irina Rosenbaum, also ex-Soviet Union years ago. The scrub nurse (operating nurse) was my old reliable—I am always given my first team—Marie Barnes, who is almost as old as me. She hands me what I need without my ever having to ask. She's from Harlem, still the largest black population in the USA.

The two operations went well, and, as usual, I was very

careful to explain the steps of the procedures and the decision-making and the techniques as I went along. When I got to the tricky part of passing the needles thru only the outer wall of the eye (this particular wall was about one-quarter of a millimeter thick) and not penetrate the wall into the eye, Dr. Shashou began explaining to the observers.

"See how Dr. Richards rests her hand on the patient's head while she passes the needle. See how only her fingers are moving while her hand stays still."

When the dangerous part was over, the young third-year resident, Carolyn Wu, asked, "Dr. Richards, how long have you been at the hospital? How many years?"

She knew nothing of the history of Renée Richards, transsexual, tennis player, ex-director of the residency program in which she was enrolled, ex-surgeon director of the hospital she was training in, ex-director of the eye muscle department, the field she was considering for her subspecialty. All she knew was what she had been told: "Come up to the operating room and observe Dr. Renée Richards do some cases on Wednesdays if you are interested in eye muscle surgery."

When she asked that question, I knew my reply would dumbfound her, but I was not above a little levity after the tricky part of the surgical procedure. I answered rather matter-of-factly.

"Let me think, this is probably my forty-first year here."

Her reply was as quick as it was predictable. "Come on, Dr. Richards. I am serious. How many years have you been here at the hospital?"

Dr. Shashou reassured her I was indeed being serious. Carolyn was taken aback. It was beyond her imagination that anyone could do anything for that long, let alone eye surgery.

In point of fact, it did happen that, in 2002, I was the oldest practicing graduate of the hospital still operating. I had come there as a resident in 1961, and of course with interruptions for active duty in the U.S. Navy, my Fellowship training, and my notorious five years off to play and coach tennis, I have worked in the clinics and in the operating room and taught the residents for five decades. To emphasize how long I truly have been at the hospital, first Dr. Shashou told the young resident the site where we were operating was not even in existence when I had started there; it was the hospital parking lot. But then, to emphasize how long ago it really was, she told the story of how, when I was a resident in 1961—and observing surgery like these young women were now doing—the patient being operated on, a 21-year-old diabetic woman, went into cardiac arrest. The anesthesiologist, Englishman Dr. Cyril Sanger, calmly took the scalpel that had been pasted to the wall of the operating room for just such emergency occasions, turned first from the operating surgeon, old Joe Laval (older than I am now at my tender age of 67), then to Joe's assistant, and finally, presented the scalpel to me.

"Dr. Raskind, we shall have to open the chest."

In those archaic days, cardiac arrest in the OR meant opening the chest and doing actual massage of the heart—nowadays replaced by closed cardiac massage from outside the patient's chest. He presented the scalpel to me, the youngest in the room, using good judgment, because I, having just finished my rotating internship, was the closest in time to general medical training of any of those assembled.

I can imagine today how difficult it would be for me to handle a medical emergency (Carolyn Wu would be a much more suitable candidate). Anyway, I took the knife from Cyril, opened the chest wall with an incision just below the rib, as I had been taught by that tyrant of a chest surgeon at Lenox Hill Hospital, Dr. Herman Meier, chief of surgery there, and I found the heart. I have fairly thin wrists and hands. I disturbed nothing. I massaged the heart.

Cyril said, "I have a pulse now. I have a blood pressure."

I said, "Good; someone get me Donald Wood Smith up here right away"

Donald was a general surgeon from Australia taking training at the hospital in plastic surgery. A few minutes later he poked his head in the OR and said, in typical Australian fashion, "Gee, Dicko, what are you doing with your hand in that bloody girl's chest?"

Australians say 'bloody' for everything but this time it was appropriate. I said, "Donald, put some gloves on and help me close this chest."

He did. The patient made an uneventful recovery. I guess the story punctuated to the young residents how truly long ago it was when I first came to the hospital. And, as I listened to Dr. Shashou tell that story—I have recounted it many times—I thought back to my history of women at the hospital. Here we were in 2002—five women eye surgeons, one woman anesthetist, one woman scrub nurse. And how my attitudes must have evolved over the years? How Cheryl Kaufmann, who was one of my residents in the 1960s, and is now one of the best eye surgeons in the city, a few times said to me, "Renée, you were awfully tough on us women in those days."

Hard to believe, but she would not say it if she didn't feel it, and experience it. Not so tough that she didn't invite me to join her Friday clinic when I first came back to the hospital after my five-year sabbatical. That was pretty good of her to make such an offer, and I accepted. I still think of what she had said, "Renée, you were pretty sexist in those days, tough on the women."

Hard for me to believe, coming from a family where my mother and sister had preceded me into medicine, how I had listened to all the tales of my mother's struggles being a medical student in 1921, becoming the first woman resident at the Neurological Institute at Columbia Presbyterian Hospital. How indeed could I have been sexist? I, who trained more women in ophthalmology than anyone ever at Manhattan Ear and Ear. I, who encouraged young women medical students to do research projects and write papers co-authored with me. I, whose surgical assistant and half the Fellows we trained are women. Hard to believe, but I accept what I was, and I understand the evolution.

Some evolution. When I went to medical school at Rochester, there were two women in our class of 68 students. The second was there to provide company for the first. When my mother was in medical school, she was only admitted to the Women's Medical College of Pennsylvania. Now, women make up half the student body of U.S. medical schools, half of our residents, and more than half of the post-graduate Fellows. It would be rather difficult to be sexist now, don't you think?

Oh well, back to my diary...

Thursday, January 7

The first patient today was Edith Jansen. We went over her visual field—a computerized examination of her whole field of vision—and found it very constricted. Edith has had neurologic problems for many years. She has had MRIs. She's had neurologic examinations. Through all that, nothing definite has ever been discovered. Today, her visual field was so constricted you would think she would bump into things when she walked around outside. Somehow, she doesn't. Her optic nerves are pale, which means something going on in her brain affects the optic nerves. Her visual fields are contracted. I don't know whether that's just because she doesn't take the test well or because it's a reflection of some optic nerve disease.

"Do you want another MRI?" I asked. She said no.

"Do you want to see another neurologist?" Again, no. So

that means I have to take the burden of her losing visual field and her pale optic nerve heads on my own.

"Edith, come back in three months and we'll repeat the visual field to see if it might be worse."

Then I saw Shirley Gaines, on whom I operated several years ago because she had had a bad result from previous eye muscle surgery elsewhere and had gone from being a divergent misalignment to a convergent misalignment (from the eye turning out to an eye turning in). The operation I did on her several years ago had a good result. Today, she just needed a refraction for her astigmatism.

Yesterday's two post-ops came in. Sally Switzer's eyes were straight, but when I showed her the mirror she said, "It looks like my left eye is going in."

"Sally, it's only because it's been out for so many years that when it's straight, to you it looks like it's going in."

Her eyelid was swollen, and I was concerned about a possible infection. I decided to not put her on an antibiotic by mouth because her swelling was really legitimate in a patient who had twice previously undergone eye muscle surgery. I will worry about her for the next few days, and I told her husband to call me if the swelling gets worse.

Probably the most perplexing patient was Delores Constantino, a very attractive 59-year-old lady I have seen for many years. She came to me 12 years ago after she had had a cerebral hemorrhage undiagnosed as to its cause. Today, she said she has been having pain in her right eye for a week and the vision was slightly blurred. I examined her carefully. I found no reason for her blurred vision or for the pain. I could only think there was some connection to her hemorrhage many, many years ago. I also thought maybe we should do an MRI or an MRA, a magnetic resonance examination of her blood vessels in her brain, and maybe that's what we'll do. But I didn't do it on the spot and, again, it was another case where I was absorbing the responsibility of a serious problem to wait and observe and then possibly order an MRA to evaluate her blood vessels. So many times, like with Edith Jansen, I have to take the burden of the danger on myself for observation rather than going straight ahead to a thousand-dollar imaging study.

Odessa Carlin is a two-and-a-half-year-old beautiful, blonde-haired, blue-eyed little girl with the right eye turned way in toward the nose, and it had been doing that for the past month. Of course, her history gave her diagnosis. Her mother had had a turned eye, as does her older sister. Dilating her pupils revealed a large degree of farsightedness and, hopefully, the glasses to correct her farsightedness will get rid of her convergent deviation.

Alexis Weiskopf—poor Alexis Weiskopf. She has so many problems, including developmental delays, some difficulty with socialization and now, at the age of five, she is beginning occupational and physical therapy. She also has amblyopia in one eye, and her parents don't force her to wear the patch on her good eye that is so necessary to improve the vision in her poor eye. I spoke with them for an hour, explaining to them the importance of the patching, that Alexis cannot dictate to them whether she wants to wear it or not, and that the physical therapist and the occupational therapist can certainly help to get her to do the necessarytreatment.

Luke Poquiccio was a pleasure, a two-year-old boy on whom I operated for a severe vertical strabismus. He had had a bad result from his previous surgery by another experienced and competent eye muscle surgeon. Today, he looked terrific. His eyes were straight, and he had no tilting of his head. His only residual is a little swelling of his upper eyelid.

I saw several other patients during the day, including the other post-op, Angela Dillon. She was elated I didn't have to give her a transfusion, and her eyes looked wonderful.

To see these patients the day after surgery and to see them with straight eyes and minimal inflammation is a pleasure, but when there is a little bit of swelling, more than usual, I have to worry about an infection over the weekend. I just have to do that.

Andrew Betz was the last little boy I saw. He needs surgery for his left eye drifting up when he looks off to the side, but he is back to England tomorrow for the school year, and I won't see him until spring. We may catch up with him then and eventually do the necessary surgery.

I left the office at six o'clock exhausted. It was cold outside, and I hurried the 15 paces into the lobby and up to the apartment where I will stay for the night. I will get up early to drive to my country office in the morning.

Friday, January 8

I leave the city at 7:00 am on Fridays, and I drive the truck, accompanied by our Airedale Terrier, Lily, upstate to the office in Brewster. I see children in the morning in the Brewster office, where Dr. Hal Farquhar has his general ophthalmology practice all week long. A few sub-specialists come up—in my case once a week—to see our particular specialty. So, in Brewster, I only see children and people with eye muscle problems—no general ophthalmology. And it's 90 percent children.

The office is a beautiful green glass cube building on the edge of Putnam County. It overlooks the rolling hills of Dutchess County to the north and the lakes and rock formations of Putnam on the other side. It is a totally different kind of office from my little boutique on Park Avenue in the city. The waiting room is spacious in the Brewster office: there are 10 examining rooms, a laser room, a visual field room, a room for office surgery—including refractive keratoplasty—a consultation room for Dr. Farquhar, another consultation room for the other doctors who come up periodically, a large kitchen, a very large business office, a telephone operator's office, and an office for doing fluorescein angiograms for retinal work.

The office staff includes four technicians, a telephone operator, two women at the front desk, a business manager, an overall business assistant, a surgical coordinator, another receptionist, and the contact lens staff. Approximately 12 women work there in addition to Dr. Farquhar, the chief ophthalmologist, all week long. I come on Fridays for pediatric work. Richard Gibralter comes twice a month for corneal work. Bob Della Rocca comes up from the city twice a month to do oculoplastic surgery, and Mandes Kates has recently come on to do general ophthalmology with Dr. Farquhar.

It's a totally different type of business operation, too, in that it is almost all managed care, and Dr. Farquhar is on the astounding number of 57 managed care plans. Contrast that with my practice in the city, where I am on the managed care roles of only five plans. I'll have more—much more—to say later about managed care plans and how they have changed medical care.

However—if you will allow me to charge ahead to the year 2019—before I get off managed care for the moment, let's look in on Peter Weseley, an ace retina surgeon at New York Eye and Ear and a certifiable genius. In January 2019, he told me plainly that managed care has not delivered.

"Managed care is an ill-defined term that might be associated with many changes in healthcare delivery over the last 25 years. In the context of the year 1999, though, it refers to an HMO model with PCPs as gatekeepers to all care, financially incentivized to be efficient through the use of capitation and risk contracting, all created by Hillary Clinton's view of how to fix our healthcare system. While the term HMO lives on as the name stamped on most Americans' insurance, the whole model of gatekeeper/capitation/ risk-contracting is largely extinct, leaving its bureaucratic skeleton as pure friction in the system. What was sold to the American people as a mechanism to improve efficiency has had the opposite effect.

"There are huge policy and philosophical challenges created by the rapid and expensive growth in medical technologies that have occurred in the past several decades and which will continue to grow exponentially absent any market discipline to counter that trend. The leaders of all first world countries that I am familiar with have begged these larger questions, choosing instead to mold the perceptions of their electorate before the next election cycle.

"Personally, as a physician, I feel like a pebble being thrashed by the ocean waves breaking on me. I just try to go with the flow."

The flow is taking Peter out of the game. He told me in January 2019 that he is finished with private practice and its managed care headaches. He has decided to join New York University Medical School full time.

On the flip side, Lisa Hall—Peter's life partner—is in it for keeps. Lisa is my former resident at MEETH and then surgical partner at the NYE+E for fifteen years, until I stopped operating. She has been director of pediatric ophthalmology at NYE+E for many years. We are still very close friends.

"For me, managed care has been a way of life as a doctor," she wrote to me. *"By the time I started my practice in 1997, I needed another Fellowship to learn about billing, coding, referrals and appeals; all a part of practicing medicine in this new climate. The days of practicing medicine when you could be well-trained and hard-working, allowing you to hang a shingle and provide quality care, were over.*

"I feel the transition from traditional insurance, which relied upon the judgement and ethics of the provider to appropriately care for her patients, to insurance being controlled or managed

by a CEO or government agency, had a profound effect on every aspect of my becoming and continuing to be a physician.

"As a training MD—during my years as a resident and Fellow (1992-1997), my mentors were all struggling with how to handle the transition. Although I benefited from their teaching me about the science of medicine I was very influenced by the constant reminiscence about the good old days and comments like, 'I hope my grand kids go into banking.' Surrounded by seasoned physicians griping about paperwork and the need to fire loyal and longtime staff was demoralizing to say the least. I was entering a profession where job satisfaction was going through the floor. The fact I had left a career in nursing after eight years and struggled through pre-med and medical school, incurring substantial debt, definitely caused me to question my choice.

"Because of the millions being made on Wall Street and in the tech industry I think we had a generation of physicians comparing their declining incomes to their peers' exponential growth in income.

"I was not influenced in a way that made me seriously consider quitting. I did not go into medicine to be wealthy. I wanted autonomy, intellectual stimulation, to work with and help people and job security. I was 100 percent successful in achieving all of these things and feel financially stable as well.

"My ongoing career which now spans 20 years since completing Fellowship continues to challenge how I counsel young people considering medicine as a career choice. I remind myself of the sour attitudes I encountered and try to be objective but realistic. I have made choices which have led to reductions in my income to be able

to practice medicine in a way that optimizes quality of care and job satisfaction. Had I larger debt or a family to support on my own, there is no question I would be practicing sub-quality care in order to keep patient numbers up and make an adequate living.

"After trying to run a practice on my own, I joined a group of other pediatric ophthalmologists. Although I would see more patients and earn less, all of the billing and scheduling and handling of staff would be taken care of. Keeping up to date in 2008 required a ridiculous amount of time dealing with electronic records, managed care contracts, etc. Joining a group allowed me devote a larger percentage of time to actually take care of my patients.

"I will add that this has taken a huge toll on the physician-patient relationship. This topic could have an essay of its own. Patients do not really understand the reason for longer waits, shorter visits, copays, etc., when they see the doctor. They are frustrated and the quality of care is suffering.

"Lastly, and most recently, the hospital where I am affiliated, [have] been a department head, and taught residents for 20 years has made huge changes to stay afloat. The pressure to recruit sicker patients requiring longer hospital stays, and has caused many of us to be pushed out and work elsewhere. Nursing staff have lost housing for new inpatient facilities and overall morale is rock bottom."

Lisa is, as I said, a good friend, and I fear her take on sinking morale is a common thread among today's doctors and staff. Anyway, like I said, much more about managed care later.

In the office upstate at Brewster, patients are brought into the examining room with the technician who pre-examines them, does many of the same things an ophthalmologist might do, and gets the patient ready for the ophthalmologist, who examines the patient, gives instructions, and then goes to the next room, where another patient is sitting, waiting, having been pre-examined, to do the examination in that room, and so on.

In the city, it is totally different. I have only one main examining room. I escort the patient in myself. I do everything that has to be done except for the eye muscle work my orthoptic technician does before the patient gets to me. In terms of general ophthalmology cases, I do everything myself, including such technical things as taking the pressure and instilling the drops and doing the vision. I even do the refraction for glasses. In the Brewster office, most of those things are done by skilled technicians.

My practice in the Brewster office, however, is not all that different from my practice in the city, even though the office itself and the practice of the other doctors there is very different. I still see only one patient in one room, and patients are escorted in and out without my going room-to-room. In addition, my own orthoptic technician—Ricky Cohen—joins me every Friday, coming up from Long Island, where she works the rest of the week for a pediatric ophthalmologist. She sees the children in her office next to mine the same way Barbara does in the city, and when she has examined the patient's eye muscles, the patient is brought into my room.

Today, I saw 20 patients between 8:30 am and 12:30

pm. In order to see 20 children in the city, it frequently takes me six hours, from 8:30 am to even 2:30 pm. To see 20 patients in Brewster, I can be guaranteed of walking out of the office at approximately 12:30 pm if I start on time at 8:30 am. The population is different; the complexity of the problems is frequently different; and the absence of seeing very many adults makes it go much quicker as well. In the city, I see so many children and adults who have had previous eye muscle surgery, who have had visits and care by other ophthalmologists, who have had consultations with two or three other specialists before they come to me. In the suburban office in Brewster, frequently I am the first one they have been referred to, although, on occasion, I am called for second opinions up here as well.

Most of the patients today had fairly routine problems such as convergence insufficiency or a weakness in converging the eyes on a near target. The problem sometimes requires exercises and sometimes glasses. We have been following a few patients for treatment of amblyopia with patching of the better eye to improve the lazy eye.

Probably the most difficult patient was little Brady Rawlinson, who has a big strabismus we have to operate on. He's complicated because he had cryo surgery for retinopathy of prematurity three years ago, soon after his premature birth and the oxygen therapy required to keep him alive, and some developmental problems.

He is extremely nearsighted; he has the residue of retinopathy of prematurity, with dragging of his retina and abnormal macular development in one eye. His eyes shake, a condition called nystagmus, and he has a combined horizontal and vertical misalignment of his eyes. His grandmother brings him, and, after I see him, I always have to call his mother at her office to report Brady's condition. This time, I called her and said it was time to operate on him for his eye muscle problems and to try to straighten his eyes by eye muscle surgery. He also has to continue doing some treatment of amblyopia, but I don't think his lazy eye is so much related to his strabismus as it is to the abnormality of his retina.

Surgery will be planned for this spring, and care will be taken to address his pulmonary problems because he has bronchopulmonary dysplasia as well. Children who are born prematurely have problems in all areas, and this is true of little Brady. His eye muscle surgery will be a challenge.

The first time I saw Jeanette Wilging she was a little girl. She is no longer so little. I operated on her in the city many, many years ago. She is now 19, and she comes with her father for periodic check-ups because the family lives in an upstate town now and no longer in the city. Frequently, we see patients in the Brewster office who, at one time or another, we took care of in the New York City office.

Jacqueline Duvin is two years old, and she wears the same hat every time she comes in. It's purple wool with a brim that turns up, and I think she wears it to sleep. She wore it when she came in for her eye muscle surgery two months ago at the hospital in the city, and she wore it today. But this time, beneath that little hat, two straight eyes instead of a pair of badly crossed eyes stared happily at me.

At 12:30 pm I walked out of the office and into the freezing cold of a wintry storm. My mind—suddenly free of patients—turned to hitting golf balls, and I fell flat on my face on the ice in the parking lot. The wind whips across the hills from Dutchess County toward Putnam and can quickly turn the roads and the parking lot into a sheet of ice. No harm done, thankfully. I picked myself up and carefully drove to the golf dome, a gigantic bubble covering a practice range—my godsend for the wintry months upstate. It is five minutes from the office.

I drove home late in the afternoon with Lily, our little Airedale Terrier, and made my own dinner because Arleen stayed in the city to do some work in the office. I shall pick her up on the train at Brewster tomorrow. It's going to be a wet and icy weekend, but I have no commitments and, as long as I don't get any calls from the patients I operated on Wednesday, it should be a relaxing weekend.

Saturday, January 9, and Sunday, January 10

Spent a quiet weekend at the house upstate, essentially snowed in and iced in. We had to walk to the house from way out by the tennis court. The four-wheel-drive Chevy truck couldn't even get down the driveway near the house. But it was okay; college and professional football fill the TV, and I caught up a little on some reading. I was happy to stay in the house and look out at the kids skating on the lake below.

Monday, January 11

This afternoon, Arleen and I drove into the city from the house upstate. I was left off at MEETH to go to my surgeon directors' meeting at five o'clock. The surgeon directors are comprised of three plastic surgeons, six ophthalmologists, and five ear, nose, and throat specialists along with our medical consultant, our head of anesthesia, and our head of pathology. The board of surgeon directors meets several times a year to discuss matters related to hospital performance of both medical and non-medical activities. We are separate from the board of governors of the hospital, called the lay board—made up of businessmen and women who have an interest in the welfare of the hospital. The administrator of the hospital—the executive director—administers the business activities of the hospital and is a liaison between the lay board and the board of surgeon directors. Recently, conflict arose between the board of surgeon directors and the administrator, and for this reason our last meeting was a combined gathering of the board of surgeon directors and the lay board—something that has never happened in all the years I have been connected to Manhattan Eye, Ear and Throat Hospital. The meeting today was back again to our regular group, the board of surgeon directors only.

We talked about the problems in operating-room staffing and the technical assistance the surgeons require for complicated cases, and we went over the problems relating to the skill and efficiency of the technical support staff in the operating room. Each time we meet, we get a report from the executive director and a report from each department head, and then we have a section for old business and new business and anything else that might pertain to the operation of the hospital.

Most of the time, we don't have much input into what the administrator does, but recently we have made our voices heard and some of the more serious problems of the running of the hospital have been brought to the attention of the administrator and the lay board. No one at the time foresaw the serious conflicts about to rain down on us.

Tuesday, January 12

Office hours started as usual at eight o'clock and, between 8:00 am and 1:00 pm I saw 15 patients. Professionally, an uninteresting day because my specialty is strabismus and pediatric ophthalmology and the patients today (it just happened that way) presented very few strabismus problems and many general ophthalmology problems, ordinary and time-consuming without being of great attraction to me.

Firstly, Harland Pettigrew didn't show up. That got me off to a good start to begin with. Harlan has an eye muscle problem (I operated on him as a child), but he is now 37 years old and comes in every few years to have me check on his status.

I did see Laurie Caban, on whom I operated for a paralyzed vertical eye muscle following an automobile accident. I was annoyed to begin with because Harland hadn't shown up and I guess I showed it to Laurie, who still complains of seeing double. When I questioned her about when she sees double, she put her head in such an absurd position that almost anybody would see double if they were tilted as far back and looking into such an extreme gaze as she showed me. I reassured her she was indeed doing well and she couldn't expect to not see double when she did a contortion while lying watching television on the couch with her head tilted way over to one shoulder. That good I'm not, and her paralyzed muscle, although much improved, is still a little a bit weak and shows itself with double vision in an extreme position of gaze.

Teresa Elander really tested my patience, however, because she is a lady whom I saw for the first time today. She is nearsighted and at the age of 50 has a little problem seeing up close as well. It is a perfectly normal physiologic loss of the ability to focus up close that all people over 40 have. She does not really want to accept this and she has gone to great lengths to do things to her eyes to undo this normal loss of focus with age. One thing she did in the early 1980s was to undergo orthokeratology, a non-surgical procedure using specially designed contact lenses to gently reshape the curvature of the eye to improve vision. After that, she complained of fluctuating vision, which of course she would because her cornea began to reassume its normal shape after having been flattened by the contact lens. Pilots used to do this when they wanted to take their pilot's vision test, which has to show 20/20 vision without glasses. They would wear contact lenses for 24 hours to change the shape of their corneas and then run in to do the test the next day with the flattened corneas and no nearsightedness, only to have the nearsightedness return when the corneas resumed their normal shape. I told her if she was interested in doing that, she could consider the new laser therapy that permanently changes the shape of the cornea and has made orthokeratology a very obsolete practice. I don't think she really accepted what I said and she left probably as skeptical and unbelieving of her true situation as before we started.

Sometimes I just know I'm not going to get anywhere with certain patients. I give it a try, but I won't be adamant, as I might have been 20 years ago.

I was happy to see Judith Frejan because I gave her some prisms to alleviate a double-vision problem following cataract surgery, and she is totally happy with the alleviation of her double vision. She was one refreshing small portion of the day's schedule. I have seen a lot of post-cataract double-vision problems, and I have helped many of them with prisms and sometimes surgery.

Abner Randolph got me going too. He refused to see my orthoptist, Barbara, for the pre-examination. He was convinced that, many years ago, an orthoptist had given him a prescription for glasses which he did not like. That is flatly not so because orthoptists don't prescribe glasses. He apparently mistook an orthoptist's examination of his visual acuity for an examination for glasses. But I was not about to argue with him that the orthoptist he saw years ago did not indeed prescribe his glasses. He was convinced of it.

And then I saw William Lawhorn, who lost his eye in childhood from a tumor and has been wearing an artificial eye ever since. He came in to have the socket behind his artificial eye checked and to have his good remaining eye examined. I did all that but was not particularly happy because people with sockets and artificial eyes should go to a specialist for particular care of that problem. That's where he really should have gone instead of coming to see me. This happens, though, and I told him I would be happy to take care of him and assure his good eye remained healthy, but I referred him to Dr. Lisman to attend to the problems of his socket.

A new patient was 10-month-old Jeremy Glassman, a beautiful little boy whose tiny finger would touch my light and put it out, and when I turned it on again his tiny finger would touch my light and put it out again. Jeremy came in for suspicion of amblyopia, but did not have amblyopia and was not likely to get it. He has an obstructed tear duct which probably needs to be probed and opened in another month or so. I used to do these all the time and I do them well, but I don't like doing them anymore and I much prefer one of the oculoplastic surgeons to take over my probings.

Frequently, I am persuaded to do the procedure myself, and I probably will end up doing it on Jeremy if he doesn't clear in a couple of months.

Now it's off to the clinic to work with the residents and the pediatric Fellow and then to grand rounds at five o'clock.

Wednesday, January 13

Wednesday, as usual, is surgery day. I arrived at the hospital at 7:15 am and changed into my scrubs. I went into the holding area to look at Nancy Gronkowski sitting with her father, who was in a hospital jumpsuit because he was going to bring Nancy into the operating room. Nancy, 10, is extremely nearsighted, a -10.00 myope in each eye, which means that, from the standpoint of operating on her eye muscles, the wall of her eye (the sclera) is very, very thin. Because of that, it is a risk to pass a needle through the outer portion of the wall and not penetrate to the inside of the eye. That could cause a retinal hemorrhage, a retinal detachment, or an intraocular infection. She has strabismus, with her left eye drifting out and her left eye standing lower than her right eye, and she needs to have her eyes straightened by eye muscle surgery on her left eye.

She is even a little more complicated because she had an operation five years ago when she was cross-eyed, and now she requires surgery to bring the left eye back in because it had drifted out and down. That meant isolating a previously operated muscle and doing the appropriate strengthening procedure on it at the same time as loosening the outer muscle that was pulling the eye too far out. And then an adjustment would have to be made for the vertical problem, as well.

I checked on my anesthesiologist, and he was one of my favorites, as usual, but then I learned the nurse anesthetist was someone with whom I was not familiar—a Russian expatriate,

Irina Rosensweig. David Silver, the senior anesthesiologist of the group, assured me she was an excellent adjunct to Dr. Tannenbaum, the anesthesiologist. I always feel more confident when I know not only the anesthesiologist but also the trusted nurse anesthetist who helps the anesthesiologist. As it turned out, Irina is excellent, and I could only marvel at this woman, who must have had much training in her home city of St. Petersburg and then had to do that training and certification all over again, with new techniques to boot, when she came to this country.

Irina and Dr. Tannenbaum placed an LMA (a laryngo-mask) in Nancy's mouth to serve as an airway. This new type of anesthetic device sometimes is used instead of the endotracheal tube. Although it carries fewer serious respiratory risks than the endotracheal tube, it does have some risks of its own. In experienced hands and in the appropriate patient, it is a very nice avenue for instilling the gases into the lungs of the patient because it does not disturb the vocal cords and the trachea. I exposed the lateral rectus muscle—the muscle that pulls the eye out—and I put a suture in it, disinserted it from the eye, and re-attached it in a more posterior location so the muscle would have less effectiveness and not pull the eye out. The amount of millimeters of moving the muscle to get the right location was based on the measurements of the number of degrees of drifting out we had made before surgery and also is based on the condition of the eye, the size of the eye, the condition of the muscle, and also simply on intuition from 40 years of doing this. We then exposed the medial rectus, which had previously been operated on, and found it to be very little involved in scar tissue. With no difficulty, it was isolated and shortened to strengthen it and advanced anteriorly by 1 mm.

My assistant, Dr. Michelle McLeod, our pediatric Fellow in training, is a graduate ophthalmologist. She completed her residency at Montefiore Hospital and is spending a year with us to learn the sub-specialty of strabismus and other facets of pediatric ophthalmology. We adjusted the position of the medial and the lateral rectus in a superior location to help with the lowered position of the left eye. This was based on my old mentor Phillip Knapp's contribution to strabismus of moving the horizontal muscle in a vertical direction to help with vertical misalignment.

Considering Nancy was very nearsighted with a very thin-walled eye and she had had previous eye muscle surgery, we felt good about what we were able to accomplish without a serious problem. Now, it remains to be seen whether the procedure we did was appropriate for her misalignment. We watched carefully as the anesthesia team brought her out of anesthesia. They left the LMA in place to be removed in the recovery room, and they transferred her to the portable stretcher to be taken to the recovery room, where she would stay for at least a half hour before being brought up to her parents. I am still working on getting the parents to be allowed to be in the recovery room and, so far, we're only doing it on selected patients whose parents have requested it.

At the point we were assured Nancy was coming out of anesthesia and waking up safely in the recovery room, Dr.

McLeod and I went up to the sixth floor to talk to her parents.

"Gronkowski? Anyone here for Nancy Gronkowski?" I announced as we walked into the waiting room where patients' families are sitting anxiously awaiting word from their surgeons. Mr. and Mrs. Gronkowski popped up and, as I walked over to them, I said, "Fine, fine, she's fine," which is what I always say, right off the bat, before I say anything else to the parents. That's the most important thing to tell them: the child is fine. After saying that, I then tell them what we did at surgery, what we found in the way of any unusual aspects to the muscles we operated on, and how we felt about the result on the operating table. We also assured them that anesthesia had been smooth and that she was waking up comfortably in the recovery room and would be up in a half hour. Then we gave a few simple directions, such as to leave the patch alone until I see her tomorrow and to get the prescription for drops filled in the hospital pharmacy so that they could be started tomorrow.

Then we went back down to the operating room to check the second patient in the holding area before his operation to follow. Robert Puccelli is an optician who has had a misalignment of his eyes since childhood and also has had previous surgery on his right eye many years ago. There were many possible choices of procedure to correct his residual cross-eyed condition and, after many sets of measurements in all different fields of gaze at distance and near, we decided to do a procedure on his left eye, the eye that had not been operated on in childhood. The procedure went well and again at the conclusion of surgery the position of the eyes under anesthesia was satisfactory, and hopefully the result tomorrow when the patch comes off will confirm that we did the right amount for the right number of degrees of misalignment.

The third patient was a 72-year-old woman. We don't frequently do eye muscle surgery on patients of that age, but sometimes when there is a condition of double vision and it is impractical to use big, thick prism glasses to try to correct for it eye muscle surgery might be indicated, and in Mildred Rutherford's case that was the situation. She had significant cross-eyed misalignment when she looked into the distance, with relatively little misalignment looking up close, a so-called divergence insufficiency that some older people get. It can be progressive and very disabling. They are unable to drive; they are unable to watch television; they are unable to walk looking more than five feet away from their bodies without seeing double. The surgery involved strengthening the outer muscle of each eye by cutting a small length of muscle out and re-attaching the muscle to its original location, thus shortening it and rendering it stronger; just like moving a belt in a buckle to a tighter notch. The surgery was relatively easy in her case. There had been no previous surgery, and in adults it is very easy to isolate the eye muscles; they don't have the thick layer of connective tissue around them that children have. But the tricky thing in a 72-year-old, just like with a little child, is the anesthesia and, fortunately, her anesthesia was performed easily and she was even waking up on the operating table before being transferred to the recovery room, which is always nice to see.

I ate lunch in the hospital cafeteria with a few of the residents and, of course, listened to some of their problems as we ate. One of our excellent young residents lamented the fact he was having so much difficulty scheduling surgery on patients through the clinic because he had to deal with approval of their insurance or lack thereof. Getting the hospital and the insurance companies together to agree on the need for surgery and the appropriate paperwork is a very large task for a young resident in training who has no experience in the business aspects of medicine. And sometimes the residents will lose a potential operative case because of the paperwork and difficulty in scheduling. I said I would see what I could do and I would look into the problem. Some hospitals employ a surgical coordinator for the residency cases the same way private doctors have office managers and surgical coordinators to do it for them in the private sphere. Of course, this costs money, and one has to balance the potential loss of cases for the hospital and the residents against the cost of increased efficiency of paying for a hospital surgical coordinator. Most hospitals in the 21st century have fulltime personnel for all such jobs.

I left the hospital in the early afternoon. I won't think very much about the surgical day. It was uneventful, and only tomorrow morning will I become interested and anxious to see how the work of the day turned out.

Thursday, January 14

Winters in New York can be beautiful. They can also be ugly. This morning began with a snowstorm that turned into an ice storm, and the city is paralyzed. Ten patients canceled office visits for the afternoon. Fortunately and importantly, the three post-ops from yesterday were able to make it to be checked.

Seventy-two-year-old Mildred Rutherford took the train with her husband from White Plains and then walked the five blocks to the office from Grand Central. She looked wonderful. Her eyes were perfectly straight and, after I cleaned up some of the residual ointment and crusting from her eyelashes, she looked very, very good indeed. No more double vision, and very little inflammation in the corner of each eye where the incisions were made to approach the muscles. I instructed her how to put her drops in four times a day to help prevent an infection and promote healing and told her to come back next week for follow-up. She had already gotten a new pair of glasses with no prisms, anticipating she would no longer need prisms. I was pleased to say she did not need them.

Nancy Gronkowski looked good also. Her father had taken the patch off last night because it upset Nancy and he cleaned her eye with a little saline on a moistened cotton ball. I could do little except look at her eyes, which were in good alignment, especially horizontally—with no misalignment at all—but she still showed a very small vertical misalignment with the left eye slightly lower than the right. That was not unexpected. I did not think the positioning of the horizontal muscles in an upward direction would be enough to get rid of the entire vertical imbalance. Overall, she looked very good and, unless I measured her with a prism and cover, I could never tell she had anything but straight eyes. We might try to get her to fuse and use both eyes together as she heals, but for the time being she is only to put in her drops four times a day—no gym, no recess, no rough-housing, no shampoo for at least a week.

And Robert Puccelli, whose mother was so worried when he did not come up from the recovery room as soon as she thought he would, looked good also. In fact, he was fusing. He was using both eyes together and wearing his new glasses with no prisms.

With all the cancellations, I had an abbreviated afternoon in the office. I did see Jack Hazen, who is going to Jerusalem next week for his bar mitzvah. Jack has congenital stationary night blindness and an eye muscle problem for which I operated on him a few years ago. He still has a small residual drifting up of one eye, and his best corrected vision is 20/40 and 20/30 with a pretty strong nearsighted correction. He wants contact lenses, but he can't have them until he gets back from Israel. Even then, it might be a little bit of a problem because he's on a few medications to calm him down from hyperactivity. I hope that won't impact his contact lens fitting. He's a handsome young man, and I would love him to get into contact lenses and get rid of his thick, myopic spectacles. We shall see.

I operated on David Ribb Schuss three times for a superior oblique palsy and a very severe head tilt to one side. Since his last operation one month ago, he has been perfect. I happily conveyed that to his mother, but she is still worried he's going to need another operation.

"Never again," she said emphatically.

Fortunately, as of this afternoon, he doesn't need any more operations.

Daniel Weisbard is two years old and can give me a numerical vision on the chart at 20 feet away and, fortunately, he's got equal vision in each eye. His droopy eyelid on one side has not caused any loss of vision in that eye.

Angela Dillon was so happy with her surgery last month she brought in 12 beautiful roses today to celebrate her gratitude for having straight eyes. A dozen roses certainly brighten the office on a dreary winter's day.

I'm glad it was a short day. In spite of the snow and ice, Arleen and I are going to drive to Forest Hills with my father's girlfriend, Ruth (aged 85—a retired lawyer) to celebrate his birthday today—99. It should be quite a celebration with my son, Nick, and his girlfriend, Oxana, there as well.

Friday, Saturday, and Sunday, January 15, 16, and 17

Friday, I was supposed to see my usual 20 children at Northeast Eye Care in Brewster. I usually go up at seven in the morning from the city to the Brewster office, but because of the ice storm that covered the Northeast we canceled the office hours in Brewster. For the first time in 12 years, we did not make it up to the Brewster office to see the children. In past times, no matter how bad the weather, we always managed to get there, but the city was covered with ice and no way could we make it up to Brewster. The appointments will be rescheduled for next week and the following week.

Instead, Arleen and I slowly made our way up in the afternoon and arrived at the house in Carmel to find our driveway completely covered in ice. I remember the time I fell after getting out of the car one wintry Saturday night a few years ago and broke my nose and cut my eyebrow open down to the bone on the ice on the dirt road close to our house. That was quite a saga and will be a tale for another day—how my son, Nick, walked in pitch black on the black ice through the woods to summon help to take me to a shelter for a few hours before we could make it to the hospital.

At any rate, this time, on Friday, we were just simply careful and we practically crawled down the driveway and the stairs to the house. The weather warmed up Saturday, and the driveway was sanded and salted so we could make it in and out with care. We were even able to get out Saturday afternoon to go to the movies in Jefferson Valley and then out to dinner with Ken and Fran Piersa, two young friends from the golf club at Sedgewood where we live. They had just lost their elderly dog the same way Arleen and I just lost Barrett, and we all commiserated on losing our wonderful old dogs. Sunday, I was mostly a couch potato, although I did get to hit a few balls at the golf dome before the two football conference championship games on TV. I watched the Jets almost pull it off against the Broncos, but untimely turnovers kept them on the short end of a 23 to 10 score.

Monday, January 18

The winter weather turned bad again. On our way out of Sedgewood, we found the bridge over the reservoir closed because of ice. We had to turn around and come back and wend our way through the club, an extra 20 minutes to get out onto the highway to head down toward the city. Today is Martin Luther King Day, and most of the schools are out, so we have 20 kids to see in the city office starting at two o'clock.

First, I saw Alec Sher, who has an eye muscle problem. He also has a chalazion—a cyst of the eyelid like a sty, a little bump on the eyelid margin. A chalazion is more difficult to deal with because it doesn't always break open like a sty with hot compresses and sometimes has to be surgically opened and curetted. Alec actually let me unroof the crust on the chalazion in the office, which is pretty good for a little four-year-old, and we are going to treat him with ointment and hope to avoid having to bring him to the hospital to get rid of it under general anesthesia.

Elyssa Haversham has an unusual condition called Williams syndrome, and such children have a particular kind of appearance, somewhat elfin-like. They have precocious language development but sometimes have some mental/developmental problems. I operated on Elyssa when she was a baby, and she is now 11 years old and going to school. Considering her Williams syndrome, she is doing very well.

Melissa Lansbury suffered an eye wound while fencing in

college. A foil entered her right orbit, slid right past the eye, and went back to the apex of her orbit, causing a hemorrhage where the muscles and the optic nerve all come together. She has done amazingly well and is left with only a very slight limitation of elevation of the right eye. She doesn't quite understand that she suffered a devastating injury and she could have lost the sight in her eye completely, and she could have lost the movement of her eye entirely. She wants it to be perfect like it was before her injury, and I've tried to explain to her that the foil entered the apex of the orbit and damaged the optic nerve and the muscles. She is very lucky she has come out of it with only a very small limitation of movement in one direction of her right eye. She wants me to authorize acupuncture for her. I said this was my limit, my boundary. In my old age, I'm beginning to demonstrate my boundaries. I never used to have any. I would do anything, and if a patient asked me to authorize acupuncture, I would do it. But not this time.

"I don't object to the acupuncture if it helps with the discomfort of your orbit that is a residual of the accident," I told her. "By all means, do it, but I'm not authorizing it."

Maria DeCarmo is 50 years old. She's from Portugal and she doesn't speak English very well, but she knew enough to come back to me years after I operated on her eye for double vision because now she's having a problem with glaucoma. She has an episodic loss of the visual field of her right eye, especially when she watches television. We are going to have to study this.

Jed Simon is a nine-year-old boy with a large degree of farsightedness. He is the son of an ophthalmologist colleague of mine. I see a lot of children whose parents are physicians, and many of them are ophthalmologists. It's a special thing to take care of a child of an ophthalmologist, a special privilege and a special challenge as well. Jed is a very smart little boy. He goes to the Horace Mann School, my alma mater. I went there more than half a century before he did. No matter. The school hasn't changed much.

Simone and Isaac Steinberg came in with their nanny, and there was some problem about how much of an examination the nanny wanted us to do on Isaac. I think she was worried about paying for two examinations, one for each child.

"That's okay," I told her. "We'll examine both children and you only pay for one."

Twenty patients. That's a lot of kids to see. They all had to be dilated. Some of them had problems. Stuart Bradford had a birth injury and is developmentally delayed, and I have been taking care of him since he was a little boy. He's now 20 years old. Many times, two siblings will come in—one will be perfectly normal and the other child will have a severe developmental problem. It's hard and it's so interesting, and it's nice to see the normal sibling taking care of the one who has the developmental delay.

Gerald Dornau always wants to know if he still gets the "drips" if he gets the chart right when we test his vision 20 feet away. I told him today he gets the "drips" anyway, whether he gets it right or not. He's got such a big astigmatism, the only way you can evaluate it is to paralyze his eyes with the drops... excuse me, "drips," and then see exactly how much astigmatism he has. He didn't do too well on the word recognition test either, so he might have a little learning disability to go along with his large astigmatism. We shall see.

Tuesday, January 19

Today in the office, we saw 20 patients starting at 8:30 am and finishing at 1:30 pm, straight through. To see 20 patients in the New York office takes at least an hour longer than to see 20 patients in the upstate office. The New York patients are all complicated problems and require much more time and much more consultation than the children we see upstate. And when I finish with 20 patients in the New York office, I am exhausted.

We started with George Preble, who is 39 years old and works for a hospital. In the past few years, he has developed a thyroid problem in which his eyes are exophthalmic (protruding). I have to measure that, and I have to measure his eye movements because people with thyroid trouble often get thyroid myopathy and double vision. But I remembered him mostly because of the telephone call he made at 9:00 am on a Sunday morning to my answering service years ago. He insisted it was an emergency and told the service to get in touch with me immediately. The service reached me and I called him back at 9:30. The emergency was that he wanted the name of a good optician so he could buy his glasses. I think it was one of the worst emergency calls I've had in 40 years.

Hasida Walfish is an eight-year-old girl from an Orthodox

Jewish family. I operated on her a few years ago and immediately ran into a serious hitch. She has an allergy to latex materials—latex gloves, latex anything—and it's so severe she could go into a respiratory obstruction from swelling of her tongue and her larynx if she touches or is exposed to latex. When I operated on her, we had to turn the hospital upside down because everything in the hospital has some latex on it—the IV tubing, the syringes, the covering for the syringes, the covers on the bottles of medication, the anesthetic mask, the anesthetic tubes, the gloves we wear in the operating room, all the articles in the recovery room, all the materials the nurses use in the ambulatory surgical center. Everything had to be switched to latex-free. It cost the hospital thousands of dollars to make that reclamation project, but at least now it is in place for future patients who have a latex allergy. Hasida was operated on successfully, and she just came in today for her usual yearly check-up. She's now nine years old. Her parents don't have a clue what had to be done to make the latex-free environment for her operation.

Leo Schneid is 86 years old and a refugee from Hitler's Germany. A very wise old man and the father of a tennis friend of mine, Jay Schneid, who strings the racquets for all the pros. Leo has lost one eye to a vascular accident, and his remaining eye is developing a cataract. He was all excited today because his doctor has put him on an anti-cholesterol medication, and he knows this medication can sometimes increase cataract formation. In the last few months, he's sure his cataract has gotten worse because of the anti-cholesterol medication.

It took a long time to consult with Leo and to tell him the risks of his high cholesterol are worse than the acceleration of the cataract, and we're not even sure the cataract is being accelerated by the Zocor because he is 86 and his cataract is getting worse anyway. But he says he only has one eye, which is correct, and maybe the cataract wouldn't increase if he wasn't on the Zocor. So we went back and forth and down and around on the issue. I gave him my opinion, and he's going to make up his own mind whether to continue with it. He'd better.

I operated on Joseph Kanek's eye muscles for a cross-eyed condition last year, and his parents are always, always questioning me about how much stereo fusion he had. His eyes are straight, and he has some rudimentary stereo fusion, but he will never have 100 percent stereopsis because children who are born with an eye muscle problem almost never get that. But he's doing very well. The fusion will serve him well throughout his life. No, he won't be perfect, but for all intents and purposes he has some use of both eyes together and straight eyes and good vision in each eye, and he will keep it.

Cathryn Chen, a little Chinese girl from Chinatown, was only eight months old when I started to operate on her for a very severe head tilt due to a superior oblique palsy. I operated on her once; the head tilt came back. I operated on her a second time; the head tilt was better but not perfect. And now, at the age of 10, she has no head tilt anymore and a perfect result from superior oblique palsy. It's the kind of case where the parents just have no idea how difficult it is to eradicate a head tilt from a totally paralyzed superior oblique from infancy. First, I resected the superior oblique. Then I tucked the superior oblique. Then I recessed the antagonist inferior oblique. Then I went over to the other eye and recessed the inferior rectus. And now, she has a perfect result, which her parents, of course, expected all along. Expectations of surgery are so funny.

Bertha Dillingham came in because she couldn't use the contact lens for near vision that we prescribed for her five years ago. Amazing. I mean, she hasn't been seen in five years and she's disturbed that her mail order contact lens from the prescription I gave her five years ago is going to still be all right for near vision at the age of 51.

"Bertha, things change," I told her. "And besides, you should have been examined between five years ago and now, anyway. You're very nearsighted. You might have retinal tears or retinal holes. You can't just keep using the lenses that you have and re-ordering them for five years without being examined. Besides, the prescription has changed."

She got the message.

And then I saw Beulah Rostein, age 61. She's a -18.00 myope. This is so nearsighted that anything beyond two inches in front of her face is totally blurred, and she wants me to operate on her because she sometimes sees double. She does have a convergent strabismus. She could benefit from eye muscle surgery, but she isn't really aware of double vision very much and she's lived with it all her life. To run the risk of a retinal tear or a retinal detachment in such an unhealthy eye, with only a small chance of fully eradicating her double vision, is really not a good surgical risk. If I correct her for distance, I've done too much for what she needs at near; and if I correct her for near, I haven't done enough for what she needs at distance. At least she understood it. She's an Englishwoman; she's been to Harley Street consultants in London, she's been to our retinal specialists here in New York, she knows the risk, and she knows the presumed possible gain versus the retinal risk she carries with surgery. I put her off, and she wasn't unhappy with that. We'll keep checking her. If she shows a different clinical picture in six months, we might reconsider it. But I'm happy I could persuade her not to be operated on.

I've always been a reasonably aggressive surgeon with almost any kind of eye muscle problem. I have it fixed in my head that I can help anyone whose eye muscles are not just right, but sometimes being conservative is the better course of management.

Jennifer Snider came in for the first time. She is 51, a violinist with a severe thyroid condition. Thyroid patients are absolutely the worst. Her eyes were so exophthalmic, so proptotic she had to have an orbital decompression to give her more space in her orbit without causing damage to her optic nerve. As a result of the orbital decompression, her right eye dropped down in the orbit and is now in a lower position than the left eye. In addition, the right upper eyelid is retracted so you can see all kinds of white space above her eye between the eye and the right upper lid.

"It looks grotesque," she said. "Why can't you just elevate the right eye to bring it up higher so that it gets closer to my upper eyelid?"

I explained that if I did that, I would give her more vertical double vision than she already has, which is small. I spent almost an hour explaining to her the difference between an eyeball that's dropped down in the orbit and a vertical eye muscle imbalance with the muscle pulling the eye down, pointing in a downward direction. It's a very difficult concept to understand. She's got a little bit of a vertical misalignment, but she also has an eyeball that's lower in her orbit as a result of the decompression. She also has a horizontal misalignment. To examine a thyroid patient with eye muscle problems takes a very long time. I can't imagine how this is done in offices where the ophthalmologist sees 60 or 70 patients a day and can only spend 30 seconds with each patient. I sometimes have to spend an hour with each patient. The more patients seen, the more income.

I finally convinced her I was going to try some prism glasses because her actual misalignment is so small and it could be managed with prisms. Of course, she would rather be cured without having to wear any glasses with prisms in them, but in her case we have to try the prisms first and then see. If her misalignment is any greater, we might consider doing some surgery. So there she is—the eye is proptotic, the right upper lid is contracted, the eyeball is down too low in the orbit, and she has double vision in a horizontal and a vertical direction.

Eleanor Peterson still has an obstructed tear duct, even after I irrigated her tear duct two weeks ago. I shouldn't have to deal with her tear duct problem anyway because I operated on her for an eye muscle problem and, coincidentally, now I seem to have taken over her general eye care too. I did the tear duct obstruction and now I'm kind of stuck managing it. So today, I took a punctum dilator and opened it up on each side again a little bit, and we'll see how she does with that.

Marvin Ingram, 20, had a congenital cataract we removed and a divergent eye we straightened. He comes in for his periodic check-up because his good eye is nearsighted and we have to periodically refine his prescription. He's happy and he's studying and trying to make up his mind whether to go to medical school or to law school. I told him to stay with the law.

Ralph Roland, 80, wants me to operate on his large convergent misalignment. He's a retired doorman in New York City, and he has so many medical problems I really don't know about operating on him. I had him scheduled once before, only to cancel him because he was on an anticoagulant and I couldn't operate on him because of his thinned-out blood. If I did, I would have uncontrolled bleeding during the operation. He's only on Imdur and Bufferin and Furosimine and Zeroxoline and Cadur and Amiodurone and Digoxin and Cinometh and Reqif and Colase and Alprazalo—and some vitamins. He's got Parkinson's disease, he's got heart disease, he's got early colon cancer, he's got prostate cancer, he's got severe heart disease— and he wants me to operate on him for his eye muscles. I told him I would do it, and we will do it under local anesthesia and he'll have to stop his aspirin for two weeks before surgery. So here I've turned down Jennifer Snider for her thyroid myopathy and Beulah Rostein for her severe myopic retinal degeneration, and now I'm thinking of doing Ralph Roland with all his medical problems at the advanced age of 80.

Anyway, I saw a few other patients during the day, not of as much import as the ones I mentioned. I finished the day looking at Carol Hall, who's 10 months old and is scheduled for surgery tomorrow morning. She was born cross-eyed the same as her sister, and I operated on her sister last year. When I saw her in the waiting room, she was teary-eyed, and her nose was slightly runny. That meant she would be scratched for tomorrow morning, in spite of the fact the grandparents had been requisitioned to come to town to help take care of her, that the parents had to take off from work, and that all the arrangements had been made for surgery. But if there's a runny nose in a 10-month-old child, there isn't going to be any operation tomorrow morning. No one in his right mind would perform an elective operation on a 10-month-old child if even the slightest suspicion arose that she was developing a cold. Carol will be rescheduled in two weeks. The worst, most devastating thing that can happen is a respiratory cardiac problem in a little infant under anesthesia. Even in the best of circumstances there is a risk of a serious problem, so she was canceled on the spot.

Wednesday, January 20

We had only one patient on our operative schedule—Sarah Pache, from the upstate office. Her parents wanted the operation done at Manhattan Eye and Ear. Sarah is a very nice 10-year-old child from some Central American country who was adopted by parents living in a small town north of Brewster. I see this a lot—children from Korea or India or Romania who are adopted by white, middle-class American families. Sarah has an intermittent divergent deviation so well controlled it's difficult to elicit it on examination and to measure how large it can become. But at home sometimes, when she's relaxed, it becomes very large. This makes it difficult to decide on how much surgery to do because, if too much is done, she's going to be over-corrected and then she'll be cross-eyed because she will utilize all that control she's been using up to now and she won't know she doesn't have to do that anymore, but, if we don't do enough, the eye will drift out just the same as it always did when she's tired. So I did a small to moderate amount of surgery on her, the appropriate amount for what I thought she needed—4 mm on the lateral rectus and 4 mm on the medial rectus, hoping to not over-correct her. I won't know the result until I see her the day after tomorrow. I'm going to check her in the Brewster office rather than in the New York office the day following surgery as I usually do.

As I left the operating room, Marie Barnes, my trusted

surgical nurse who has been with me for many years, told me one of our other standby, stalwart nurses in the operating room, Louise, is retiring, and I gave her a little contribution for the retirement party. It seems that many of the staff have left or retired, and Manhattan Eye and Ear is certainly not what it was many years ago. Some nurses have been fired, a few like Louise are retiring, and the turnover in the staff, especially in the operating room, has given many of us on the board of surgeon directors some discomfort about the efficiency of the operating room staff.

I had plenty of free time this afternoon, so I came back to the office, and Arleen and I went through all my bookshelves and my desk to clean them up. It had not been done in 20 years, and the reason we did it was because my new computer—my first computer—is coming tomorrow morning and we had to get space ready for it on my desk. I am totally computer illiterate, and it is going to be a very, very nervous thing for me to enter the computer age. Many doctors my age have never gotten into computers. It might be one of the reasons several are in early retirement. I'm not there yet, and it's important for me to be on the internet, to become proficient online for things I want to look up, and to use e-mail. I'm going to be tutored by the man who is making the computer for me. The way I see it, if my sister, age 69, can learn to use a computer, then I think I can too.

Thursday, January 21

Usually on Thursday morning in the winter I run over to Chelsea Piers to hit some golf balls before we start in the office at one o'clock. I was ready to go this morning at 8:00 am. The phone rang. Little Jeremy Gross was horsing around with his brother and took a knee in his right eye. He was in a lot of pain and he was seeing black dots. So that was that for my hitting golf balls at Chelsea Piers. I told his mother to bring him right over to the office and I would see him when they arrived.

Fortunately, he did not have a hemorrhage inside his eye and did not have a fractured orbit. He did not have a dislocated lens, but he had a very severe corneal abrasion. I put some antibiotics in his eye and a pressure patch on his eye and told him he had to be seen tomorrow.

Two hours later, the phone rang again. Mrs. Gross reported that Jeremy had taken off his patch.

"Bring him back right away," I instructed her.

So Jeremy came back. He still had the corneal abrasion, but he doesn't like to wear the patch. So I gave him a prescription for artificial tear drops and antibiotic drops to use instead and I'll see him in a few days.

Then, we started our usual schedule at one o'clock with Alan Perkus, whom I've taken care of since he was a little child. He's now doing physics for the government at Los Alamos in

New Mexico.

I asked, "Alan, are you making any bombs yet?"

"No, they don't let me do that yet."

Then I saw Robert Puccello, whom I operated on last week. His eyes are straight, and he's using both eyes together. He is delighted.

Mildred Rutherford, also operated on last week, is doing well and does not have double vision anymore.

Mitchell Lavermann is a little bit of a problem. He's got the retraction syndrome, but hardly any turning of his face in order to use both eyes together. He's really doing very well, but his parents are extremely nervous and they transmit that to Mitchell. Well, I guess I know what being over-protective is like. He's doing fine. No more glasses, no more patches, no operation.

Dorsey Jenkins had an unfortunate problem following cataract surgery when the needle for the anesthetic used to numb the operated eye injured one of the eye muscles and caused the right eye to be in a contracted downward position. She has been seeing double ever since the otherwise uneventful cataract operation. I am considering surgery on her for her restrictive vertical imbalance and double vision, but she actually looked better today, so I'm going to put off the surgery and work with her orthoptically with some exercises and prisms for a while longer.

Ricky Stephens, age seven and one-half, came down from Albany for a second opinion because surgery was recommended for his convergent strabismus. I spoke to his mother for a long time and explained to her what he needed and that both eyes had to be done. A slight vertical problem needed a little attention, as did the cross-eyed condition. I told her the surgeon who would do the procedure in Albany was a friend and a colleague and an experienced surgeon. I hope I reassured her. I had no reason to suggest she do anything different.

Scott Hammon is 40 years old, and he had an automobile accident at the age of 20 that left him with a left hemiplegia and a partial IIIrd nerve paralysis of his left eye. He would like to have his eye straightened because the IIIrd nerve paralysis resulted in the eye being way out and way down. I'm going to consider the corrective surgery for him.

I saw a few others in follow-up—a few I'd operated on recently, a few who were operated on a few years ago. No real problems, except for Nancy Gronkowski's mother, who is worried about Nancy's eye being smaller as a result of surgery. Well, her eye isn't smaller, but she has a residual vertical deviation where the upper eyelid is a little bit lower because it follows the lower position of her eye. I could do nothing about that when I corrected her divergent deviation two weeks ago. As it is, it's so small nobody can really notice the eyelid is in a slightly lower position, except for her mother. I tried to reassure her Nancy was doing fine, which she actually is, and she no longer has her eye way out. She should be able to wear contact lenses and present herself to the world as a normal person pretty soon.

Next, I was very mad that one family who had made five appointments canceled because a couple of the kids are sick.

That left a gap of five appointments on our schedule. We hate to schedule more than two patients in any family, and I don't know how Amy got talked into scheduling five Farhadians, but they were canceled because two of them had a cold. Actually, I feel punk myself because I've got a cold, so I don't mind finishing up a little bit early. I'll go upstairs and try to nurse my cold, with Arleen's assistance.

My computer is installed. It's sitting in front of me on my desk. It's not on. I wouldn't have any idea even how to turn it on. The man is coming Monday to give me my first lesson.

As I walked out of the office Thursday evening, the young man who had been in the automobile accident was sitting in his wheelchair in the waiting room. He saw me as I was about to leave.

"Dr. Richards, I just want you to know it's a privilege for me to be taken care of by you," he said. He spoke with a slight stutter.

I looked at him, taken aback. "It's a privilege for me to be able to take care of you. I hope I can help you."

I went up to the apartment upstairs and I got right into bed. I was coughing almost every minute and feeling sicker and sicker as the evening went by. I knew I had picked up the flu virus from one of the kids who had been in on Monday, three days ago. I was just hoping it wouldn't be a bad case.

Friday morning, January 22

I felt awful. After breakfast, I managed to get into the truck and drive up to Brewster to start seeing patients at 8:30 am.

There were 22 children on the list for the morning. I couldn't stop coughing, no matter what I did, and the 22 patients were not easy to get through.

I started with Lizette Tompkins, who has had half of her brain removed for uncontrollable seizures from a congenital vascular abnormality of her brain and of her right eye—the Sturge-Weber syndrome. Lizette is never easy to examine. She is now seven years old. She has a visual field defect. She has optic atrophy in each eye. It is difficult to get her to read the eye chart and to try to show me what area of her visual field she can see from and what she can't. It's impossible to do a visual field test on her and it took quite a bit of time and energy to see her. And she was only one of the 22 patients.

I saw Sven Smith, grandson of one of my neighbors in the Sedgewood Club where I live up in Carmel. He's typical of many of the kids I see up in the Brewster office, because I know the parents and I run into the families in the store or in town and it's kind of a small-town practice.

Then I saw a little boy named Jimmy Malloy. I am the eighth doctor his father has sought out for his son. He got my name from the Best Doctor List in America and from his pediatrician, but he chose to see seven other doctors before eventually coming to see me, which has to tell me something about where I stood on his list of preferred choices to take care of his son. He came in and was very difficult. He didn't want my orthoptic technician to look at the boy, and he was rather defensive. He had a big belly, he was wearing a baseball hat, his pants belt was way below his belly and he was wearing a T-shirt. I explained to him that his son had low vision and nystagmus, which is shaking of the eyes, and he really needed to be worked up with an electroretinogram and other electrophysiologic studies. I told him it was not a good idea to keep taking his son from one doctor to another for radical treatments that had been recommended for his shaking eyes. I hope he took my advice, and I hope we can schedule an ERG on his son to try to figure out what's going on with his eyes.

I saw Michael Yeats, on whom I operated twice for a head tilt, one of the most complicated things we have to deal with. I saw Serafina Calafiore, who has juvenile rheumatoid arthritis, and sometimes such children can get an episode of iritis in their eyes. I look at her every three months to make sure she has no iritis. I saw Annie Brauner, daughter of one of our orthopedists in town, and we're working on her amblyopia with great co-operation.

When I finished, I was so sick I was beginning to shiver. There had been no cancellations, and I had seen 22 kids. I left the office at 12:30 pm and picked up Arleen at the train station at Brewster North, and we got home about 1. Climbing down the stairs from the driveway to our home wore me out. I was shivering so much I didn't think I would be able to make it into the house. And when I got upstairs and got into bed, I had shaking chills most of the afternoon. My hands and feet were so cold that not even an electric blanket could keep them warm. My temperature was over 102. I was coughing so badly I saw flashes of green light every time I coughed, and my headache screamed so that nothing, not even codeine, could help it. I couldn't sleep, and I just lay there in bed, miserable. At 11:30 at night, I got the message that a patient of mine whom I had seen during the week was at the New York Eye and Ear Infirmary with an acute attack of glaucoma. I had to deal with that on the phone.

Saturday, January 23

Arleen's birthday. It wasn't much of a birthday for either of us. She was about to become ill with the flu and I was already in the full throes of it, with no sleep, a terrible headache, no food, coughing, seeing flashes, and on the phone with my internist several times during the day. He prescribed Tylenol and codeine and Biaxin and a few other medications, and I was miserable. I spoke on the phone with the resident at the New York Eye and Ear Infirmary who had seen my patient with the acute glaucoma the night before. I told him to go ahead and do a laser iridotomy on the affected eye.

I was exhausted. In bed the whole day, I kept getting one phone call after another—from my son, Nick; from my friend, John Poster; from my friend, Herb Fitzgibbon; and now Arleen was sick and I was upstairs in bed, unable to get out of bed, and she was downstairs in her bed getting sicker and sicker and trying to take care of me. It was a horrible day.

Sunday, I was still unable to get out of bed. I was on the phone with my internist, Jeffrey Glick, several times. I couldn't eat, I was nauseated, and the headache was unbearable.

Monday, January 25

I spoke first thing to my associate, Scott Greenbaum, and told him about the patient with the acute glaucoma over the weekend and arranged for Scott to see him that morning. I called Amy and told her to cancel the office for Tuesday and to cancel surgery for Wednesday. It was the first time in more than 30 years I had ever had to cancel office hours or surgery because of illness. I had been scheduled to operate on the daughter of one of our administrators at the hospital. No way could I do it. I canceled the clinic. I canceled the office. I canceled the operating room.

Monday night, Richard Lewis called. He's one of my golfing buddies from across the lake at the club, and his son is a patient of mine. His son had been hit with a snowball in the eye, and he wanted to know what to do. I was lying in my bed in Carmel, and he was on Central Park West in New York City. I told him to put a patch on the eye and to take him to a colleague.

I was still far too sick to accept the invitation to the annual Super Bowl party in Great Neck. Every year, my close friend, Abby Siegel, has a Super Bowl party for all the old ex-tennis players, and we gather and watch the game and have a good time. This is the first year I had to miss it. I stayed home Sunday and watched the game from my armchair and wondered how I would be able to operate the next morning.

February

Monday, February 1

This would be the first day I had done any work in eight days, and I was scheduled to operate with Dr. Steven Greenberg, my young associate, up in Putnam Hospital, on two children. One was a patient of mine with a very divergent eye that does not see well because of optic nerve dysplasia. The other was a little girl Steven had sent me to see the week before who still required more surgery. We operated on both of them and got through it.

I wasn't sure we would be able to operate on the little girl because she had had a runny nose the day before, but she was clear at the time of surgery, and we went ahead with the procedure. I then drove into the city and saw some patients Monday afternoon, but I was exhausted. It really was too much for me to operate on two patients at Putnam and then drive into the city and see patients in the office in the afternoon, but I had missed so much that we didn't want to keep getting farther and farther behind.

The first patient was a very, very complicated little girl who had previous surgery elsewhere and had a vertical misalignment and a horizontal misalignment. She clearly needed more surgery, but even at my best it would take me a while to figure out what was going on with her ocular motility.

And I didn't have my orthoptist, Barbara, today either. So I had to see all the patients myself, which meant putting in the drops and doing all the things she usually does to help me, including getting the history and the visual acuity. I got more and more exhausted and a bigger and bigger headache as the afternoon wore on.

I saw an adult patient who keeps coming back with a contact lens-related problem. I don't deal with contact lenses anymore, and it was just a complete drain on my energy to have to help her with a persistent contact lens problem unrelated to anything I'm doing these days.

When I finally got through the trying schedule, I made it upstairs to the apartment and collapsed. I stayed in bed for 13 hours, until Tuesday morning.

Tuesday, February 2

I came downstairs at 8:00 am and started our regular schedule, 17 patients from 8:00 am until 1:30 pm. I soon grew totally exhausted. Several patients were children, some of them with severe neurologic abnormalities.

Philip Krumel has a trisomy chromosomal abnormality and significant neurologic deficit, and Adam Reifsnyder has a head tilt and needs an operation on his superior oblique tendon.

Sylvia Hollander, 75 years old, has an eye muscle disorder with double vision, swelling on one side of her face, several unconnected symptoms, and signs which might require an MRI or might require other diagnostic tests. I take it upon myself to not order every test in the book on her, although

I'm never sure; maybe I should order something that might uncover a problem. On the other hand, she's had most of these things for many, many years and seems to still be quite healthy, so I take the burden of her undiagnosed conditions upon myself rather than put her through every expensive test there is.

When I finished, I came back up to the apartment and slept through the afternoon. I had a very important surgical schedule for Wednesday, and I wanted to get as much rest as possible. I didn't go to the clinic. I didn't go to grand rounds. I didn't do anything except go upstairs and rest.

Wednesday, February 3

I was to operate on a 10-month-old child whose sister I had operated on for a convergent strabismus a year ago. Ten months is very young to do a child with strabismus, but they have to be done early in order to give them any chance to develop binocular fusion. So we do them at about 10 months of age, although the anesthetic risks are much greater in infants than in older children. She is the little girl we had canceled because of a runny nose last week. I called the anesthesia department, told them I wanted one of the best stalwart, experienced anesthesiologists. Happily, I was sent Paul Dilecki, who has a great deal of skill and experience. We operated on little Carol Hall, and the procedure went beautifully until the very end.

I had finished and had taken my gloves off, and was just

sitting watching the end of the anesthetic as Dr. Dilecki was skillfully bringing her out of anesthesia. In spite of all precautions, she went into a laryngospasm, and her oxygen saturation went straight down from 100 percent. He held her in hyperextension with her chin up and the mask up and broke the laryngospasm. I don't think I took a breath for the next few seconds—which seemed an eternity—although I exhaled deeply when her oxygen saturation immediately went back up to 100 percent. It's the kind of problem that can happen in spite of the greatest prevention, in spite of all precautions. A child can go from perfect into serious danger in a moment. She did well and recovered beautifully. I'm going to see her Thursday in the office. How much of this averted catastrophe should I tell her parents? Enough to forewarn them about any future surgery, not so much to put them in a panic.

The next operation was on Michael Patagliota, who had a very severely convergent eye from infancy. After that, I had to help Gupta, my second-year resident, do a service case on a five-year-old boy with a gigantic divergent deviation. So many times, the service cases are neglected, and this little boy went from being an intermittent divergent deviation to being a constant one. He really should have been operated on while he was still intermittent. In the private sphere, he might have been, but sometimes clinic patients do not have as good an attendance record and don't get the care prescribed at the optimum time. At any rate, it wasn't too late, and I helped Gupta operate on this little boy to straighten his eyes. Surgical patients from the clinic often have some insurance, which helps pay the surgeon's fee, usually less than the ordinary private fee. Sometimes they do not, in which case the attending surgeon receives no fee. This system has had little change until the past few years. Now, because large corporations have taken over many voluntary hospitals, the financing of clinic patients operations is different, and different with each of the governing corporations.

Gupta is on the eye muscle service now, and I supervised his surgery (I'm the responsible surgeon and he is the resident, and I supervised and helped him to perform the procedure; I do whatever is necessary myself, if required). Gupta is an excellent resident with excellent hands, and he is going to become a very fine eye surgeon in short order. Fortunately for me, he was the resident today, because some residents are not as capable and I have to do a great deal of the procedure, and I have to be on such guard against a mistake that surgery becomes a very tedious situation. If the resident has good hands and good surgical instincts, it's a pleasurable experience supervising in surgery. But if the resident does not have good hands and does not have good surgical instincts, it can be a very, very trying experience. I'm sure I had more patience 30 years ago than I do now, although I have more experience now, but sometimes it's a good situation and sometimes it isn't. Fortunately, on Wednesday it was good.

After surgery, I came back to the apartment and collapsed again and went straight to bed. I got out of bed at five to go over to the City Athletic Club because my friend, Leslie Pollack, a big organizer of the American Jewish Historical

Society, Sports Division, was hosting a big cocktail party. Dick Schaap presided. Dick is a famous sportscaster, and we're good friends. Dick had a very bad eye injury last year, and I helped him a little bit at the hospital. He was the master of ceremonies, and they introduced a bunch of the more famous Jewish athletes of the past and the present, and they included me. A lot of my old friends were there, and it was the first time I had really been out of the house, except for doing some work in the office and the operating room for a couple of weeks, since my illness. Everybody said how thin my face looked, and I guess it did because the flu took 10 pounds from me.

By Thursday I was feeling a little bit better and more like my old self. Maybe I was feeling better because Wednesday night at the Jewish Historical Society party I had had my first drink of vodka in 10 days. I usually never go a day in my life without having some vodka with my dinner. Maybe I'm on the mend.

Thursday, February 4

Amy called me upstairs at noon to say that Michael Patagliota was already here. We operated on him yesterday for a very large convergent deviation. I came downstairs early and saw him, and when I took the patch off he became light-headed and felt like he was going to pass out.

This sometimes happens. It's a vasovagal reaction, a fight-or-flight reaction, and sometimes the patient can lose consciousness completely, so I laid him down flat and made him take some deep breaths. Fortunately, his eye looked very good and was in good position. He's no longer so horribly cross-eyed. I sent him home with some drops and some ointment and I'll see him next week.

Carol Hall, the 10-month-old child on whom I operated yesterday, looked like she had never been operated on as far as any swelling or redness goes. That happens with 10-month-olds in comparison to older children and adults. Her eyes were absolutely straight. Her parents came with 12 beautiful yellow roses for me, and they are truly very grateful we brought her through the surgery safely and her eyes are so perfectly straight the next day. This is what it's all about. This is what we do this kind of work for and why we keep on doing it, so I was delighted she looked as wonderful as she did.

Then I began to see the usual schedule of patients and, although I had reasonable energy in the beginning, by 5:00 pm I was wiped out. I guess it just shows me I'm not totally recovered from this devastating flu just yet.

I saw Leonard Lehrer, the famous American artist, who needed a slightly stronger prescription. I had to study him because he's recently been diagnosed with diabetes. However, his eyes are not suffering from any diabetic changes.

I saw Marlo Goodman, who is 27 years old and really should have her intermittent divergent deviation operated on because it's too much for her to handle on her own. Whenever she relaxes a little bit, one eye or the other drifts way, way out.

Esther Ringel is a six-year-old girl with a lot of farsightedness and a small amount of convergent strabismus.

Another ophthalmologist suggested she have surgery. She could have some surgery, but I think it's more important right now to work on her vision and have her wearing the appropriate glasses and do the appropriate patching for a small degree of amblyopia.

I saw several other kids, none of them with any significant problems. I finished the day at five o'clock, again ready to go upstairs and collapse. I'm not looking forward to tomorrow. I looked at the schedule up in Brewster, and there are 20 more kids to be seen in that office in the morning.

March

Thursday, March 4

Barbara Schneekloth, our orthoptist, is on vacation this week, so I had to see all the patients myself. I have to do a lot more work in Barbara's absence because I have to do everything on them. It's exhausting.

At one o'clock, I saw Steven Hammon, on whom I operated yesterday, and when I got his left upper eyelid open (it was quite swollen) I found his eyes in good alignment, so I was very pleased. Of course, I wasn't happy he had so much swelling, but anytime you work on the superior oblique tendon there is always a lot of swelling. I have him on an antibiotic by mouth. He had no corneal abrasion. He looked fine, and all in all I was pretty pleased with the way I saw him on the first day after surgery.

Then I saw 20 patients by myself, among them Jennifer Wallin, on whom I operated for Duane's syndrome (both eyes). Jennifer is unusual because both she and her sister have Duane's retraction syndrome. We might want to get some blood from them and see if we can find the gene on which Duane's syndrome is located. Lucy Barnhart is one year old and now she needs the same operation for Duane's syndrome because she's got a big turn of her face to the left side.

Thelma Rattner is 69 and was in my sister's class at Forest Hills High School. I have taken care of her for a long time too. And then I saw Joanna Land and Rachel Thompson. Both

Rachel and Thelma have had surgery twice. They looked good.

It was just exhausting to see so many patients in a row and to have to do it myself, but we finished at 5:30 pm. I'm by myself tonight because Arleen took the puppy and Lily up to the country, so it's take-out time—rather, delivery take-out time. I'll just relax and drive up to see 20 more kids at Putnam Hospital in the morning.

Steven Hammon's father brought in the medical reports from his accident 20 years ago. The accident occurred on Route 6, right in Carmel, in the town in which I live.

Amazing. Three different doctors told his father there was little hope for Steven, but his father persisted and Steven is now walking with some help. He's having other things attended to, such as the eye surgery I just performed. Steven owes a lot to his father for doggedly pushing his rehabilitation.

Steven's father had been told by some people just to put Steven in a nursing home and forget him. His father wasn't about to do that, and Steven's made a lot of progress in the past 20 years. His father also brought in an article from the newspaper with pictures of Steven and him and some of the steps along the way in his long rehabilitation. I'm glad I was able to help him a little bit with his eyes.

Friday, March 5

I drove up at 7:00 am in the morning to start seeing patients in Brewster at 8:30 am. The first patient was Steven Marcello, on whom I've operated twice—once for an esotropia in early childhood and the second time for a secondary exotropia when his eyes started to drift out. Steven's doing well. He doesn't have much fusion, so his eyes are a little divergent for distance, a little convergent for near, but essentially straight, and he's got good vision in each eye. He only needs to wear glasses for reading because of his astigmatism.

I saw Daniel O'Connor, a young man on whom I operated when he was very little and then on whom our pediatric Fellow and I operated on recently in the city because he only has Medicaid now at the age of 21. He's doing well, except he's now got a conjunctival cyst in his right eye as a result of the last surgery we did. I'm just going to watch it. If it's not any smaller in six months I'll have to go after it.

The most difficult patient was Carlton Roseboro, the young man with a tumor of the cavernous sinus which we've watched for several years. About six months ago, at the age of 13, he underwent neurosurgery. In the effort to take most of the tumor (which turned out to be a meningioma) out of his cavernous sinus, bleeding occurred at the carotid artery and at a little aneurysm behind the carotid artery. He was left with a hemiparesis on the left side and some difficulty with speech. This was the first time I had seen him since his neurosurgery. His speech has recovered, but he still has a little bit of left-sided weakness in his arm and his leg. He has been getting rehab, and I hope he continues to improve.

There is still residual tumor in the cavernous sinus. It's still entwined around the carotid artery and he is still being evaluated by several different specialists, including a neuro-ophthalmologist and neurologist at New York University, the neurosurgeons at New York University and at New York Medical College, and he's been seen in consultation with several top neurologists and neuro-radiologists on the East Coast. I might present his case again at our dinner at Manhattan Ophthalmological Society, where I presented him three years ago.

I left the office at one and went to hit some golf balls. The weekend promises snow, so I tried to get outside for a little while before the snow came.

Tuesday, March 9

We started seeing patients as usual at 8:00 in the morning. Maria Bolles is a college professor who had the sudden onset of what sounded like a cerebrovascular accident some months ago. One neurologist said she had an abnormality of her cavernous sinus. Another neurologist said she had a hemorrhage. She got better on her own, with no treatment, and she seems to be doing well.

Young Yale Shonzeit complained of seeing blobs in front of her eye and also blurred vision. She said she saw things floating by—not exactly floating but going along wherever she looked. She's only eight years old and it's sometimes hard to evaluate a child's symptoms. What might be vitreous floaters or might be a scotoma of some kind or another is very difficult to elicit by history. Most of the time, you don't see anything when you look in, so it's difficult to make the diagnosis. Her mother was the photographer for my book on strabismus and is back in the business of photography after having four children.

The daughter of my dear friend Len Rosen came in. She is upset with me for some unknown reason even though I helped her out during an emergency with her eyes. She's 30 years old. She's in graduate school and is a wonderful young woman, but it annoys me that she is mad at me and I don't know why. Len is the most irascible human being I've ever met. How he has three such nice daughters and a wonderful wife nobody seems to be able to understand.

Paulina Patel, only a year-and-a-half old, came in with an obvious Duane's syndrome and no ability to move her left eye past the center position and a face turn to the left. She's seen two other ophthalmologists. One said she had a Duane's syndrome and one said she had nothing. I am often the third one to make the judgment.

It's a very common situation. They see two or three others before they end up seeing me and then, finally, when they see me I tell them the same as maybe one or two of the others have, and then they're satisfied that's what the child has.

Rachel Adler wouldn't let me put the drops in her eyes, which is a little bit unusual for a 13-year-old. She should have the drops because I have to do a complete exam on her. She's got double vision and a turn of her eyes. She was tough. Sometimes 13-year-old kids can be tough.

I had some soup at my desk, and then I went to the clinic at the hospital to help the residents see a few patients in the muscle clinic. A very nice young resident who came from India was very anxious to learn how to use the retinoscope properly. I took a lot of time working with him to help him master the technique of figuring out whether a child is farsighted, nearsighted, or with astigmatism just by shining a shadow across the retina. He was very appreciative of the time and experience I gave him to help him learn how to use the scope.

I didn't stay for grand rounds. Instead, I came back to the office and frustrated myself for an hour trying to work my new computer. For someone my age, it's like learning a new language. I sat there trying to get on the internet to a chat room with other ophthalmologists, and I couldn't do it. I need a little coaching.

Wednesday, March 10

This morning we only had one case—Sam Kramer, 47, whose eye could intermittently go out 60 prism diopters, which is a gigantic turn, and then he can control it and pull his eyes straight. Most of the time, he walks around not controlling it and his eye is way, way out. I operated on him. He was scheduled for surgery three years ago and he chickened out, deeply nervous about the possibility of double vision following surgery. My pediatric Fellow, Michelle McLeod, helped me do the case.

It was a little bit complicated because he had had a

tracheotomy in childhood and his trachea was very, very small, with a stricture. An adult endotracheal tube couldn't be passed into his trachea to administer anesthesia. It took a great deal of effort to push vigorously a much smaller tube past his stricture into his trachea. The case went well, but I'll be anxious to see what he looks like post-operatively because he had such a big misalignment and he had such good control over it.

I hit a few golf balls at Chelsea Piers and got back to midtown in time to keep my appointment with my internist, Dr. Jeffrey Glick. I hadn't had a check-up in a few years and it was time for me to be checked over. Medical offices are so much different today than 10 years ago. A receptionist greeted me; a nurse took me into a room, blood work was done, along with urinalysis and chest x-ray; and then Dr. Glick came into the room and we sat and talked for 15 or 20 minutes as he tried to elicit what problems I might be having medically or otherwise. The biggest problem he came up with was I seemed a little bit depressed, and we talked about the possibility of going on one of the antidepressants, like Wellbutrin.

His partner, Steve Fochios, the president of our medical board at Manhattan Eye and Ear, came in and we talked about golf a little bit and also about the possibility of my being on something to help my decaying mood these days. I think my mood is primarily related to finances. I haven't sold the house, and it's a big nut to pay for the expenses of that house with the diminished income we're experiencing. I'm still one of the most respected eye muscle surgeons in the city, and yet, with the reimbursements being so low, with everybody being on managed care—having to go to the doctors on their plan—and the dwindling down of private practice, I just don't make enough money to comfortably live a normal life and pay almost $70,000 to maintain my house.

My chest x-ray was okay; my cardiogram was okay; my echocardiogram was okay; my mood is not so great.

When I got home, Arleen showed me a book of drug interactions. The book warned against taking these antidepressants combined with alcohol. Well, I have two vodkas every night, religiously, and I'm not going to stop that. I don't want to get a seizure either—one of the remote complications of Wellbutrin—so it looks like I'll have to deal with my mood without specific serotonin re-uptake inhibitors. We shall see.

A reflection on managed care:

"We do more, and our codes provide less remuneration. I am thinking of dropping out of Medicare, but I can't give up on so many patients I have had in my practice for so many years. That is a potential downside. I do want to maintain our practice because (my son) Nico will be joining us in about a year and three months. He will be part of VRMNY (Vitreous, Retina, Macula Consultants of New York), but I think he aspires to be more like Stan Chang than me... surgical, not medical, retina. To date, he has written 56 papers, virtually all in prestigious, peer-review journals. (My *name is only on two of them.) So, he is headed for an academic career, and managed care will be more meaningful to him than to me. My approach to all changes in the medical and economic environment is influenced by our partnership and practice. My solution is avoidance behavior. I try to insulate myself as much as I can from the burden of code interpretation and regulation and stick to teaching, research, and patient care. My motto, which I pass on to all our Fellows, is, "Only consider doing what is in the best interest of your patient... always."*

Lawrence A. Yannuzzi, MD

Larry has published hundreds of scientific papers and 14 textbooks. He has won every medal in retina in the world. He is director of the Retinal Research Center of the Manhattan Eye, Ear and Throat Hospital and founder and president of the Macula Foundation. When he was a resident, he came to me one day and said, "Dr. Raskind, do you think we can start a fluorescein clinic here at the hospital?"

What he was talking about was a new modality that involved injecting fluorescein dye into the venous system of a patient and then to image the vasculature in the retina—the beginning of understanding macular degeneration.

I said, "Go for it," and we had some of the first fluorescein angiograms in the world.

For this section on managed care, I have called on a number of my colleagues for their input. Their thoughts on managed care are expressed in their own words. Managed care is a critical issue facing the medical world, the insurance providers, and the patients. I do not pretend to know what changes are coming, but changes are coming, for better or for worse.

What I know most about managed care is that it has affected the financial aspect of my private practice of ophthalmology (however, hopefully not the actual examining and treating of patients). During my entire life in medicine, I never knew much about the financial compensation I received for my work—not as a training resident, nor when I was in the U.S. Navy Medical Corps, nor when I was in private practice. Someone else always gave me a check and that was it, even when I owned my own practice and was the employer, and especially when I eventually became an employee. In my own practice, fees collected for service were transferred to the bank; my office manager, Arleen, and my accountant, Paul Grayson, put together my taxes. Arleen paid the bills and made sure money was in the bank for me to spend as I wished—until there wasn't any.

Call me an *idiot savant* if you like. It is not that I don't like money—I just have no aptitude for the financial side of my medical career. Would I have been better off as a salaried employee from the start? Probably yes. However, when I started to practice ophthalmology in the 1960s, the norm was to go into private practice, and so I did. I only learned about the business of medicine when I had to, and when managed care came along I had to learn something about it. Not that I hadn't heard of the concept. I had because my father was involved in one of the earliest managed care organizations. It just did not apply to me when I started my first private office in 1968 on Park Avenue at 63rd Street in New York City, two blocks from my hospital—Manhattan Eye Ear and Throat

Hospital on 64th Street—where I had trained.

Managed care simply means prepaid healthcare. It is not exactly health insurance in that it does not protect from financial loss. The term emphasizes the care provided. In the early years of the past century, long before this diary of 1999, there were two types of managed care, both created by providers' desire to protect their income.

One was the HMO (health maintenance organization) that charged a pre-set amount of money per member for services performed at its facility and at the doctors' offices. It was called capitation.

The second was early Blue Cross and Blue Shield organizations started for teachers, with services provided by contracted community doctors and hospitals. Blue Cross (each state in the USA has its own) started in 1929 and provided hospital-associated in-patient care—prepaid. Blue Shield paid doctors' fees and other services. Both BC and BS relied on independent private practices rather than employing physicians.

In the beginning of prepaid medical group practices, doctors were expelled from their county medical societies for joining. My father did not get expelled from the Queens County (NYC) Medical Society for joining one in the early 1940s, but he never became president of the Society, on which track he was slated for election.

The most famous and one or the earliest prepaid medical practices, and still in operation in the 21st century, was the Kaiser Foundation plan, also known as Kaiser-Permanente in California. It was started in 1937. On the East Coast, Group Health Association, a non-profit consumer cooperative, started in Washington, D.C. Both engendered expulsions from medical societies and revoking of physicians' hospital privileges. However, by the 1960s, Kaiser had survived and was more accepted by doctors' societies. When I was the resident instructor at Manhattan Eye and Ear in 1967, when almost all graduating residents went into private practice, two of my residents opted for careers with Kaiser—Arnold Smoller in the group in San Francisco and Peter Rosen in the one in San Diego—no hassle with private practice, no hiring, firing, billing, collecting, fighting with insurance companies. Both enjoyed long careers with Kaiser.

In 1942, Congress passed the Wage Stabilization Act, which set wage and price controls. The Hospital Insurance Plan (HIP) was formed in New York City to provide medical coverage for New York City employees. It was regulated by the State of New York. My father joined it as an orthopedist in order to see more patients with orthopedic conditions. He did not get many referrals in the private sector from other physicians because he had never taken an orthopedic residency and was not board-certified. (Note: see my reflections after the July 28 diary entry for an explanation). In HIP, he took care of only orthopedic patients. He joined two groups in HIP—one in Flushing, Queens, and another nearer his office in Long Island City, Queens. Being in HIP afforded him a large orthopedic practice. However, the price he paid for joining a prepaid medical group was dear—socially, among his peers, and the majority of his community's doctors; more about that in my reflections after the July 28 diary entry.

Early HMOs like HIP had their own medical staffs. In the 1950s, a new form of HMO started—the IPA (Independent

Practice Association). In the IPA, the HMO contracted directly with private physicians. HIP has continued, however, and is alive today, having joined together with Group Health Insurance as Emblem Health.

Big changes in healthcare delivery came just when I finished my training in ophthalmology in the 1960s. These changes were huge but hardly affected me because I was in the Navy on active duty from 1963 to 1965 (a real managed care delivery of healthcare, one might say) and then in 1966 I was taking my Fellowship in strabismus (my expenses paid for by a private organization, the Heed Foundation). It wasn't until I returned to MEETH as resident instructor and started to see private patients as well that I became just a little aware of the huge milestone in healthcare that had started in 1964, created and organized by President John F. Kennedy, and then after his death, by Lyndon Baines Johnson—MEDICARE. First, Medicare for the elderly, and then Medicaid for low-income patients. Both hospital and physician services were included. It was the start of the third party payment system that severed the financial link between provider and patient. And it was the start of healthcare cost inflation with both an increase in price and utilization.

I don't remember many details of that era. There were lots of amazing stories in those days. One of the residents' jobs was to collect eyes for the Eye Bank. When somebody would die, we would rush over to the funeral parlor or the home, wherever, take out the eye, and bring it to the Eye Bank. Often we were running around the city with bottles of eyes in our cars.

I remember one time making rounds with Byron Smith. Like in the old London hospitals, the doctors would walk around in single file behind the chief. When I was his resident, I would escort him to the door on Friday nights when he left. "Good night, Dr. Smith. I'll see you on Monday," was my usual send off.

Residency in ophthalmology in my time might not have been too different from the present—outpatient clinic supervised by an attending surgeon. The training by these doctors was the best in the country:

Byron Smith, the father of oculoplastic surgery; Dr. Charles Kelman revolutionized cataract surgery with his work on phacoemulsification and replacement of the cataract lens; Dr. David Sudarsky taught the new scleral buckle operation for retina detachment; Dr. R. Townley Paton, who did the first corneal transplant at MEETH and started the first eye bank in the country, and Dr. Harold Whalley Brown, director of the Eye Muscle Clinic and my first professor in strabismus.

I would badger him on exactly what procedure I should do on the patients scheduled for surgery and he would say, "You take the muscles off the eye, you set the eye straight, and you put the muscles back on."

Byron Smith did his first experiments on blowout fractures in the surgical dissection area in the basement at MEETH. A blowout fracture occurs when a batted or thrown ball blows out a hole in the floor of the orbit and creates a fracture. Bryon was the first to describe it.

I do remember that era was the beginning of pre-certification. For the first time in the '70s, when I was building my practice, doctors were required to get a treatment or an operation pre-certified by a third party (MD, staff, or agent of an insurance company). Like a second opinion, but for financial approval. When some of my patients had Oxford Insurance, Arleen had to ask for approval from an Oxford ophthalmologist, who was usually a general ophthalmologist—most of them cataract surgeons who knew nothing about the surgery I did on eye muscles—hired by Oxford to make these decisions. One time after getting a refusal from Oxford, I called up the Oxford consultant and suggested in semi-polite, for me, language that he was duplicitous. He reversed himself and gave the approval. Arleen remembers that once a secretary at Oxford in charge—not the hired Oxford ophthalmologist—refused approval for surgery on a patient with double vision and severely misaligned eyes.

First, the secretary had said, "Did you try everything else?"

Arleen said, "Yes."

She told Arleen, "Well, maybe he can get used to it."

If that same secretary had ever had to see an ophthalmologist for that same problem and he had told her to just get used to it, I wonder what she would have said.

Pre-certification was one part of the problem of increased healthcare costs in the '70s and '80s, with the rise in managed care. Some HMOs became prepaid medical group practices and preferred provider organizations. Hospitals and MDs were trying to control the costs of healthcare. The third-party payment system was severing the financial link between the provider of service and the patient. By the end of the '70s, Medicare, Medicaid, or private insurance provided most healthcare.

When I started to write my diary of 1999, some MDs had already started to move away from solo practice to form private groups of physicians. And hospital consolidation occurred, with rises in hospital prices. Hospital and health system mergers grew. In this environment, the financial struggles of my hospital, MEETH, increased—leading to the crisis involving its impending demise. Consolidation included firms becoming multi-state instead of just one-state—like United Health Care—and, importantly, converting from not-for-profit to for-profit organizations. By 1999, patients involved in managed care had increased from three million to 80 million. Integrated delivery systems had become established. Even Blue Cross and Blue Shield had become for-profit.

I had little awareness of these changes in healthcare delivery in 1999. All I knew was managed care was shrinking my income and making solo private practice a losing financial proposition. Its most significant effect was this: When I started private practice, the patient was responsible for the fee for service. If the patient had insurance, he or she would communicate with the insurance company for the recovery of part or all of my fee, but it was the patient's responsibility. In the era of managed care, it was my office that had to communicate with the patient's insurance company to recover the fee. If the service was approved, whatever fee the insurance company stipulated for that service was what I received. In the days before managed care, the fee for an eye muscle operation on a child with crossed eyes might be $4,000. That was the fee, regardless of what the parents' insurance, if they had any, would pay them. The amount actually paid was between the doctor and the patient. In the days of managed care, where the insurance company's fee would be accepted as total payment, if I were on that plan—for instance, Oxford—my fee of $4,000 usually came to be $1,000, which Oxford dictated for that operation. And that is what I was paid. That much about managed care I knew.

How much does managed care differ from doctor to doctor?

I remain very close to Steven Greenberg, first a postgraduate Fellow with me in pediatric ophthalmology at MEETH, my surgical partner when we operated at Putnam Hospital, and junior author of my textbook on strabismus surgery. Steve is an excellent tennis player (it was said I selected only Fellows who were good tennis players). He joined WestMed, one of the largest group practices with many specialties, a few years ago after many years as a partner in a small group practice. He just sees the patients now. Everything else is done for him. He suffers through having to do all electronic chart and record keeping; otherwise he loves it.

"I basically grew up in the managed care era," Steve told me recently. "I remember the staff meetings at United Hospital when I first went into practice where the established physicians were seeing the demise of medicine with the entry of managed care. As a participant with plans early on, it did not take long to establish a busy practice. I was never one to dwell over managed care contracts, or pick and choose."

He is now happily in a large group that does all that for him.

That coin has another side.

"Private doctors are being put out of business due to stupid bureaucracies," Larry Parsont told me. "We cannot afford our medical offices, which are only zoned for medicine. We need rent

stabilization if you expect us to accept Medicare or insurance. Soon, institutions which run impersonal clinics will take over. Did people think NYU dropped tuitions for medical student altruistically? Really? They are a business and now have well-educated young doctors to run their clinics at a bargain salary. System broken. I could fix it with a Medicare-for-all system, but it will not be free."

Like Larry, my friend David Haight—one of the preeminent corneal surgeons in NYC—doesn't mince words when he talks about his feelings.

"Managed care has severely disrupted the normal doctor-patient relationship," he says. *"We now have insurance company bureaucrats deciding what treatment and what medications are appropriate for our patients. In effect, they are practicing medicine without a license and forcing the physician providers to comply with their rules. In recent years, they have also shifted a substantial portion of the financial responsibility to the patient. Many patients now have extremely high deductibles, which, on top of the monthly premiums, make it almost impossible for patients to actually seek medical care even if they are nominally insured."*

David is no fan of government interference, which he says has made things even worse.

"The Affordable Care Act has prevented many of my established patients from continuing under my care. With the institution of the ACA, their existing plans were canceled because they were non-compliant with the ACA rule. The insurance companies created new replacement plans, which they forced the patients to take. In many cases, however, the insurance companies excluded me from participating in these plans while at the same time retaining me

as a provider in their commercial lines. Clearly, this was a form of discrimination aimed at controlling utilization in the lower-cost ACA plans. Many patients are now worse off under the ACA than prior to its existence. The ever-declining reimbursements for healthcare providers coupled with the continued upward spiral of overhead costs is rapidly destroying private practice medicine as we know it."

Larry Turtel, a former Fellow and still a close friend, runs a private practice in New Jersey. Larry is often on the state's Best Doctors list, and he wrestles daily with managed care.

"We've been with it so long," he said. *"Every single patient that comes in has a discussion about their insurance. This has become routine, so we are used to it."*

The years that he has been in managed care have not made the plans less erratic and confusing.

"Is the visit covered by their eye insurance—VSP, Davis, whatever—or their medical insurance, or both? Accommodative esotropes have the exam covered by medical and the refraction through their vision plan. Nobody really understands it, and the insurances are inconsistent.

"When patients don't have vision insurance but do have medical insurance, they get angry if we diagnose myopia and don't create a medical diagnosis. So you either are a creative liar or have an unhappy patient.

"When patients have a lower copay for their vision care plan than their medical, they ask you to not code their diabetes or whatever and just go with a vision plan diagnosis. So we need a whole team of people to deal with this.

"It's never really clear whether to use consult code, medical code, or vision code. I mean, how do you code an autistic child who nobody else can examine, who ends up being well?"

A problem that comes up a lot is ineffective communication.

"A patient calls the insurance company," Larry said, *"and asks if routine vision is covered. The insurance company answers yes. The patient comes in for an exam, but we don't accept that particular vision plan."*

Who does the patient blame? "The patient always gets upset with us."

Another problem is trying to decipher meaning. For example, he said Horizon has a zillion different plans for which the particulars are not specified on their cards. *"Takes forever to figure it out."*

He has emerged victorious in numerous battles, but it is a never-ending war. *"I have been audited several times, won each one, but I have had to spend many hours writing letters."*

He said just getting approval for special testing (such as MRIs) can take him and his staff hours. He said he once spent an evening getting approval for a retinoblastoma.

"The managed care in this area is impossible to communicate with," he told me. *"They will not negotiate or answer you unless you send a letter of resignation... I could go on and on."*

So could Richard Gibralter. The "rock doc" has had two aces in golf, like me, so we address each other as Ace and Ace Two. He is in private practice in New York City—an outstanding cataract and cornea specialist, graduate of residency at MEETH, then on the board of surgeon directors with me. He is in charge of the history of MEETH—recently published—which delves into the crisis of the hospital failing. That's a story we'll get to in a little bit.

Larry and Ace tell the same story. Their stories are like mine, only they know the details. I always had someone—Arleen when we were at 40 Park, and then the business manager for Harvey Rosenblum when I was at 220 Madison Avenue, and then Hal Farquhar in Brewster, and now Dawn Rush in Yorktown Heights. I always leave the business end of my practice to someone else. Always.

"Managed care has driven a wedge between the patient and the treating physician," Richard said. "It has been a failure at containing costs and has degraded the physician's ability to act as an advocate for the patient. Pre-authorizations for testing and procedures, as well as approval for medications, are tedious and take additional resources."

Again, communication is an issue in this high-tech age.

"Several pharmaceutical plans approve only their panel of drugs for coverage," Ace told me. "This information is often difficult to access.

"Often we are called, with the patient telling us the drop we prescribed is 250 dollars but we can substitute the equivalent with two drops with no copay. Alternatively, we are called saying there is no coverage for a rather basic medication previously approved. Electronic medical records were supposed to provide better linkage of information among hospitals and doctors. Now physicians spend more time inputting data into templates. The systems do not communicate, are expensive, and require constant upkeep

and support. EMR has been said to be responsible for increased physician burnout and a decreased satisfaction with a doctor's chosen profession."

Robins Tien, one of my former Fellows at MEETH and, like Steven Greenberg and Larry Turtel, an outstanding tennis player, is the chief of pediatric ophthalmology at the University of Rhode Island Hospital in Providence. His father is Chinese, his mother English. He and I presented a paper together at the AAPOS meeting some years ago, and more recently he coordinated with AAPOS and the People's Republic of China Medical Society to bring pediatric ophthalmology to China for the first time and to set up training of pediatric ophthalmology specialists in Beijing and throughout China. His experience with managed care in Rhode Island is very much the same.

"Managed care, ugh. Lifespan, the hospital corporation/chain that dominates Rhode Island, is attempting to become a soup-to-nuts health system complete with its own employed doctors, or rather providers. For a private practice like mine which depends on referrals, the Lifespan in-house pediatricians are required to refer to Lifespan's in-house ophthalmologists, thereby decreasing referrals to my practice. In the last four years, Lifespan hired two just-trained pediatric ophthalmologists, doubling the number of pediatric ophthalmologists in Rhode Island. They are very unbusy but well paid. New doctors are flocking to these types of jobs with good pay and easy work—about 1/2 to 1/3 the patient volumes seen by my partner and me (they do so little surgery I wonder how they can keep their skills up). For the time being they are sitting pretty, but eventually, I assume, the diseconomies of scale will catch up

with them and salaries will be cut. Experience, reputation, talent, and surgical skill mean nothing. One credentialed provider is as good as the next.

"Another feature of managed care is that some insurers carve out exclusive products with provider groups that impose a financial penalty on patients who see doctors out of network; this is another problem for a small independent practice and a constant administrative headache.

"Anyway, fortunately or unfortunately, I'm getting to the twilight of my practice years and am happy I was able to have a busy and successful private practice where I could use just about all my medical and surgical training, do some teaching, and contribute to a few good clinical research projects.

"It is disheartening that what attracted many smart and ambitious people to medicine—the opportunity for independence and financial rewards for the energetic—is fast disappearing. Derek Sprunger told me they are now all employees in Indiana—at the stroke of a pen, the hospital took over their practice. A cousin, an orthopod in Ann Arbor, says private practice is extinct in Michigan, too."

Robins' wife, Alex, is also an expert in the area of managed care. She has greatly helped me try to understand the complexities of this monolith of the medical world.

She wrote this for me:

"Managed care plans are a form of health insurance in which a third party contracts with a panel of health care providers and facilities that provide medical care for a reduced fee with the goal of controlling not only cost, but also utilization and quality. The

term 'narrow networks' describes the trade-off: decreased consumer choice for a reduced price. However, the idea that utilization and quality are similar to those of health plans that do not substantially limit choice is unclear, as managed care plans can be either for-profit or nonprofit, and can also vary widely in quality.

In the first twenty years since 1999 we have seen:

Physician loss of autonomy;

Push to utilize electronic medical records and other health information technology;

Rise of mid-levels;

Off-loading risk to physicians and patients, in form of value-based reimbursements and high deductibles and copays;

Corporatization of health care, death of private practice, move toward employed physicians."

On the other hand, there's Jack Dodick, one of my residents when I was the residents' instructor at MEETH. One time when he was a resident, he had a patient who had cataracts, and the cataract in one eye became swollen and caused an acute glaucoma. The pressure in the eye went way up. The cataract had to be taken out, not just for vision but to save the eye. It happened at the end of the afternoon. Jack called me at home and said he had a woman whose lens (cataract) was intumescent, a swollen lens, and acute glaucoma had resulted.

"How old is she?" I asked.

"She's 95."

"What do you want to do?"

He said, "Let's operate."

He had never done a cataract extraction before. So I came

over and at midnight we took out her swollen lens, and he said, "Should we do the other eye?"

One never does both eyes at the same time, but I said, "Go for it," and we did the other eye too. Jack called me in my office the next morning to report our patient was sitting up in bed reading the newspaper with her temporary reading glasses. Jack went on to become one of the most famous cataract surgeons in the world.

And of course it was Jack and Larry Yannuzzi who simply said, "Dr. Richards is back," when there was some resistance to my coming back to the hospital after changing my name and being away for five years. Their words settled that—by then they were the directors of the hospital.

Jack is professor and chairman of the ophthalmology department at NYU Medical School. He also served as chief of the surgeon directors at MEETH, which figures prominently in this story. Jack has operated on many luminaries throughout the world, but his take on managed care is simple. Jack never accepted any managed care patients.

I don't know, maybe that makes Jack the smartest of the bunch.

However, Jack had plenty to say when I pursued him about managed care.

"The sun is setting on the warm know-your-patient Marcus Welby Care," Jack wrote me.

"Once was a time patients placed great trust in their doctor and the physician took time to listen, taking pride in this special relationship. The physician, in turn, felt a strong sense of responsibility to deliver the best quality of care he or she could

deliver. The term physician burnout had not been invented. The contract was between two parties—patient and physician. The third party called medical insurance was in its early infancy.

"I believe the change began about 50 years ago with the advent of Medicare under the presidency of Lyndon Baines Johnson. This was probably the inauguration of the largest universal health care insurance program covering our nation's aging population. Initially, this change was skeptically embraced, as fees offered by this program were fair. But this was really the beginning of the end. A third party was now in the mix.

"Of course, we all know what ensued. Most physicians enrolled in Medicare and once in they witnessed a steady ratcheting down of fees. They were forced to do more for less to cope with declining revenue and increased expenses. The phenomenon of physician burnout was born.

"Concomitant with the rise of Medicare, another change occurred. General medical insurance was in its infancy. Insurance companies initially acted as a third party, paying some or all of the patient's fees. The major carrier was Blue Cross/Blue Shield. What followed was a proliferation of new insurance companies that realized an industry could be formed with profit potential by owning both the patient and the physician. The companies formed panels and doctors signed on, in great part feeling they might be left out and lose patients. The same thing occurred here as with Medicare. Ratcheting down of fees to the participating doctors. More expectation of doing more for less. More physician burnout.

"The next step in this story is the realization by hospital administrators that they could exclusively own the patients, the

doctors and in some cases be the insurance carrier. Hence we saw the birth of faculty group practice. Initially, the doctors were graduates of the institution and happy to get a job. The hospitals, however, began to realize they could add many more patients to feed hospital services by acquiring established practices. Established doctors saw this as an option to deal with dwindling revenue.

"The formula for acquisition was fairly uniform. A lump sum was paid to the physician or practice that usually matched their average net in the immediately preceding years. This contract usually was for two years. When the contract expired, a modification of the terms of salary based on Relative Value Units (RVUs) usually followed. This most often resulted in a ratcheting down of salary with payment contingent on the number of units of service performed by the physician. In other words, the two year honeymoon was over and relative discontent ensued.

"More recently, especially in the field of ophthalmology, venture capital discovered in this specialty a potential for profit and hence another option for ophthalmologists occurred—the phenomenon of aggregation. Companies formed with an eye toward the buyout of high volume practices or practice groups. This is still in its infancy, but it appears that formulas for acquisition are similar to those of hospital faculty group practice.

"The sun is setting on private practice, except, perhaps for the moment, in remote rural areas.

"I believe the quality of care will remain good, because that is how physicians are wired. However, physician burnout will occur earlier and patients will perceive doctors as providers rather than compassionate caregivers. The advent of electronic medical *records with loss of eye contact has not helped this phenomenon."*

For myself, I know that twenty years ago, faced with growing managed care, I had a feeling 1999 was an important punctuation point in medical care—one of the reasons I decided to document my practice of each day that year.

It was important, too, because it marked the end of the century and the millennium. Not as important as 2010, but that would take another large book to document. I leave that for other students to decipher—the Affordable Care Act of 2010 (Obamacare). It is 1,000 pages long. This much I know: health benefit plans must cover dependents to age 26, HMO coverage cannot be excluded for pre-existing conditions, exchanges are created where individuals and small businesses can buy insurance from private plans, and expansion of Medicaid occurred—the four tenets of Obamacare. Not easy to comprehend its detail, even one of the most brilliant Supreme Court justices of all time, Ruth Bader Ginsburg, admits to staying up nights studying Obamacare to be prepared for challenges to its legality.

Managed care is not an easy subject. For emphasis, here's another comment from Larry Yannuzzi.

"Essentially, I used to be a one man show for the partnership and the foundation (along with its teaching and research activities). I no longer contribute to administrative consumption, but simply teach five to nine Fellows at a time each year. I have written about 600 papers in peer reviewed journals and a dozen books, one the most successful ever for an ophthalmic text by Elsevier. Publishing companies are fewer from perishing and merging, as Jack has reminded me, 'Nobody reads books any longer.' I have a small library of retinal books I have

assembled since residency. It needs to find a safe and usable home... where? In any case, I just see patients and insulate myself from the dilemma of managed care. I get paid and bonused and focus on what is in the best interests of my patients. I read all of the journals, which cuts into leisure reading. I have mastered the art of good health, although muscles, bones, urinary tract events have surfaced without much in the way of function, and I still enjoy myself. An exception is awakening on a Monday morning and asking myself, "What am I getting up for?" only to enjoy the rest of the day once I get rolling.

"Regrets: never a good tennis player... wish I took a golf lesson... never learned enough about genetics. Highlights: awards... appreciation by an array of Fellows... advances in AMD... family... friends. Future: Nico will be joining our group (his idea)... maybe development of a way to get rid of drusen (yellow deposits under the retina)... grandchildren with accomplishments in their chosen areas (very diverse)... a better president.

"So the short answer to my question on managed care is AVOIDANCE behavior. Surround yourself with colleagues you respect and trust, and above all, be in a position in which you do not have to see patients to make a living."

I will leave the final word on managed care to my friend Alex Tien, who offered these predictions (the thoughts in italics are mine, for what they are worth):

Increasing corporatization of healthcare, as might makes right (and is also more lucrative due to increased market share). *Me: As to that, I can only say that, unfortunately, Alex is probably right. Will universal healthcare save it?*

Nurse practitioners take over primary care due to persistent doctor shortage as well as insurers. *Me: Nurses will be called physician assistants. Doctor shortage reminds me that big business (pharmaceutical companies and insurance companies) are already watering down the concept of "physician." "Healthcare provider" is the new term. For my whole life since medical school I have been "Doc" to my friends—at the golf course, in town, in my neighborhood, everywhere I go. What will I be called in the new age of medicine? "Hi there, healthcare provider."*

Desire to spend less for healthcare services; more states pass legislation allowing nurse practitioners to practice autonomously. *Me: Gosh, Alex, I hope not.*

Payers continue to off-load risk to physicians and patients in the form of value-based reimbursements, high deductibles and copays. *Me: Absolutely; it is already ongoing.*

Clinical judgment is out, and managing patients by algorithm is in, leading the way to increased use of artificial intelligence in healthcare, some of which will be embedded in the electronic medical record. *Me: Truly a dire prediction, Alex, so let's hope not.*

Medical school is shortened to three years as medical establishment realizes belatedly that something must be done to decrease the cost of medical education in the face of anticipated lower future earnings and competition from autonomous mid-levels, but this measure does not go nearly far enough to address the magnitude of the problem. *Me: There are already six-year programs leading to combined MD-PhD degrees, so it is not beyond possibility that traditional medical school might be shortened to three years. A number of MDs are already opting to get BSA degrees (administration) from business schools after medical school.*

Best practices in medicine will increasingly be used to justify restricting patients' options for medications and treatments. *Me: A gloomy thought.*

Genetic sequencing will continue to be used in healthcare, including by insurers to calculate risk; the pharmaceutical industry will resist efforts to rein in the cost of medications, aided by a lack of political will, in turn fueled by hefty campaign contributions; more states will create legislation to deal with this problem, including obtaining medications from Canada. *Me: Now we are on to something. One of the two biggest problems for future healthcare is the pharmaceutical industry. The other? Private insurance companies.*

Alex Tien is an expert on all of the above and a professor at the University of Rhode Island. I am just an old-time doc, more in tune with 1999 than 2020. Trust Alex. Don't go by me.

Oh well, back to my diary...

Thursday, March 11

Started off at 12:30 pm by seeing Sam Kramer, on whom we operated Wednesday. His alignment looked pretty good, and I think he'll get used to the fact he doesn't have to pull his eyes in anymore. He looked okay after surgery and needed a little bit of reassurance he's not going to see double for the rest of his life, because he won't.

Our doorman, Thomas Watson, came in complaining he saw a flash of light from his computer and has seen a spot in his eye ever since. I dilated his pupil and he's got a maculopathy, worse in one eye than in the other, like an early macular degeneration in a young man of 26. That terrible condition has nothing to do with his thinking he saw a flash from his computer. That's just what made him be aware of his macular pathology. We'll have to study him, get intravenous fluorescein angiography, and maybe he'll have to have a laser. I don't know.

In Gabriella Barrett's case, she has looked good since I operated on her. It's amazing. I did the same operation on her mother 30 years ago that I did on her.

And then I saw Emily Dewhurst, who needs surgery. She was done uptown by someone else and still needs some more done, vertically and horizontally.

Michael McCarthy brought me a present for operating on him and straightening his eyes, but actually he's beginning to drift out a little bit. I hope he doesn't drift too much. He brought me a beautiful pen and clock for my desk. It was very nice. A sweet little six-year-old boy.

Anyway, it's off to Putnam tomorrow morning. It's still freezing in New York, and I wish the winter would be over.

Friday, March 12 'Putnam County at 8:30 am

We had to drive up from the city in the Jeep because the garage people were so smart they smashed in the back window of my truck when they were trying to wash it and it's still in the garage in the city. So, we have one vehicle for the weekend with a major storm forecast.

Anyway, we got through 20 patients at Northeast Eye Care. Nothing exciting, except Karen Niswander. I operated on her to correct a bad result she'd had from surgery elsewhere, but she still might need a little more surgery. Her mother was very, very concerned about what had happened in the first operation. Although she's not litigation-minded, she thinks the doctor should be reprimanded, and I got caught between a rock and a hard place—yes, he should be reprimanded, but also he shouldn't be sued. He was in over his head. He really never should have done the procedure. It was the wrong procedure done by the wrong guy. It wasn't his field of expertise. It's a bad situation. I told her just that.

A few of the kids I operated on when they were about three are now 13 to 14 years old. It is always interesting to see them as teenagers. Lauren Mauer and Ashley Nevin (I saw Ashley's three children in the office in Yorktown Heights last week—January 2019. How do you like that?), both wear contact lenses because they are quite myopic, and, now that they are 13, they don't want to wear their glasses anymore.

As I look at the list, I see there was no one of any great interest—ophthalmologically, only Terence Davinski, who is now 13 years old. His parents are going through a divorce, his uncle was killed in a car crash, and he sleeps 12 hours a day and gets headaches. We have to decide why he's getting headaches. Is it related to the lymphoid tumor I took off his conjunctiva five years ago and now is recurring in his head, or is it because his parents are getting a divorce and his uncle was killed? Probably the latter.

We saw two little kids who have seen Dr. Deborah Rachmil, down the street, and had surgery recommended to them. And, yes, they did need surgery. One child had a Duane's syndrome, and the surgery for that is not exactly like doing a tonsillectomy, but it's almost impossible to tell that to the parents. They're ready to proceed with surgery by the doctor down the street because she's on their insurance plan and that seems to be perfectly okay to them. Indeed, it might turn out to be the case. They have an out-of-provider proviso in their insurance plan, so they could have me do the surgery if they wanted to, and would only have to pay 20 percent for that privilege. They don't really understand. They're not sophisticated enough to really understand the significance of one surgeon doing this procedure versus another. If they don't have that knowledge and understanding, it's not my part to try to explain that to them. It's just not done, and would be fruitless anyway if they don't already understand it.

That's a problem in the mechanics of the third-party system. I had seen the child originally at the age of two and said the child would someday need surgery. Now the child is four, and the surgery is needed. She has been taken to another doctor because she's on that doctor's plan, and yet they come back to me because they want the final word. I give them the final word, and they're still prepared to go back to the doctor who's on their plan to do the surgery. I can't say anything, and I just wish them well.

The weekend was quiet until the storm hit Sunday afternoon, the 14th, and left a foot of snow on our property, which had to be plowed out Monday morning. Fortunately, I'm going to Florida on Wednesday for six days, which should be a nice escape from what has not been a pleasant winter.

Jeffrey Glick called me over the weekend to say all my lab tests were good. My cholesterol was good, thyroid studies were good, my hemoglobin is good, everything is good, except I am still feeling low, and he thinks I ought to go on Wellbutrin. We shall see. I think if we sold this house and I was in a financial situation where I could breathe easier, I might not have to go on Wellbutrin.

Monday, March 15

I have the day off. We're still up at the house, shoveling out from a storm that left a foot of snow and turned the satellite television set off. A couple of people looked at the house over the weekend, but still no bites and no offers. If we could sell this house it would take a big load off my mind because we're not earning enough in the practice anymore with the reimbursements cut as much as they've been and the income down. Managed care echoes keep ringing in my head.

We're not earning enough to really keep our heads above water. If we sold the house, it would make all the difference in the world, and then we could get a smaller house without such a big yearly expense. It's the beginning of the downsizing of the lifestyle.

It's true, this is my dream house—nine acres, professional

tennis court, 400 feet on the lake, my own dock and my own boat and tremendous privacy, within the Sedgewood Club. But we can get a little house within the Sedgewood Club. We don't need the court anymore. We don't need 400 feet on the lake, and we don't need nine acres. And we don't need a big mortgage and big taxes. If we could sell it and buy a smaller one, or build a smaller one up here, I would be delighted. It's a tough sale, though. It's a pretty unique kind of house, and we're asking a lot of money. We shall see.

Tuesday, March 16

Starting at eight o'clock we saw several patients, some we operated on and some who need surgery. Janet Ambrose looked very good after her lateral rectus resection for an incomitant esotropia. That's not an easy thing to accomplish without disturbing her primary-position normal muscle balance.

Lois Carpathia is still a diagnostic problem. She's got something on her MRI that might be a brain tumor or might be inflammatory. My recommendation is still to follow her, to do serial MRIs, and, if there's any sign of change, to act accordingly. Her lateral rectus palsy is getting better.

After seeing 22 patients, I went to the clinic and saw some patients with the residents. The day ended with our Manhattan Ophthalmological Society dinner, which we have four or five times a year. A group of supposedly-esteemed New

York City ophthalmologists have a little dinner club, and we meet to have dinner and cocktails and present patients to each other. I presented Carlton Roseboro, the young man who has a tumor in the cavernous sinus. We finally operated when Carlton was 13, after we watched it, having known about it for nine years. It got so big it involved the carotid artery and the neurosurgeon could not resect it completely, and Carlton sustained a thalamic infarct with a hemiparesis on the right side and slurred speech. The speech has improved. Carlton still has a little weakness on his right side from the neurosurgery, and he's still got the remnants of a mass in the cavernous sinus. Now he's got a metal clip on the posterior communicating artery, which makes it hard to do any MRIs on him. We talked about him at the dinner society meeting, but I didn't get any really good advice on what to do.

It's primarily a neurosurgical problem, and the ophthalmologists discuss it, but they're not the ones who make the definite decision about further surgery, or perhaps fractionated, stereotactic radiation—a new modality—to try to get rid of the remaining cavernous sinus tumor without disturbing any more vital functions in his head.

Wednesday morning, I'm due to fly out of here for my five-day spring break to see some baseball games. That'll be welcome after a difficult winter and even a difficult day Tuesday.

Trip to Florida

I flew out Wednesday morning and got to Tampa in time to play a full 18 holes. I left by myself a day earlier than my closest friends, who joined me Thursday afternoon, Les Pollack and his wife Yvonne and Steven Greenberg—my pediatric ophthalmology associate and former Fellow—and his son, William, the designated kid, who is nine years old. He's the one who gets all the autographs on his ball, and the coaches and the players always throw him balls at the games. He's terrific.

The first game we saw was at Legends Field in Tampa, and George Steinbrenner, the owner of the Yankees, got the tickets for us because of my friendship with Dick Savitt, who is good friends with the Yankees' owner. Dick is grateful because of how I've helped him with his eyes and the problem he had with retinal detachment. Because of all this connection, Mr. Steinbrenner got us fantastic seats for the Yankees games. We saw a great game Thursday night, and then we saw three more games, culminating in the wonderful game Sunday against the Atlanta Braves.

I also played some golf with Steve Greenberg's brother, Larry. We played a little tennis and we had a lovely time. We do it every year. Spring training every year with the Pollacks, the Greenbergs, and me.

It was my second trip to Florida within a month and the last one until probably the fall.

Tuesday, March 23

I arrived in Newark at midnight, got home at 1:30 in the morning. Fortunately, Amy and Arleen had rescheduled the patients to start at 10:00 am instead of 8:00, so I was able to get a little sleep before starting in again.

I was very happy to see Ralph Roland, the 80-year-old man who is on so many medications and has so many heart, vascular, and cancer problems. It's been three weeks since I operated on him. His eyes are perfectly straight. No prisms, no double vision. Absolutely wonderful results, and he knows it. He's a pretty sharp old guy. He's a retired doorman. He knows his way around, and he knows we did a pretty good job in fixing his eyes. He's right on for distance and near, and he's delighted.

I saw Adam Reifsnyder, whom I've been following for a head tilt. He's now two-and-a-half years old, and it's time to bite the bullet and do a tuck of his left superior oblique, one of the more difficult operations we have to do on a little child. It's the only operation that's going to help his head tilt.

I didn't stay for grand rounds. The subject was glaucoma, and I was tired anyway because I didn't have much sleep, having arrived so late from Florida. I came back to the apartment to have dinner and rest.

April

Tuesday, April 20

S tarting at 8:15 am, we saw 20 patients. Casandra Riggis, the 10-month-old daughter of an ophthalmologist, Idella Riggis, was first. Casandra has a significant convergent strabismus, as well as nystagmus, a head tilt, head-bobbing, and spasmus nutans. Her mother really should get her an MRI because of the few cases of spasmus nutans associated with lesions of the chiasm. It should be done, and then I'm going to have to operate on the little girl because she's got such a big esotropia. I am concerned about her visual potential because she's got very significant nystagmus since infancy.

Edna Wong, a 63-year-old Chinese lady, had a complete lateral rectus paralysis of one eye, partial in the other eye, from an automobile accident. I've operated on her once—on all four horizontal muscles because her deviation was gigantic. Now it looks like I might do a little more surgery because she's got a residual face turn, although she's much, much improved from what she was originally. She could hardly see out of one eye because it was turned in so far toward her nose.

I saw my dear friend, Gene Scott, just for a routine examination. Gene's a famous tennis player who went to Yale just after I did. We've been friends for more than 30 years. He's the publisher of *Tennis Week* newspaper. He's still playing tennis and still one of the best in the world, even with two new hips at the age of 60.

Fokis Andiros, 24, is going to need further surgery. He had

two procedures by another doctor for exotropia, and now he has an esotropia with limitation of abduction of his left eye. It's going to be a little bit difficult exploring his left eye and figuring out what to do to get him straightened out.

Adam Reifsnyder was back. I was very happy about the superior oblique tuck I did last week. The little fellow looked so great the day after the surgery. He came in today, and he's tilting his head again. Sometimes these tucks hold for a short period, and then they loosen and the head tilt comes back. It looks like he's tilting again, so we'll let him sit for several months. He might need further surgery to try to help him with his tilt. It was disappointing because for the first few days after surgery he looked terrific.

Then I saw Alva Lippert, who has a very, very large right exotropia, and he's terrified of surgery because somebody told him he's going to see double if he has it done. Whenever patients have the fear of double vision implanted by someone, they become very reluctant in adulthood to have anything done. He needs to have this surgery because he's got such a disfiguring deviation, but he's very, very fearful of post-operative double vision.

Shirley Bart, who has prisms for her lateral rectus paralysis—or palsy, rather—was next. We're going to have to operate on her. I told her to stop her medication for myasthenia because I don't think she has myasthenia. I think she's got a lateral rectus palsy from her hypertension.

We finished with Anthony Michaelopolos, a Greek child who has an intermittent exotropia that needs surgery. His parents have seen a few other doctors, but I think they want me to do the procedure. We're going to do it in a couple of months, before the family moves back to Greece.

I went to the hospital and saw several patients with the residents, including a few who are going to need surgery. That will be an interesting experience because I'll have to supervise the residents doing the surgery and, depending on how capable the resident is, it is a pleasurable or decidedly unpleasant experience for me.

Wednesday, April 21

I played golf with Art Leonard and Larry Parsont out on Long Island, and we walked 18 holes. I raced into the city to get to Bellevue Hospital at 4:30 pm for a lecture by David Guyton on dissociated vertical deviations. It was very, very well attended. He's a professor at Johns Hopkins and a very well-known strabismus and optics expert. He has some very revolutionary ideas about dissociated vertical deviations, all of which I'm not quite sure I agree with, but it was very stimulating and interesting to listen to him. I didn't go to the cocktail party and libation at the Water Club because I'd been on my feet enough, walking 18 holes in the morning. I decided just to come home and put my feet up after the lecture instead. I had already socialized a little bit with most of my friends and colleagues at the lecture. People came from all over the city to hear Dr. Guyton speak.

Thursday, April 22

We started out seeing Agripina Savas, a 30-year-old woman I operated on when she was an infant, and then again when she was 10 years old. Now she comes in because she wants plastic surgery on her eyelids and the surgeon is worried about doing an incision that might cause injury to her inferior oblique. He wants to know if I operated on her inferior oblique before.

I'm not sure because her records are 10 years old and we no longer have them. She still needs more eye muscle surgery anyway, and she wants me to tell her whether they should do the plastic surgery on her face—whether she needs it. I spent an hour with her going over, around and about, and over and under whether she should have the plastic surgery. It ended up that she's going to have it and then she'll come back for more muscle surgery if she wants it in the future.

Patty Fox is so delighted with her surgery now, five years post-op. I was the only one who told her one eye should be operated on. Everybody else told her both eyes should be operated on. We got a very good result and she's delighted.

I saw a 79-year-old man with double vision with horizontal and vertical and torsional components. He's got some maculopathy and a membrane peel in the left eye and doesn't see well in that eye. He's got a developing cataract in the right eye. He wants me to fix his double vision, which is very hard to do with gigantic horizontal and vertical prisms, which will not help his torsion, anyway. He's a very sharp man from Woodbridge, Connecticut, sent down by Dr. Joel Silverman from Yale. I spent a long time with him and will try some prisms. If that doesn't work, we might have to operate on him.

Menachem Rappaport is five years old with a very large esotropia he's had for his whole life. His mother doesn't understand why he needs an operation and when it should be done. I explained we should do it and we shouldn't wait until he's much older. Hopefully, she will schedule the surgery.

We saw several other patients, some of them post-ops, some of them pre-ops. Malcolm McCain is now seven years old, and it's time to operate on him. I told his parents, "Don't delay things. Stay put. Don't do anything. You've sold your house. You've bought a new house in Bronxville. You moved your kids to a new school. Don't do anything until you hear from me later this weekend."

Of about 20 patients, we ended up scheduling four or five of them for surgery; some of them that should have been done long before now and the others when it is appropriate to do them since it's only the first or second time I've seen them. I can't be accused of not doing the surgery when it was indicated.

I am done with patients today, but I have phone calls to make. I needed to call several friends who are surgeon directors and who went to the meeting Wednesday that I didn't go to because I went to David Guyton's lecture. They all had the same sad story. Sure enough, the residency program at Manhattan Eye and Ear has been canceled and nobody knows what's going to happen to the hospital. The lay board won't talk to the board of surgeon directors. The lay board members won't comment on whether the hospital has been sold either.

This is the most famous eye specialty hospital in the country. It's been in existence since 1869. It has the highest reputation for training eye, ear, nose, and throat, and plastic surgeons in the country. It's one of the few specialty hospitals remaining extant, and now its residency program has been canceled. The lay board won't talk to the board of surgeon directors, and the administrator is calling all the residents and telling them they are going to have to find new positions. This is a truly chaotic situation.

Surgeons at the hospital don't know if the hospital is going to close, if all the patients they have scheduled for surgery are going to have to be canceled, if they have to find new positions on the staffs of other hospitals in the city in order to do their work. Nobody knows what's going on and nobody's talking and nobody can get to the lay board, this group of imbeciles that has managed our hospital into oblivion.

Friday, April 23

We started at Northeast Eye Care in Brewster with the usual 20 patients, and my mind was hardly on it because of what was going on at Manhattan Eye and Ear, but in between phone calls to the other surgeon directors I got through the schedule of patients. Rick Gibralter was there with me. This was his last day at Northeast Eye Care because he's quit going up there. He's a corneal surgeon and was a little bit upset to learn a new doctor hired in the practice is going to be trained in refractive surgery and is going to be doing it. So there's not much need for Rick to come up there anymore. So his last day was today.

We saw several patients, the usual Northeast Eye Care schedule of children, some with strabismus, and some just with more simple problems. One adult was post-op and had a good result from an inferior oblique recession. The two pre-ops were going to be done on Monday up in Putnam Hospital.

After seeing the patients and spending half the morning on the phone trying to reach some fellow surgeon directors to see what's going on with the hospital, I went back to the house, picked up Arleen and the two puppies, and drove into the city. I had a dinner Friday night at the United Nations— the Eastern Tennis Hall of Fame celebration honoring the induction of Dr. Reggie Weir, the first top black player to play in a competition open with other players and a very good friend of mine until he died some years ago. Two of my best friends, Herbie Fitzgibbon and Dick Savitt, were there, along with several other old friends. We spent a wonderful evening celebrating the induction of Reggie. Herb and Dick had long ago been inducted into the Hall.

We came up to the country on Saturday morning, a dreary drive. Arleen informed me on the way that we are in bad financial straits. We have not paid our taxes on this house for this year; we owe money for the malpractice insurance; we owe money for the dues at the Sedgewood Club; and we're about $20,000 short of being able to pay some of these expenses. I don't know what I'm going to do to raise $20,000. The money doesn't come in that fast from our practice, but we have to pay the taxes and we have to pay the malpractice insurance, so…

"Where's all the money that we're earning, that we're working so hard to make to pay our expenses?" I asked.

"Well, the reimbursements are low. Oxford pays us $90 on a $400 bill, sometimes $55 on a $125 bill. Surgery that would be $4,000 they pay $900 for, and our expenses don't get less, they get larger."

It's a good thing we're selling this house because we'd be further and further in debt every month if we didn't. We have the inspection Monday, and I hope it goes through because we've got to get out from under. We can't afford to live at this level, with these kinds of taxes and these kinds of expenses with the income we are earning. Now, with the problem at the hospital, things are even worse. I don't know where I'm going to operate if the hospital closes. I'm not on any other staff in the city. I used to be at Cornell, but I'm not anymore. Everything seems to be coming to a head all at once. This is quite a week: April 1999.

Well, I'll try to enjoy the weekend as best I can, but I'm sure I'll be on the phone for most of it with my colleagues concerning the hospital issue. As far as our personal financial problems are concerned, Arleen and I will have to scrounge around on our own.

It used to be the only thing I had to worry about was how a patient was doing. Now, it seems there are many more things to fret about, mostly involving money and the status of medical practice and my profession.

A reflection from 2021:

Looking back, I see how complicated it has been.

Until the early 1950s, there was no sub-specialty of ophthalmology called "pediatric ophthalmology and strabismus" (confusingly uniting an age group with a condition in the title). In fact, there was hardly any sub-specialization. Eye surgeons did everything related to eyes—cataracts, trauma, glaucoma, eye muscles (strabismus), retinal detachments, etc. For me that was true, too, having been trained in the early 1960s. I did everything when I was in the Navy at St. Albans Hospital and even during my first ten years in private practice (except the retina, which I gave up after my tour in the Navy). I decided to do only eye muscle surgery in 1982 when I came back to medicine after being away for five years. In the present day, ophthalmologists specialize right after residency and take Fellowships in their chosen fields— retina, glaucoma, neuro-ophthalmology, oculoplastic surgery, etc. So in the present I am called a "pediatric ophthalmologist: (shortening the title from the added-on "strabismus") by some, an "eye muscle specialist" by others, and just "ophthalmologist" or plain "eye specialist" by others still. In fact, my training was as an ophthalmologist from my residency at MEETH and as a strabismus specialist because I took a Fellowship in strabismus and eventually confined my surgery to eye muscles. But I did do cataracts and retinas and glaucoma and corneas and oculoplastic surgery for years, and since strabismus occurs often in children, and because the present-day Fellowships are in pediatric ophthalmology and strabismus, and our local and national organizations are the Greater New York Pediatric Ophthalmology and Strabismus Society and the American Association for Pediatric Ophthalmology and Strabismus, I am known in 2020, and have been for some years, as a specialist in both. I consider myself a strabismologist—for children and adults—a pediatric ophthalmologist, a general ophthalmologist, and a dinosaur in the field of ophthalmology. I would venture to say I am one of only a handful in AAPOS whose post-graduate training was just in strabismus.

As I said, "It's complicated."

Complicated in definitions for sure, but that's nothing compared to how complicated the subspecialty of strabismus itself really is. I used to badger my first professor in strabismus—the white-haired old giant of the world of eye muscles when I was a resident, Dr. Harold Whalley Brown—to tell me how many millimeters to move the medial rectus muscles on a cross-eyed child whom we had just presented to him for consultation at a muscle conference held monthly at MEETH.

He would say, "You take the muscles off the eye, you set the eye straight, and you sew them back on."

A little euphemistic; he would then tell me what to do, the instructions still often indecipherable to a fledgling strabismologist. It was then I decided I needed to learn more about strabismus (the misalignment and problems of the two eyes working together) and I would require a Fellowship in that area of ophthalmology. Twenty-five years later, when I published my book, *Strabismus Surgery: Text and Atlas*, I put as the frontispiece:

"You take the muscles off the eyes, you set the eyes straight, then you sew the muscles back on. Harold Whalley Brown." Not so complicated.

When I was a young ophthalmologist newly returned from my Fellowships in strabismus and was the resident instructor at MEETH, I was invited by Dr. John McLean, the chief at Cornell Medical School-NY Hospital, to join his ophthalmology staff. He had been my civilian consultant at St. Albans Navy Hospital. His strabismus expert, Dr. Ed Dunlop, was soon to retire, and I took over the job as chief of the pediatric eye and eye muscle clinic. At that time, only a handful of experts in strabismus worked in the USA. In the present day, the American Association of Pediatric Ophthalmology and Strabismus has more than a thousand members. The number was once so small they formed a club— the Squint Club (Strabismus Club, actually)—and met once a year in different locations in the USA for a three-day meeting. There were only about ten in the club. In 1975, they held their meeting at West Point, the US Military Academy on the edge of the Hudson River about an hour north of NYC. Dr. Dunlop was a member—he invited me to come as his guest and to deliver a paper on some research I had been doing on the superior oblique muscle, the most complicated of the eye muscles. I went and brought along my three-year-old son, Nicholas, and his nanny for the weekend. He had much fun watching the cadets, climbing over the cannons and other armaments overlooking the Hudson River right where General Washington had encamped some years earlier. I presented my paper and listened while Dr. Marshall Parks, already one of the few top leaders of the group, critiqued it. And then I listened to Harold Whalley Brown critique it. My paper concerned a taut superior oblique tendon which limited its elongation and caused double vision in upgaze. The condition had first been described by Dr. Brown some fifteen years earlier. It was called Brown's syndrome. At the Squint Club meetings, the experts, with decades of experience in studying eye muscle disorders, would often disagree about what measures to take for various conditions, and lively discussion would result. When Dr. Brown would give his opinion, that would usually be the end of the discussion on that particular case.

And so it has come to pass that I have been practicing ophthalmology for nearly sixty years (the last day of 2018, I saw a patient in my office in Yorktown Heights whom I have been taking care of for 50 years). And I operated on eyes for fifty-five years, but now that number starts getting complicated too. I might have forgotten when I actually stopped operating—2016? 2017? As I said, "It's complicated."

Oh well, back to my diary...

Sunday, April 25

The announcement came with no warning in today's Sunday *New York Times*, in the Metro section. The hospital was going to be sold, and the lay board was going to use the money to open some satellite clinics in underprivileged neighborhoods. This is the board's spin on the fact it has mismanaged the hospital into its demise. The board didn't tell anyone it was being done. The only warning came when board members told the residents last week they would not be able to finish their residencies and told new residents not to show up. They didn't tell any of us on the board of surgeon directors. They simply announced in the *Times* that the hospital was being sold because it was in financial distress. Here's the most prestigious eye hospital in the city—one of the top 10 in the country, providing training, research and care in ophthalmology, ear, nose, and throat and plastic surgery for 130 years—and this inept board is closing the doors. After 130 years, Manhattan Eye and Ear will be no more.

I have been on the phone the entire weekend with Jack Dodick, Steve Fochios, and my friend Les Pollack, who is also my financial advisor, to try to figure out if there is any way to save the hospital from being torn down and replaced by some real estate development. The anger and the resentment we feel toward this lay board is so overwhelming it's almost impossible to describe. It is unbelievable how that board has mismanaged this trust and misinformed the doctors and the community—and now, in the newspaper, the entire city. And now, board members have the gall to turn around and say they're actually do-gooders because they're going to use the money to open up clinics in underprivileged neighborhoods. It's just mind-boggling.

Anyway, now we are trying to find a power-broker, someone with connections to the mayor, to the governor, to the press, to see if we can force the board to sell the hospital to another hospital that will continue to run it as an eye hospital, someplace like Beth Israel. But the people at Beth Israel are so different from the people on the lay board that they can't even get together to talk things over. This is all going to cost a lot of money, too, and we don't know where the funds are going to come from to pay for such a power-broker, somebody with enough influence and skill to force this board to make the right deal for the hospital to survive rather than to sell it off outright.

In the meantime, the residents are crying. They don't know what's going to happen to them.

The incoming residents are beside themselves. Several of us on the staff have no other hospitals where we work. The patients who come to the hospital have been left in the lurch. The doctors who operate at the hospital believe they have to quickly try to get on staffs of other hospitals in the city. This is the worst crisis the hospital has ever faced, and it is imminently closing unless we mobilize some resource to force the board to keep it open with a merger.

Monday, April 26

On a personal side, we are having our house inspected today as a prelude to the bidders who made an offer we accepted. If all goes well today, the next step will be the closing and then, after 15 years, we will look around for a new place to live. Of course, we'll miss this house because we love it, but it's time to move on and time to downsize and time to make it so that we can pay our bills. We haven't paid the taxes on the house for a year. We owe money for the malpractice insurance; we owe the club dues up here—which are only $3,000 a year—and we don't have the funds to cover these expenses because our reimbursement from the managed care companies is so low we just don't make enough money in the practice to stay even. I can't deal with this too much longer. I'm going to go out and hit some golf balls.

Tuesday, April 27

In the midst of the furor over the impending disaster of the hospital being sold, we saw 22 patients, starting at 8:00 am in the morning and finishing at 2:00 pm in the afternoon.

Laura Campanis is just beginning to walk now. Her speech has returned. The tumor is gone from her cerebellum, and her VIth nerve palsy is getting better. Good progress so far.

Leonore Stroman was taken care of by another ophthalmologist for amblyopia and told to patch all day long. Since February, she's been patched morning, noon, evening, and all night long—a disastrous thing to do. One never patches 24 hours around the clock. She's had this patch on for three months solid. Fortunately, she's seven years old, and the other eye is not going to get weak but, in a little child, it can be disastrous. It's called occlusion amblyopia. When they took the patch off today, the child saw double because her two eyes had been separated from each other, dissociated from each other, for three months. I gave her a new prescription.

"No patching for a month," I told her parents, "and come back and we'll see what's going on."

Nothing exciting in the rest of the patients we saw, a number of them old friends of mine, including Carol Gertz and Marilyn Siegel, both of whom I've known for the past 30 years at least.

It's actually harder to see my old friends than it is to see new patients. My old friends require much more time because we want to get up to date. When I've got only a few minutes to see each patient and the waiting room is full, it's tougher to see my friends than it is to see new people. However, it's so nice to see friends that I sit and talk for a little while with each one. That's just the way it is.

Now, I turn my attention to our problems at the hospital and trying to find a power-broker attorney so we can broker a deal with the lay board and get the board to stop plans of turning the hospital into bricks for money. But, if we hire a power-broker attorney, we're going to have to muster some money to pay him, and this is going to be a problem. I just got a call from Joe Conway, one of our incoming residents. He has no idea what to do, and I told him to sit tight because we hadn't given up on the hospital yet. In the meantime, even though we're not giving up, some of us are making our own application for a staff appointment to the New York Eye and Ear Infirmary, just in case our efforts fall through. Arleen is going to take the completed application down to the Infirmary this afternoon. I've already spoken to the head of their eye department and their administrator and a friend of mine who's in touch with the president of their board of surgeon directors. Everybody is scurrying to leave the sinking ship—a ship we're still trying to save from sinking.

This morning, Les Pollack called Ken Bialkin at Skadden Arps, probably the most powerful law firm in the city, to see if we could interest Bialkin in representing us. If he does, that's going to cost money.

Wednesday, April 28

I operated on Doyle Conners, who is HIV-positive, this morning and did a recession of his left inferior oblique. It's always difficult to operate on a patient who has AIDS because, if you stick yourself with a needle or an instrument, you might contract the disease. Everybody is very, very careful in the operating room with waste products and with surgical instruments, and we take things very, very slowly. We got through the inferior oblique recession without difficulty.

Then I helped a young resident, Melissa Leung, do two inferior oblique recessions. She's not done much surgery, especially on oblique muscles, so it took a little bit longer to do it but the operation went well. It was on a patient from the clinic on whom we had operated twice before, but Melissa had nothing to do with his previous operations.

Following the surgery, we continued deliberations on the problem with the hospital and on trying to obtain a power-broker attorney and a publicist to counter what the lay board has done to destroy our 130-year-old institution. I was on the phone most of the rest of the day with Jack Dodick and with Les Pollack, who's trying to get an attorney at Skadden Arps. I think we've settled on an attorney and a publicist to help us.

Now, we have to raise some money to pay for them. The surgeon directors have been designated team captains, and we each have a list of members of our hospital staff we have to call to plead for the money we need.

Thursday, April 29

We started at 1:00 pm and we saw the HIV-positive patient we operated on yesterday, being very careful with taking off the patch and putting it in the hazardous waste area. He looked good. He wasn't seeing double, and his eyes were straight. That was one good thing for the day.

The pediatric Fellow, Dr. McLeod, came to observe for the afternoon and saw the patients with me.

The first patient was Avery Dorman, an old high school classmate, which is always difficult. And then we saw David Schuss, on whom we've operated three times for a superior oblique palsy with significant head tilt and right hypertropia, and, amazingly, now his eyes are straight and he's doing quite well.

Ann Rosenberg is 79, and she can fuse with her prisms, but she's getting cataracts.

Doris Bell, on whom we operated, came up from Florida. Her eyes are in good alignment and her headaches have disappeared since we operated on her. We questioned whether her headaches came from glaucoma or from her eye muscles. It turns out they came from her eye muscles because the headaches are now gone.

Casey Schwartz was a diagnostic problem because he's nine years old and he's complaining about a pushing feeling on his eye. We could not find anything in his examination, so we'll simply have to observe him.

And then we saw Kirk Flynn, a young optometrist who's had an intermittent convergent strabismus his whole life. He's done a lot of visual training, but now he realizes the only option for a definitive cure is surgery, which we're going to do shortly.

Elizabeth Candiotti had a combined horizontal-vertical deviation operated on up at Columbia and still needs more surgery. She's wearing some prisms, but she's only 10 years old, and she's not going to wear prisms the rest of her life, so we're getting ready to do more surgery on her. One more measurement will probably be all she needs before we do it.

Alexander Moss was in. His father was Jeff Moss, a writer, composer, and lyricist on PBS-TV's *Sesame Street*. His father died last year and Alexander still needs to have surgery for his divergent deviation, which I hope we are going to do shortly.

We saw a few more patients, and then I got back on the telephone, making calls to try to raise money to pay for our attorneys.

As if I didn't have enough problems, I got a terrible letter from my office landlord because we looked at another office we didn't know was owned by our landlord. Now he's mad at us because somebody else showed it to us and we can't take that office because of something about restrictive rules between competing real estate brokers I never understood. Now he doesn't want to renew our lease in this office. I have to talk to my attorney about it, and it's a big mess to add onto everything else we're dealing with: the hospital, now the lease to the office, the house we're selling—an inspection turned up a number of things we have to fix before it can be sold—and the house we're looking at because we have to keep raising the offer. I told them my last offer was as much as I could afford. Anyway, I have to get back on the phone.

Friday, April 30

We saw about 16 patients—okay, maybe 18; who's counting?—at Northeast Eye Care, starting at 8:30 am.

It was a typical Northeast Eye Care Friday morning. Most of the patients were fairly routine—nobody with any complicated problems, except Harry Sofer. He was operated on four times, and now he needs more surgery because he's got a big divergent deviation and a vertical, as well.

I left at about 1. And then I had to start calling all the people on my list from Manhattan Eye and Ear to ask them to raise money. We're asking for $2,500 from each staff member for the hospital rescue fund to save the hospital. We've hired a publicist, Howard Rubenstein. We've hired a high-powered lawyer, Charlie Stillman. We have about a week to prevent the lay board from turning the hospital over to a real estate developer and destroying it. If it's longer than a week, everybody's going to start fleeing. People are going to be looking for other jobs; residents are going to scatter; OR staff is going to fly; and it's going to be the end of the hospital. So we are trying our best to do something significant during the next week to prevent this from happening. I called about 20 of our staff and explained the situation to them and asked them for $2,500 to be made out to the Hospital Rescue Fund. I hate calling friends of mine for money, but I'm doing it because I'm trying to save the hospital. So that was the rest of Friday.

May

Saturday, May 1

Today, I played golf and tried to forget the problems of the hospital. I tried to forget the problems with the lease on our office in the city, where the landlord is mad at me because I spoke to another agent for the building next door. It is ridiculous for the landlord to be upset because the other agent's name was on the door. Now my lawyer, Stu Byron, has gotten involved. He said I should have called our landlord instead of the name on the door, but I didn't know any better. So that's another thing I have to worry about.

And then, of course, I'm worried about my son because he's still living in Forest Hills at his grandpa's house, and it's about time he moved out. I don't know what's going on there. We have all the problems with the house we have to try to fix before it's sold, as a result of the inspection, and then we have the problems with the house we want to buy because they won't agree to the offer we made. So, it's not an easy time. My mind is hung up on these problems, like a needle stuck in a vinyl record. The Manhattan Eye and Ear disaster, the lease on our office in the city, the house we're selling, the house we're trying to buy, my son still living in my father's house in Forest Hills without a true career at the moment, and I don't know what's going on—I'm trying to practice ophthalmology and do my thing and carry on as best I can. This is a very difficult time.

Today, I tried to relax and play some golf, and I enjoyed it very much. I played with Marty Connolly and Jerry Rattigan, my two buddies, and I won eight bucks and played very nicely. And then, Saturday afternoon, I tried to practice a little bit and take a lesson over at Centennial. Practice was horrible. I could not hit a ball, which put me in a panic because we will have our first event of the season at the club Sunday, and I knew I was going to be a disaster. Everybody expects me to play pretty well, even though I was a professional tennis player and not a professional golfer. I was just in a state.

I had too much to drink Saturday night and was up all night. I felt sure I was not going to play well in the mixed scramble. I went out and played beautifully, and my team won. So, it goes to show—what? I don't know. Lose your swing, have too many drinks, don't sleep, and you'll play great. Arleen says she has to go through this every single year with me.

Monday, May 3

A nice Saturday and Sunday got me in the mood to operate today in Brewster. I operated with Steven Greenberg. We did two cases. One was a little complicated because the patient had had previous surgery and the same muscle had to be re-operated and an inferior oblique had to be done. I was a bit skittish about the operation because we had a new anesthesiologist, which always makes me nervous. I was assured he was trained at Mt. Sinai and was reliable. Turned out he was, but I hate anything different from what I'm used to.

The second case went okay, and now we're heading down to the city. Tomorrow is a busy day in the office, but, more importantly, we're having a big meeting of the entire medical staff at the hospital at 5:00 pm and will go over the whole problem of saving Manhattan Eye and Ear. I've been on the phone all weekend long—except for my golf adventures—calling people, telling them about the meeting, asking them to contribute money to the Hospital Rescue Fund—give what you can, $10,000 for the heavy-hitters, $2,500 for the ordinary ones, to pay for our lawyer and our publicist—to help us try to hold off the lay board's efforts to sell the hospital out from under us.

In the meantime, everybody is scattering, trying to get on staff at other hospitals. It's really a terrible crisis—just terrible. It's a horrible situation for all of us, but ghastly for me because I am right in the midst of trying to sell the house, trying to buy a new one, worrying about what Nicky's going to do for his career, and worrying about the office in the city because the landlord is so mad at us now because we didn't call him first when we checked out another office. We'll have to leave the office in August. Since a megalith called Clarity took over the Brewster office, two of my close friends have left, Rick Gibralter, the corneal surgeon, and Bob Della Rocca, the oculoplastic surgeon. I'm the only one who's survived up there in the Brewster office over a period of 15 years, and I don't know how much longer I'm going to make it up there. So we might even have to get a new office up there, in addition to a new office in the city, and a new house, and a new hospital, and worrying about my kid and what he's going to do for the rest of his life.

Otherwise, things are just swell. As someone once supposedly asked Mrs. Abraham Lincoln: "Other than that, how did you like the play?"

Thursday, May 6

I drove down from the country with the two Airedales and hit a few golf balls along the way. We started in the city office at about 12:30 pm with all the paperwork and all the dictation I had to do. Two patients for surgery were being measured by Barbara in the other room, and they always ask me to see them and to answer questions. I keep telling everybody that's the day for their measurements and they're not to see me. It really gets me mad because I come in to do my work—dictation and paperwork—and not to see patients, and then they're always asking me to talk to these people who are there for their measurements only. This time I said no. Maybe they'll explain to the patients this is not the day for them to see me, it's the day for their measurements.

We started seeing patients at one o'clock.

Daniel Levine, five months old, came up from Chevy Chase, Maryland. I know his grandfather, who's a doctor. Daniel has an eye that won't move past the midline, probably a Duane's retraction syndrome, but it conceivably could be a VIth nerve paralysis. Even if it were a VIth nerve paralysis, it would be congenital and probably not due to something ominous in his head. I told the parents we would not do an MRI. That put the responsibility on me in case he has something threatening in his head. But I don't think he does. I think he's got a Duane's syndrome, and we'll just have to watch him for a face turn and any induced astigmatism and amblyopia in that eye.

I was troubled by Adam Reifsnyder. I did the superior oblique tuck on him, and his head tilt was gone for a week afterward and then re-appeared. Disturbing, because it was such a perfect operation and he had such a good result initially, but now he's starting to tilt his head again. I tightened that muscle as much as I could, and if I take him up and to the right, it's limited in going up there, a sure sign it's been tightened plenty. I couldn't have done any more of a tuck on him than I did. We're just going to have to watch him now and, maybe in another year, we'll try to figure out something else to strengthen the superior oblique a little more. He has no vertical deviation, but he must have some torsional component that makes him tilt his head.

We saw several other patients—a lot of little children. Alexandra Lerner, 10, wears contact lenses for astigmatism. I wanted to look at her lenses on the slit lamp microscope, but the right eye lens was missing and she wasn't even aware she didn't have a lens in her eye. Her mother started looking all over the waiting room floor.

"Stop looking for that lens," I told her. "It's a little piece of plastic. You're not going to put it back in her eye, anyway.

She's going to have to go get a new lens."

Damien Guardino is now 14 years old. I operated on him at the age of one, and the day after surgery his father was swinging him around his head in the waiting room until I came out and suggested politely he not swing his kid around his head in the waiting room the day after he had his eye muscles operated on. Anyway, Damien's 14 now and all grown up.

Michael Abrams is no child. He's a very big 35-year-old policeman from Long Island. I had twice operated on his eye muscles. He came in having just recently had a keratorefractive procedure on his right eye, and he's seeing haze. We hear all these advertisements about people with perfect results from these keratorefractive procedures—no haze, no problems, a five-minute procedure. Everybody's having it done. Well, here's a guy who's a policeman and has to shoot straight and had the procedure done on one eye. He can see okay, but not perfectly, and he's got haze. So, it's not a perfect procedure, this lasik, and people ought to know that. Not everybody's absolutely 100 percent perfect. In the other eye, which wasn't operated on, he uses his contact lens and he sees 20/20 and he has no haze.

Anyway, we saw about 18 patients, including the post-op from Wednesday. We had operated for a very, very tight medial rectus muscle and a neglected Duane's syndrome he'd had from infancy. He looked very good. He still can't get his eye to the midline, but he can use both eyes together with his head practically straight instead of what he used to have to do— turn his head 45 degrees in order to use both eyes together. I consider it a good result. I couldn't have done much more on that medial rectus.

I was too tired when we finished today to drive up to the country, so we stayed overnight, planning to drive up in the morning to see patients in the Brewster office.

Friday, May 7

The Friday schedule was typical of the Brewster office, almost 100 percent children, some of them with problems, a lot of them routine.

The two post-ops came in from Monday, Thomas Donnelly—we operated on his right eye Monday morning, and it looked pretty good considering three muscles had been done—and Vincent Striano—on whom we waited until he was eight-and-a-half to operate, and he looked good too.

Jolene Lassiter has 12 diopters of farsightedness in each eye. Her glasses are so thick they look like ice cubes. I'm trying to encourage her to think about contact lenses, but she's only 10, so we'll wait another year.

Samuel Tobias has nystagmus, and he turns his face to dampen his nystagmus for best vision in right gaze. I won't operate on him for that because it's not bad enough.

Serafina Calafiore came in again to be checked because she has juvenile rheumatoid arthritis and sometimes such kids get iritis in addition to their arthritis. I check her every three months for that.

Hal Farquhar, who owns the Brewster office, came in to

the office while I was seeing the patients and talked to me about Clarity and the takeover of his practice by this titan organization, which has bought up practices and then manages them for the doctors. The doctors still run their own practices but have to give back 20 percent to the company. I don't understand why it's worth it to him to do that, but he feels it gives him more contracts with managed care companies and better management of his practice. (He can't handle the number of patients he sees anyway.)

"Hal," I asked, "what are you going to do if you get more managed care contracts from Clarity managing you?"

"Well, then we'll have to hire another doctor." Then he says to me, "How would you like to work a couple of extra hours a week, or maybe another day's session?"

"Why should I? I don't make any money doing it the way I do it. I have to give you 50 percent of the office visits I see because of the overhead, and then I bring my own orthoptist up with me when I see the patients anyway, whom I have to pay the fee for her services. And at surgery, I have to give you a third of every operative case I do, and I have Steven Greenberg assist me, and we don't get reimbursement for the assistants anymore, so I have to pay him something to assist me. So I don't earn any money up here at all. I only do it for community service and so I can start my weekend a day early. Why should I want to work a couple of extra hours and ruin my entire Friday, rather than just the Friday morning?"

He got the picture.

I left the office as I usually do, exactly at 12:30 pm, and

went over to Centennial, a beautiful public golf course five minutes from the office in Carmel. I took a lesson with Lynn Slobin, whose father-in-law was captain of the Miami tennis team when I was captain of the Yale tennis team. Lynn's trying to help me with my game. It was great because I could forget about the problems at Manhattan Eye and Ear, the problems with the leasing of the office in the city and with Rudin Management, the problems with the office up in Putnam where I'm not happy and I'm not earning any money, the problems with the house we're trying to sell and the people who are holding us up and not going to contract but keeping it so we can't show it to somebody else, the problems with the house we want to buy that we can't buy until we sell the first one, and the problems with my son, Nick, who's in limbo as far as a really permanent career is concerned. So it was good to be out on the golf course taking a playing lesson and worrying about my alignment and completing my backswing and completing the follow-through. I didn't think once about these other problems for the three hours I was out there.

This weekend, I'm going to have to get on the phone and make more calls to my colleagues in the city. I have to know what's going on with the residents. Even if the hospital does fold, which it might, we have a commitment to these residents, especially the ones coming in and the ones who haven't been completely trained. What are we going to do with them? These young people have chosen Manhattan Eye and Ear out of all the hospitals in the world, practically, because it's one of the 10 best eye training centers in the world. They could have gone anywhere, and they chose Manhattan Eye and Ear, and we chose them, and now the hospital is threatening to close. So we have to place them in other hospitals. We have to do something to keep their training and to start the training of the ones who are just coming in.

This hospital is 130 years old. It started in 1869 on 34th Street in a little brownstone. It moved uptown to 64th Street, where it is now, rebuilt the building in 1925, and became the pre-eminent eye hospital in New York City and one of the most distinguished in the country. Those who work at MEETH are leaders in their fields of ophthalmology, ear, nose, and throat, and plastic surgery. The Eye Bank started at Manhattan Eye and Ear—all the basic retinal work and cataract surgery and corneal surgery and eye muscle surgery. Experts worldwide worked at Manhattan Eye and Ear, saw their patients, treated them, operated on them, and trained residents and Fellows to follow in their footsteps. And I am approaching my 40th year at Manhattan Eye and Ear and, suddenly this year, watching it threaten to go into extinction.

I came there as a resident in 1960, after Gene Scott had introduced me to Townley Paton, chairman of the ophthalmology department and the president of the board of the hospital. He introduced me to Dr. Paton at Southampton when I was playing in the old invitational tennis tournament in the summer. Dr. Paton, who had been captain of the Princeton tennis team in 1926, took a liking to me and has been my benefactor and my patron ever since. He was the president of the lay board as well as the president of the board of surgeon directors. There was no conflict in those days between the lay board of governors and the doctors. It was one and the same. He was the chief of both, and that's why the hospital ran in harmony at that time and didn't split until many years later when the lay board became distinct and separate from the surgeons.

I had my residency at Manhattan Eye and Ear from 1961 to 1963, and then I was away for three years, two in the Navy and one on my Fellowship, and I returned to Manhattan Eye and Ear to become the residents' instructor and director of the Residency Training Program in 1966. I've been there ever since, as assistant attending, surgeon director, and director of the eye muscle department. I've taught more residents how to operate on an eye muscle than any other doctor in New York City, certainly. I've helped more residents learn the rudiments of diagnosis and treatment of eye muscle disorders in the clinic than anybody else.

And now it looks like all of this is going to be gone unless we can do something to keep the lay board from selling the hospital.

We had a meeting Tuesday, after the strabismus conference, of the entire membership of the medical staff, and all these issues were discussed, along with all the possibilities for resurrection. We've hired a high powered lawyer. We've hired a publicist. We're trying to fight the lay board legally, but that might not work because the board might have a legal ground for selling the hospital. The board owns the charter.

A lot of possibilities would save it. The lay board could

sell the hospital to a real estate developer who could turn it into a high-rise and keep the first eight or nine floors for the hospital. Or, we could be taken over by Mt. Sinai/NYU, which would own the hospital and use it along with us for surgery and for clinic visits and for training residents and Fellows, and we would be part of the Greater New York University/Mt. Sinai complex. Or, the doctors could take over the hospital and several of them could have their private offices in the hospital. We could sell one of the three buildings, and then we could run the hospital from the remaining building and have some of our offices there, as well.

There are a lot of possibilities for saving the institution. Whether any of them will come to pass, I think we'll know in a few weeks.

Monday, May 10

The prospect of this evening's board of surgeon directors meeting rattled my uneasy mind as I drove into the city this afternoon. I had reason to be uneasy. The hospital administrator, Dr. George Sarkar (not an MD doctor), completely wasted our time at what turned out to be a terrible meeting. Steve Fochios, the head of the medical board, Jack Dodick, head of the ophthalmology department, David Adelstein, head of ENT, Sherell Aston, head of plastic surgery, and the rest of us board of surgeon directors pushed for answers but got no satisfaction.

We asked Dr. Sarkar pointed questions. Is the hospital

closing? Has a deal been struck to sell it for real estate? Will Mt. Sinai buy it, or perhaps Sloan-Kettering? What will happen to the residents? What will happen to the hospital? All we got in return from Sarkar was double-talk. Every answer he gave us was double-talk.

He said if the quality of medical care suffers, he would close the hospital, which he has nothing to do with. He told us he would have to say to the board of health that the hospital could not continue. It was all a contrived, diabolical scheme on his part to expedite the closing of the hospital, which he knows is going to take place. We asked him repeated questions about what the deliberations of the lay board were with Mt. Sinai, with Sloan-Kettering, with real estate developers. He said he didn't know. He said the consultants would have to be asked. He deferred further questioning to the president of the lay board. Sarkar wheedled his way out of every question we asked. It quickly turned into an exercise in futility. It insulted us to listen to his double-talk non-answers to our questions.

What's going to happen to the residency program? He knows the residency program is over. He's admitted he called the incoming residents and sent them letters that they're not going to be taken in as of July 1. He said he couldn't promise the first- and second-year residents would have positions. He knows full well they won't have any positions because there won't be any hospital. It was a terrible performance of one weaseling lie and deception after another.

By 6:30 pm we had had enough, and we called an end to the charade. Dr. Sarkar left the room. We all went upstairs in the main building to David Adelstein's office in the ear, nose, and throat department and held a meeting of our own, informally, without the presence of the administrator. We called our attorney, Charlie Stillman. Tomorrow morning in Supreme Court in New York, he told us, a lawsuit would be filed against the lay board for all the mismanagement and for the irresponsibility of taking the hospital to the point of demise. The lawsuit lists one gross infraction after another in addition to some conflicts of interest of a very serious nature, such as contracts to build operating rooms being given to a member of the lay board who has never built an operating room before. The lawsuit details many other infractions of sensible fiscal responsibility in which the lay board has indulged and that is trying to sweep under the rug by selling the hospital to either Sloan-Kettering or to a real estate developer.

We talked about the lawsuit that's going to be filed, and we're hoping this will preserve the hospital. But the danger is that, as soon as one orderly leaves, one admitting clerk leaves, one operating room attendant leaves, one nurse leaves, the hospital breaks down. The laboratory breaks down. The requisitions for laboratory stains are not being adhered to. The appointment desk doesn't receive the calls for clinic appointments. We're concerned the hospital is breaking down step-by-step. Even if our lawsuit has value and merit, it might be too late—as soon as one small chink in the hospital care takes place, the entire thing will unravel. That's why we kept saying at our surgeon directors' meeting that the quality of care must continue at a high level. But the fact is that, if we don't have enough operating room staff to maintain the operating room, we can't operate. If we don't have enough clinical staff, we can't maintain the clinics. And then the hospital will close precipitously. So time is of the essence. This lawsuit has to bear fruition quickly. We have to have the lay board thrown out and a new one appointed. The only person who can do that is state Attorney General Eliot Spitzer. And then it becomes a political problem. So we shall see. We're all very upset.

And to add an additional terrible note, we found out tonight that Charlie Kelman, who invented the operation we all use for cataract surgery, has been diagnosed with a brain metastasis from lung cancer. At the age of 68 and with two little twins just four years old. It made all the other problems seem to pale in comparison, and yet that's what we're dealing with on a day-to-day basis.

On a more personal note, I just spoke to my real estate broker. I told her if the people who quibble about buying the house don't do it within 48 hours the deal is off, and I'm not reducing the price one cent for improvements they uncovered on their inspection of the house. So we're either selling it by Wednesday or we're going to stay in it.

What a trying day. I'm whipped.

Tuesday, May 11

We started at eight o'clock with a phone call from Larry Levine asking me if I want to play golf with him. It's a beautiful day. "No," I had to tell him, "I work for a living, unlike some other people."

Joseph Kanek, on whom we operated for esotropia, came in. His parents brought in his little brother, who's showing a turn of his eye for the first time along with extreme farsightedness. He's got to be treated too.

Then we saw John Simmons, two, who got glasses for farsightedness from a pediatric ophthalmologist. Dissatisfied, his parents went to another pediatric ophthalmologist, who diagnosed farsightedness and astigmatism. They didn't know what to do so they brought Joseph to us. The child does have astigmatism in addition to his farsightedness. I said he should wear glasses for both. I gave them a new prescription because it was a little different from the second doctor's prescription, but they're worried how they are going to pay for it because I'm not on their plan. They want to use my prescription and they want me to take care of the child. It's a difficult situation.

Then I saw my friend Jerome North, who's also Leslie Pollack's close friend. North, a financial tycoon, has bad macular degeneration—a macular hole, actually, in one eye, with 20/200 vision, and early macular changes in the other eye, with preservation of 20/20 vision. I took a long time to dilate him and to study his retina and to refract him properly. It's a problem. He's a very active, important man, and he's losing his central vision.

David Denahom gave me a book he wrote about computers. He's a computer wizard. I operated on him and he's very happy because I straightened his eye after all these years. He had a gigantic deviation, and he presented me with a book he wrote about cyberspace. He's a Horace Mann boy, so a lot of his computer work started when he was a student there. Of course, he was there 20 years after I was.

Kathleen Porter came in. My friend Kathleen is the head of the ACLU, and her husband, Richard, is a big malpractice lawyer. She's a liberal Democrat, and he's a conservative Republican. They have some connection. We were talking about a certain doctor, and she said, "Oh, yeah. Richard's suing him." Anyway, Kathleen's okay. She just needed a routine check-up and a check-up for glaucoma.

Laura Campanis is slowly making progress with walking after her brain surgery, but she still doesn't walk unassisted, and she is doing better with her VIth nerve paralysis.

Shelley Bancroft came in. She's 67. I knew she didn't have myasthenia gravis. She had VIth nerve palsy from hypertension, so I took away her treatment for myasthenia and she's getting better because her VIth nerve palsy is getting better.

Jacqueline Bowen has an esotropia that might be cyclic—there one day, gone the next—and I suggested surgery. Mine was the third, or maybe fourth or fifth opinion. She has seen several other doctors. She should certainly have surgery.

Camilla Danza, now 34, had a transposition done in early childhood, and I don't think it was the right procedure because I think she had a retraction syndrome, but she's status post transposition surgery by a good pediatric ophthalmologist. Anyway, she's all right now, except she's got an elevation of the left eye when she looks to the right. I'm sure she was a retraction syndrome.

Janet Ambrose is terrific. I resected her lateral rectus, and she's doing great.

Korby Samson, the great-granddaughter of my friend, noted ophthalmologist Harald Gold, came in with her new glasses. Her eyes are straight, but she's got some amblyopia in her left eye, and we're going to have to do some patching on her.

Lastly, Seth Tracy. We operated on him last week for a disfiguring, neglected retraction syndrome. He's good, but he's not perfect, and I'm a little disappointed he has to turn his face 15 degrees to fuse. Of course, it's better than the 45-degree turn he had to do before we operated on him. While I was there, I could have done a little bit more. I could have let it slip further back.

So now I have to go to the hospital to see the residents. Because of all that's going on in the hospital, I spoke to David Guyer about what we're going to do with the incoming residents. We still have them on hold. We can't let them scatter because then we lose our residency, and there's no place for them to go anyway. They can't go to lousy programs. They were the best selected residents in the country, so they can't go to junky programs, which would be the only place they could get in at this point. Also, you have to figure out who's going to pay for their salaries and what kind of programs are going to be accredited. It's a big mess. It's May, and their residencies start in July. We don't know what we're going to do with them because we don't know what's going to happen with the hospital. We don't have the funds to pay for them to be residents elsewhere, nor the accreditation elsewhere, so we're trying to find different locations where we can train them. We're in court today with the lay board over what is happening to the hospital. The lawsuit we filed is being heard by Judge Bernard Fried this morning.

And, last night I was on the phone for an hour with my attorney, Stu Byron. I spent an hour and a half listening to him yell at me over this issue of the lease for our office and why I didn't tell the leasing company of our building that I wanted a new office instead of answering the sign in the office in the building we looked at next door. He yelled at me for an hour on the phone. Then he also yelled at me about what we're doing with Manhattan Eye and Ear, which is not exactly 100 percent under my control.

So much for another tough day.

Thursday, May 20

We saw the two post-ops at noon. Dennis Jadowski's eye looked pretty irritable because it's a very sick eye. His mother probably had German measles during pregnancy in Russia, and then he developed a cataract, and it was a small eye. It's way, way out, at least it was until we operated on him yesterday. The eye was straight today, but it was pretty hemorrhagic because it's not a healthy eye.

And the other patient, Anita Ho, the painter, looked very good. Her eye was nice and straight and not particularly inflamed at all.

Then we saw 20 patients, starting at one o'clock with Ramona Vincent, on whom we operated a few months ago and on whom I had operated when she was a year old (she's now 25), and she still feels her eyes are not perfectly straight.

Young adults and middle-aged adults who have had strabismus since childhood are so burned psychologically by their problem that, even when their eyes get straight, or close to straight, they never see them that way. They always feel their eyes are not exactly right and that people are looking at them in a strange way. It's a terrible psychological burden. Even when we make their eyes absolutely straight, they are convinced that, in some positions of gaze, people are looking at them and saying they're strange. She came with her father. Her eyes were teary. She was upset that she doesn't think she looks just right.

So, we talked about doing a little bit more and we talked about the risk of making it even worse if we did a little bit more, and then having to do more still. She and her father have a definite psychological hang-up over the alignment of their eyes.

I saw little Adam Reifsnyder, who's still tilting his head even though his eye muscle balance is perfectly normal. That's so disturbing because you operate for the head tilt, you make the muscle balance normal, and the head is still habitually tilted. It sometimes happens, and I might eventually have to do more surgery on him.

Jonathan Viningiano came in. He's 12 years old, and I remember when his father carried him like a little papoose in one of these papoose bags when he was a year old and we operated on his eyes. He's okay.

Mohammed Sarfras is from Pakistan and works in the operating room in the hospital. He's actually a foreign medical school graduate, but he can't practice here. He had had surgery for a nystagmus, which is rather experimental surgery and not particularly successful. We've largely given it up, but sometimes it's still done. He had it done at the hospital this year, and he wants my opinion about it now. At this point, there isn't much more that can be done, and I told him so.

Sam Wolf came in from Long Island. He had a retinal detachment and a retinal detachment operation and now he's got a vertical misalignment with double vision. We'll probably have to operate on him, although now there's a risk to his retina by doing the eye muscle surgery to get rid of the double vision. He either stays with his double vision, or we risk a retinal complication by trying to get rid of his double vision.

We saw a lot of patients, and I was too tired when we got finished to drive up to the country. We always say we're going to drive up after seeing the patients Thursday afternoon, and then I'm always too tired to do it. So we stayed in the city.

Friday, May 21

We drove up to Northeast Eye Care in Brewster and started seeing patients at 8:30 am, and I went through the usual schedule with my orthoptist, Rickie. We do it so quickly and so easily up there. It's just the difference between night and day, the ease with which we can see the patients in Putnam compared to the New York practice. The average time for the visit at Putnam is 10 to 15 minutes, and the average time for the visit in New York is 45 to 50 minutes, mostly because so many patients in New York are adults with all kinds of medical problems in addition to their strabismus and their cataracts and their glaucoma and their retinal complications. Most of the patients in Putnam are children with straightforward strabismus, although not always. Sometimes there are problems too.

For example, Dustin Southworth is 15 years old now and has Alport syndrome, a kidney disease, and he's subject to abnormalities of the lens of his eyes, as well as maculopathy. These children have chronic renal failure as they get older. He's also extremely nearsighted with astigmatism as well.

We finished at 1, and I raced out of the office. My friend, Hal Farquhar, saw me rushing out.

"How about extending your hours the way we had talked about it?"

He knows damned well I have no intention of extending my hours. I don't make a nickel up there as it is. I think I made

$4,000 in four months of coming up to Northeast Eye Care.

It's absurd. I mean, I do it just for community service. I give him 50 percent, and I pay my own technician, and the reimbursements from the managed care companies are just ridiculously low, so I end up making nothing, and he wants me to extend my hours.

I think we're not too long for Northeast Eye Care. I think we're going to start a pediatric group in Putnam County and separate ourselves from Northeast Eye. I should have done it a long time ago, but I didn't have the energy to do it and everything was comfortable simply coming up there to see the patients and leaving. But if we're not going to make any money at all, I might as well stay in the city an extra day of the week and see patients in our city office. So maybe we'll make something of it up in Putnam and start a real pediatric ophthalmology group.

Michele McLeod, our graduating pediatric Fellow, wants to come up, and Steven Greenberg, my associate and former Fellow, wants to start something up here with me. The three of us might start a small pediatric ophthalmology group. After all, Putnam County is the fastest-growing county in the state and the patients will only be children, so we should be able to do it. It just takes planning, and we have to get together and organize it—along with the problems of the hospital and the problems of the office in the city and the inability to pay our taxes. So nothing is simple at this particular point in time.

We owe $15,000 in taxes for our house, which is absurd in the first place because we don't use the school system, the fire department can't get to our house, we don't need any of the other services—and yet our taxes on the house in the country are $15,000 yearly. It's just crazy.

We have an attorney up here, John Porco, who is going to try to do something about our tax bill, which we haven't paid. So maybe if we started a pediatric practice up here, we might make a little more money and be able to pay our taxes.

Friday afternoon I played golf with Larry Yannuzzi and Rick Gibralter and my young friend, Dr. Rob Reiner, Leslie Pollack's son-in-law. Larry kept talking about us forming a core faculty in the city and going over to NYU or to Cornell. On each hole we played, Larry had another idea about how we were all going to join together at NYU and how we were all going to be a core faculty there. He talked about David Guyer becoming the new chief of ophthalmology at New York University, and what we're going to do with the residents, and how we have to get the residents to have new positions, but we still want to keep them together. It was just crazy listening to him. I don't think he really understood what he was saying. On the one hand, he's going to keep all the residents together and have a core faculty teach them, but we don't know where; on the other hand, he's talking about all of us going over to NYU or to Cornell and being the core faculty there, which, of course, they already have. They don't want 35 new ophthalmologists from Manhattan Eye and Ear to take over their positions and jobs.

It's just a mess. We can't take over Cornell or take over NYU, and we can't teach our residents in some abandoned psychiatric hospital on 75th Street. The hospital is going to close, the residents are going to have to be scattered to the far corners of the earth, we have to help them get positions, and then we have to go to other hospitals ourselves and get on the staff and operate there. And this idea of moving our whole faculty somewhere else—I just do not see that.

Anyway, it was fun playing golf with them, although it didn't exactly take our minds off our problems during the afternoon.

Saturday morning, I told my friend Ann Rothman and her husband, Dr. Bob Rothman, an orthopedist up here, to start looking for space for us in one of the offices near the hospital so we can start our new pediatric ophthalmology group, separate from Northeast Eye Care.

It was a rainy weekend, and not too much golf because of the weather, but a lot of time to think and organize how we are going to change our situation as the millennium approaches: the situation at the hospital, the situation in the office in the city where we're not making ends meet, and the situation up here, where we've never made ends meet. I went over the records of what we earned in the city compared to what we spend, and it was absurd. Most ophthalmologists run at a rate of 40 percent overhead and with us, it's about 60 percent overhead. We just don't keep any money at the end of the year at all. We did in 1993 because our income was double what it is now. Just double. But the expenses stayed the same. So now our expenses are 60 percent of what we make. Five years ago they were 30-40 percent of what we made. So there's no money left over to pay our bills, and especially to pay the taxes. We'll have to do something about that too. Our lease is up in the city in August, and we're going to have to make other arrangements.

This week, maybe I'll play golf with Larry Levine. I remember the last time I played golf with Larry, my limousine liberal lawyer friend who's a multimillionaire. He runs the Jewish Fund for Justice and he loves Hillary and Bill Clinton; he's a Democratic liberal who lives like a conservative Republican. The last time I played with him, we were driving down the fairway in the golf cart, going to his ball, and he said, "How's your practice going, Renée?"

"Well, Larry, it's an artistic success and a financial failure."

"What do you mean? What do you mean? You ophthalmologists make a ton of money."

"No, we don't," I said. "I don't make much money at all. I can hardly pay my bills."

"Well, my cardiac surgeon makes three million dollars a year."

"That's cardiac surgery. That's not ophthalmology."

"Ehh, you ophthalmologists make tons of money too. You do all those lasers on everybody."

"Larry, I don't do lasers. I do eye muscle surgery, and I do it on children whose families have small incomes, and its managed care and the compensation is very low."

"Aww, you do all these lasers, and that's how you can make a lot of money."

I repeated to him, "I don't do any lasers."

"What about all these consultations you do?"

"Well, you know, from Oxford, I used to charge $300 for a consultation, and Oxford pays us $90 for the same consultation. And when I operate, I used to get $4,000 for an eye muscle operation, and now Oxford pays us $1,000."

He turned to me and said, "Well, that tells you what it's worth."

I looked at him. "Get out of the cart and hit your ball."

If he hadn't had a quadruple bypass, and if I wasn't supposed to behave like a lady, he would be lying on the fairway squashed under the golf cart.

Tuesday, May 25

I looked at the schedule this morning, and the names of 24 patients stared back at me. I told Amy to cancel the last four because it was going be a very busy day and I would never get through it. It was a good thing she canceled those because we worked from 8:30 am until almost 2:00 pm. If we had kept those last four on, I wouldn't have made it to the hospital for the important conferences that afternoon and evening.

At 8:00 am, we saw Giacomo Catesteriano, an 18-month-old child with a very small convergent strabismus—easy to miss, but he definitely had it, and he definitely needs to wear some glasses and maybe do some patching.

Nobody else was a new patient, and it was a weird schedule because the patients had all kinds of different problems, most not related to strabismus. Some were, but a lot of them were general ophthalmology patients with a weird variety of conditions. Several had been operated on years ago by me and some more recently.

Among them was Laura Campanis, the little child with the brain tumor that was resected last month. She came into the office today walking, a really wonderful sight to see because she'd had a complication of a right hemiplegia following her brain surgery, and now today, for the first time, she walked into the office, and she was using her right side more normally. In addition, her VIth nerve paralysis is improving, so she's doing better on all accounts.

Riley Bowman, who had six operations for his glaucoma and then finally got a vertical strabismus from one of the injections for anesthesia during one of his operations, came in because he was concerned that, after six procedures for glaucoma, the pressure in one eye was starting to go up again. It actually was pretty low, and I reassured him he was still on the right track. I don't think he's losing any visual field, and his optic nerves looked about the same.

I left at 2:00 pm to go to the hospital and see some patients with the residents in the clinic, and we scheduled some surgery for June 23 with a first-year resident, Lisa Parks. She might not even be in the hospital come July 1, so what are we going to do with clinic patients on whom we've operated at the end of June if the residents are no longer there in July to take care of them? This is going to be some problem.

Then, at 4:00 pm, Joe Calhoun came as a guest lecturer and we presented cases to him on strabismus, and he discussed them with the staff. Then he gave us a talk at 5:00 pm, the Gershowitz Lecture on pediatric ophthalmology about the pitfalls and perils of strabismus surgery. The lecture looked vaguely reminiscent of the things I've been telling the residents for the past 35 years. Joe has the same ideas I have about keeping things safe in the operating room, and it was refreshing to hear him repeat so many of the things I've been telling the residents for years. After the lecture, a dinner was given in his honor at the Lotus Club as the guest of the New York Society of Pediatric Ophthalmology. I couldn't go because of the emergency meeting of the staff of Manhattan Eye and Ear at the hospital at 6:00 pm. The meeting lasted until 8:00 pm. So I worked today from eight in the morning until eight o'clock at night.

The meeting was a knockdown, drag-out affair with the entire medical staff present, along with our lawyer, Charlie Stillman, and his co-counsel, Mr. Bines, and our publicity representatives. Many doctors raised serious questions for our lawyer. Stillman said we would get a ruling by Judge Fried on Friday about our status as the board of surgeon directors. If we have standing, then we can petition the court for a delay in the lay board selling the hospital to Sloan-Kettering Memorial.

We talked about other strategies, including a media blitz, radio talk show announcements, letters to the attorney general, and other possibilities for press conferences and written articles to try to counter what the lay board has done in the way of attempting to make the public believe selling the hospital is in the best interests of Manhattan Eye and Ear and that the board is trying to continue Manhattan Eye and Ear in ridiculous little outpatient clinics in Harlem and Jamaica. And so we're working on publicity to educate the public and the attorney general and the judge as to the true nature of what the lay board is doing. It's preposterous the board is selling Manhattan Eye and Ear, doing it to cover up the board's mismanagement of the hospital over the past 10 years. If it is sold to Memorial, the books are never going to be looked into. If it becomes another eye hospital merger with Mt. Sinai NYU, then clearly Mt. Sinai NYU will look into the books and will see how the administrator and the lay board have seriously mismanaged the hospital into its financial difficulty.

The lay board hopes that, by selling it to Memorial, nobody will ever look at the books. We're trying to keep the board from doing that. Now we're beseeching members of the Memorial board not to go through with the purchase. Memorial board members don't even know the doctors are not in favor of selling the hospital and they've been led to believe Manhattan Eye and Ear is going to continue somewhere else. That idea is a total fabrication. It is not going to continue anywhere if it gets sold.

I need to get in touch with Sandy Weil, president of Citigroup, an old friend of mine from junior tennis days. He happens to be on the board at Memorial, along with Lawrence Rockefeller, James Robinson and Paul Marks, and several other very luminary-type people on the board of Sloan-Kettering-Memorial.

The lay board has done a lot of financial double-dealing. The board paid off the bonds of the hospital and has all this excess money now, along with a very favorable mortgage which should have helped keep running the hospital. Instead, the board paid off the bonds and is now trying to sell the hospital to Memorial or to the Colony, a real estate firm from California. The Colony plans to build a high rise apartment, and Memorial will turn the existing new buildings of the hospital over into a breast center. It's our job to convince Memorial it is not a good idea to destroy Manhattan Eye and Ear, that the breast center can be built anywhere, and we could work something out where we could share the building of the hospital with them. All these are possibilities other than closing Manhattan Eye and Ear.

We keep coming back to the same questions. If it closes, what are we going to do with all our clinic patients? What are we going to do with all the residents we were training? They have to find other positions, and they are unable to do so. Some of them have visas that allow them to stay in this country to study at Manhattan Eye and Ear. They might be deported. The third-year residents will certainly have no place to go because there's no place they can go to do the surgery they need to become trained.

What about the liabilities for the continued care of the patients in our clinic? More than 60,000 clinic visits every year—where are these clinic patients going to be taken care of?

Some of the doctors were very, very emotional. We're very, very upset with the lay board, and now we're unfortunately taking it out on our lawyers and our publicist because we want action. We want a press conference, we want spots on the radio, and we want a campaign mounted to approach the attorney general and the board of health. The lay board is not interested in keeping Manhattan Eye and Ear open and doesn't understand the significance of this particular specialty hospital.

I never got to the dinner for Joe Calhoun at the Lotus Club. I came home and had something to eat and went to sleep to get ready for surgery Wednesday.

Wednesday, May 26

First we operated on Frank Nychas, a 24-year-old man who had surgery by Dr. Idella Raggis twice for exotropia and now has esotropia with a limited ability to move his eye in abduction. Dr. Raggis watched the operation because she's very concerned about her patient. We exposed the medial rectus first and then recessed it, and then we went after the lateral rectus, which was very difficult to find because it was so far behind the equator of the eye, almost near the optic nerve. I finally found it, isolated it, and advanced it forward to increase the abducting effect of that eye. Then we had to take both the medial and the lateral rectus and raise them up because Nychas had a vertical misalignment as well. It was a very difficult surgery. It took about an hour and a half, but I think we accomplished what we had to do.

Then we operated again on Edna Wan, still dealing with an automobile accident that caused a total lateral rectus paralysis on one side and a partial one on the other side. I operated on her once and did a gigantic amount of surgery on three muscles. I brought her back this time to do a final tune-up, a little more on one of the medial rectus muscles (which was very hard to do because it's already very far back), and then to tighten up the weak lateral rectus, too. I thought of doing a transposition on her, because she really has almost no lateral rectus function. That's a dicey operation because she has hypertension, and the risk is that we diminish the blood supply to her eye and she could lose her eye. So I didn't do it. I did the conservative procedure, which will help her with her face turn, but won't give her much in the way of adduction.

I finished surgery about 11 and went to Dr. Norman Medow's office across the street from the hospital. We discussed the hospital, pediatric ophthalmology in general, and the possibility that maybe we might combine our practices into a large pediatric ophthalmology group. That would require a new office, increased staff, and a lot of business and administrative details—a gigantic undertaking. But we're under the gun because the building landlord wants me to sign a new lease on our office here and he's pushing me to sign it by the end of the week. Fortunately, it's Memorial Day weekend, so I think we can hold him off until after the holiday and then give Norman a chance to think over the possibility of joining our practices together to form Manhattan Pediatric Ophthalmology Associates. It probably won't work within the specified required period of time, so we'll probably end up signing the lease anyway and we'll see what we might do in the future.

Wednesday afternoon I went out to Forest Hills and saw Grandpa (my father) and Nicky. Grandpa didn't look exactly right to me. His speech seemed a little bit funny, although I showed him some pictures and he recognized his roommate from medical school. He remembered his roommate's name but he had not been too fond of him for various reasons, although he was supposed to have been my father's best friend. He got up and came to the door when we left, so he seemed all right, but his speech was not exactly right. Nick and I went out to dinner, and Nick told me his ideas for a new business with Oxana making crystal hair barrettes out of semi-precious stones—topaz, amethyst, rose quartz, aquamarine, and others. And I saw the little laboratory he and Oxana started up in the attic of the house, and then I came back to the city.

Thursday, May 27

I saw a reasonable number of patients in the office. The two post-ops looked very good—Edna Wan, with the VIth nerve paralysis following an auto accident, and Frank Nychas. I really did a good job of finding his lateral rectus and repairing it and doing the medial. He looked very straight when I saw him today.

We saw a new patient, Sean Dougherty, a professional boxer with double vision. He got hit in the head and has a superior oblique palsy. I told him we had operated on another champion boxer, Vito Antuofuermo. Vito had retained the middleweight championship of the world on a controversial draw against Marvin Hagler.

"Yeah," he said, "I think he lost that fight when they said he won the title."

I said, "Regardless, he had a muscle problem and we repaired it, and we're going to have to do the same for you. And then you should stop boxing."

He agreed.

Friday, May 28

I drove up to Northeast Eye Care—the Brewster office—and I told them to make my schedule stop at 11 so I could play golf with my friend Jack Dodick in Connecticut. The shortened schedule offered nothing especially exciting in the list of patients, and I walked out at 11 to drive to Wilton, Connecticut.

The one interesting thing was that, at 8:30 in the morning, when I walked in the door, my friend Hal said, "Oh, Renée, would you see a patient for me? She's a friend of my daughter's boyfriend or something."

"Sure, Hal. I'll see her."

"Well, I put her in your schedule for you."

I don't know why he's rearranging my schedule, but he put her in at 8:30 am. I looked at the records. She's my patient, to begin with. Where he gets involved in it I don't know. I have operated on her and I see her every year, and to make matters worse she didn't even show up. So the 8:30 am spot could have been used for somebody instead of us sitting and twiddling our thumbs, waiting for the next appointment to start at 9:00 am. It's one of those things that make me more and more aggravated about staying at Northeast Eye Care. I don't think I'm going to be there for too much longer.

At 11 when I left, the new manager said to me, "Oh, leaving early?" I looked at him like he was nuts.

I got to Connecticut to play golf with Jack. We hadn't even gotten on the course before we were informed about the court case, which the judge had ruled on early today. We lost the case. Unreal. Jack's the director of the ophthalmology department. I'm the longest-running, oldest member of the staff, still teaching and training residents in my 40th year, and we learn this hospital that has been our entire working life is going to close. The judge ruled we have no standing. NO STANDING. Isn't that amazing? Jack Dodick is one of the top cataract surgeons in the world. I'm maybe one of the foremost eye muscle surgeons in NYC. I've been director of the residency training program there. I'm surgeon director and head of the muscle department, but we have NO STANDING. The doctors have no standing, and the board can sell the hospital to Memorial, which is what the board is doing and that's that. We can appeal it. We can invent all the public relations frenzy we want; we can stand on our heads. We can appeal to Eliot Spitzer, the attorney general, and we are doing that. We can write letters. We can form a gigantic campaign and sign petitions and go on the radio and go on all the talk shows and do whatever we want. The hospital will still be sold. It's probably not going to stay open beyond June 30. I'm scheduled to operate with a resident on June 23. That resident will be gone by the end of that week, so I'll have to take care of that patient myself, privately. What an irony. That this hospital—the top eye hospital in the city, perhaps in the country—is going to close because the lay board has mismanaged it into financial difficulty and now wants to get rid of it and sell it to Memorial so that nobody else is going to look at the books.

The meeting we had with them Tuesday was atrocious. It was just brutal. No wonder I almost walked out.

Anyway, it wasn't too good an afternoon of golf for Jack and me, but we tried to forget the hospital as much as we could. Life goes on.

Memorial Day Weekend

I spent the weekend playing golf and taking it easy. Sunday morning, Nick called from Forest Hills to tell me Grandpa wasn't doing so well. He couldn't walk. It took a great deal of effort but Nick and Ada—Grandpa's live-in assistant—and Ada's husband, Eddie, got Grandpa upstairs into bed. This morning he was eating, but his blood pressure is down and his pulse is a thread. Arleen and I are going to drive in tonight and go directly to Forest Hills to see how he's doing. It's probably getting close to the time to call my sister and Grandpa's girlfriend, Ruth, because

I'm not sure he's going to make it for too many more days. I think he's had a stroke and, at the age of ninety-nine-and-a-half, I don't know if he's going to pull through.

This is a good time to recap all the overwhelming things that have happened in the past month. I think one of the diary tapes got lost, so I might not have an exact chronicle of what transpired, but, let me just recapitulate several different fronts on which we have been fighting.

The hospital is going under. The board of surgeons met with the board of governors, and it was a sham meeting because it was just to fulfill the board of governors' requirement to hold meetings with us. Board members said they were continuing the mission of the hospital with their little first aid stations in Harlem and Jamaica, which was just so much nonsense. They're not fulfilling the mission of the hospital that way. The mission is as an eye, ear, and throat specialty hospital in New York. And that they're killing. It's gone. At the meeting we had at the hospital of the medical staff, where everybody was so energized and animated, and some of the doctors talked about calling the attorney general and the petitions and the press, we were told to hold off until the judge made his ruling. Well, now that the judge made his ruling, I think we're going to see a bomb go off amongst the medical staff, but it's not going to do any good.

Sandy Weil never returned my call. He's on the board at Memorial. I've been trying to call our friends who are on the Memorial board to tell them the doctors at Manhattan Eye and Ear are not in favor of the hospital closing and the hospital is not moving somewhere else. The Memorial board has been tricked into thinking we're moving and the doctors are in favor of all this, which is just another one of the diabolical schemes of this lay board and the administrator.

Here I am trying to make ends meet practicing ophthalmology in this year of 1999, with a net income of $60,000. I can't even pay my taxes, and the administrator of this hospital he's administrated into oblivion gets $600,000 a year and will probably continue when the hospital is sold, as he'll administer these new sham clinics in Harlem. So much for the hospital.

On the personal front, we failed to sell our house. The guy chiseled us down to $712,000 from the $800,000 asking price. Then he went down $10,000 more because he said repairs had to be done, and we told him to go to hell. Well, we can't even pay our taxes. We have a $15,000 tax bill we can't pay because our income isn't high enough in relation to our overhead. All we can do is pay our mortgage, and we have nothing left over to pay the taxes. Failing to sell the house has put us in a pretty bad bind, financially.

Then there's the problem with the lease in the city where we looked at a less expensive office. The management of our building which also owns that building found out and told us we couldn't have that office and that we were even going to have to get out of our current office. That's how mad they were at us.

Meanwhile, we pay them more money than any other tenant in our building, and we've been model tenants for 16 years, taking care of everybody connected with the building and being the best tenant they've ever had. So Stuart Byron (he's my attorney) had to enter into the fray and speak to the agent, an intransigent hothead who manages Rudin Management, and finally got him to agree to give us a new lease. My associate, Scott Greenbaum, doesn't want to have his name on it, so we're not sure what he's up to. He might want to leave us at some point. So much for the lease in the city.

Then we have the problem of the office at Northeast Eye Care. We're seriously thinking of leaving because we're not making any money. Fifty percent we give to Hal Farquhar for every patient we see, and I have to bring in my own technician. The reimbursements are pitiful. We made only $4,000 in four months of coming up each Friday since the beginning of the year. That's an insanely small income for a surgical specialist in any specialty.

These are some of the problems we face at the end of Memorial Day 1999. The most imminent, I think, is Grandpa. And we'll see what's going to transpire with him in the next few days.

June

Tuesday, June 1

Last night we stopped in Forest Hills to see Grandpa, who was able to get up and to walk a little bit. His speech is a little bit slurred, so I think he probably had a transient ischemic episode because his blood pressure had been down over the weekend as well. His blood pressure was okay, his pulse was okay, and except for a little bit of slurred speech he seemed to be all right. I did a neurological and he was intact. I told Ada to give him an aspirin every day but not to give him any blood pressure pills. I called my sister and told her what was going on and that I would follow up.

This morning in the office was no treat. A lousy schedule greeted me—very difficult patients from years ago who are very complicated and very difficult.

I can't even touch Amanda Ormond's eyes to put drops in them because she has such an emotional overlay from the time of her ptosis surgery and multiple vertical eye muscle surgery. She's 28 years old now and she still won't let me put the drops in by myself. She has to hold her eyelids open for me to do it. And to check her pressure with the applanation tonometer is almost impossible.

Clark Sanderson is a -28.00 myope in one eye, and his status is post cataract operation and epikeratophakia in the left eye and developmental delay. It's impossible to examine Clark because you can't get near him with the applanation tonometer, and you can't refract him because he makes a slit out of his eyelid to create a pinhole effect, no matter what lens you put in front of him.

Johanna Maria Rumann is an old German woman from Argentina on whom we operated years ago, and her husband is now dead. I don't know what her background was in the old days in Germany, but they were one of the expatriate families living in Argentina after the Second World War.

Beverly Swisher came in with a corneal ulcer. Beverly had bilateral Duane's syndrome I operated on in early childhood, and she's 25 now. For the corneal ulcer, we had to send her to the hospital for cultures and scraping, start her on fortified antibiotic drops, and arrange for Rick Gibralter to see her tomorrow because I'm operating—a very complicated situation.

And then we saw Alexander Liberatore from Sao Paolo, Brazil, on whom we're going to operate tomorrow for both a divergent strabismus and a face turn for nystagmus. It's a totally impossible situation because the operation for the nystagmus is going to make his divergent deviation worse, and then we'll have to do more surgery for the divergent deviation because of that.

Wednesday, June 2

This morning we operated on Alexander Liberatore for nystagmus and a divergent deviation. He has had cataract extraction in each eye already, even though he is only 19 years old. He goes to college in the States. We operated on him for his nystagmus and his exotropia, which is a very tricky maneuver. We did a recess/resect on the right eye, which should help both the nystagmus and the exotropia. If I had operated on his left eye too, it would have made the exotropia worse, so I elected not to do that. We'll see how he does.

The other case was Menachim Rappaport, a five-year-old Lubovitcher Orthodox Jewish child from Brooklyn. He came into the operating room with a picture of Chief Rabbi Menachim Schneerson pinned on his pajamas for good luck. He was named for the chief rabbi. Rabbi Schneerson is the spiritual head of the Lubovitcher sect in Brooklyn, and he recently died, and it was thought he might even be the messiah by some of his followers. Anyway, the little boy did very well, and we did a recession of each medial rectus for esotropia.

The hospital is beginning to look like a morgue. Fewer and fewer patients are being scheduled. More and more of the hospital OR staff are asking me for letters of recommendation. Jules and Marie Barnes and some of my closest allies are beginning to ask me for letters. I am in the process of getting on the staff of New York Eye & Ear Infirmary and going through all the rigmarole of a new staff appointment, with credentials of many, many years ago, an infection control course certification, and CPR certification, and all these things required for new appointment to a hospital staff, at my ripe old age. But our hospital is failing by the minute. We lost the appeal to the judge, so now our only avenue left is political—influencing the attorney general and the board of health. We are not optimistic.

I played golf with Jack Dodick again this afternoon, joined by Larry Parsont, on Long Island. We were all crying and talking on the cell phone with lawyers as we were playing, and trying to figure out whom we know in the Republican hierarchy who can influence the governor as well as the attorney general. That's our last-ditch attempt to save this hospital, which the board of governors has so cleverly allowed to fall apart.

We think there might be several areas of wrong-doing on the board's part—which members are trying to cover up—including double-booking, not billing for services rendered, getting a conflict-of-interest construction company to build five unnecessary new operating rooms. We think the president of the lay board may have mismanaged the trust fund of the hospital in a bull market and lost $600,000 he was supposed to have invested for the hospital. It seems a comptroller we had years ago knows about all the double-dealing and the double-booking, but he's unwilling to come forward. That's one source of fraud we can't tap, although it would be wonderful if we could get him to testify. He simply won't do it.

I will add a sad note here: The lay board president was one of the corporate chiefs at Morgan Stanley, a huge Wall Street investment firm, whose staff was situated on a top floor of the World Trade Center. When the building was evacuated on September 11, 2001, 95 percent of the staff got out, but when he was told to leave he did not.

He was a good friend of my close friend Gene Scott. He was also one of the most eligible bachelors in New York. He didn't need to be on the lay board of a hospital. He did it out of a wish to be of community service. As I said, sad.

The lay board is just trying to sell this hospital so fast to a real estate developer, the Colony, or to Sloan Kettering Memorial hospital so the books will never be examined. If we were sold to Mt. Sinai and maintained as an eye hospital, the books would have to be examined, and the lay board does not want that. It also turns out our publicity agent is in thick with the real estate people in this city, and he's not going to do anything against a real estate developer. It was a terrible mistake for us to hire him as our public relations expert. Be that as it may, we're stuck with him, and our lawyers are working to try to get to the Republican hierarchy.

Thursday, June 3

Barbara, our orthoptist, attended a meeting of the Eastern Regional Orthoptics Society, so she wasn't in the office. I had to see all the patients by myself, which is always a little bit more difficult because she does a lot of the preliminary work for me—their history, checking the glasses, the measurements, the orthoptic examination, the visual acuity and putting the drops in the children. When I have to do it myself, it's a lot more work.

I saw Casey Schwartz at one o'clock. I still don't know what's wrong with the child. He keeps complaining about a pressure sensation on his eye. I finally figured out maybe it's because he's got a beginning divergent deviation of his eyes, and he's trying to control it, which I never felt was a problem with him. Maybe what he's describing as pressure sensation is muscular asthenopia of trying to keep his eyes straight. With youngsters, it's very hard sometimes to understand their true symptoms. He says his eye feels weird or he feels a pressure behind them or below them. An adult would be more capable of saying it's a pressure sensation or a muscular effort at lining his eyes up.

We saw Tyrone Wangerhals, 44, who is somehow related to Herbert Walker, former President George Herbert Walker Bush's father-in-law. Tyrone had a cerebral hemorrhage several years ago and now has a hemiplegia. We did heroic surgery on his eyes for vertical nystagmus that had required a chin-up position for dampening and reducing the oscillations and surgery for vertical strabismus with torsion, which required an adjustable Harado-Ito procedure—probably the most difficult operation we do—to split the anterior fibers of the superior oblique, move them temporarily so you're selectively strengthening only the fibers responsible for torsion, and doing it on an adjustable suture you can tighten or loosen when he wakes up, and in addition moving his eyes up to help with his vertical nystagmus.

He's done very well since the surgery. He still requires a small amount of vertical prism, but he sees well. He doesn't have to wear his patch, and that's amazing because he was constantly wearing his patch before surgery because of intractable double vision. He's very grateful for the surgery we did on him and he's had an amazing result. The Harada-

Ito procedure alone is difficult enough without doing it on an adjustable suture and doing a procedure for vertical nystagmus in addition. He had had a bilateral superior oblique paralysis as a result of his hemorrhage. We did a Harada-Ito on one side, a tuck of the superior oblique on the other side, and both superior recti.

Edna Wong is recovering nicely from her surgery. She's still the diva and the prima donna and comes in groaning and moaning, but she's actually doing just fine, and she's got no face turn anymore.

I saw my cousin Ruth Stone, who's 86 years old and was at my parents' wedding in Bryn Mawr, Pennsylvania, in 1927. We operated on her for exotropia, and we're watching her cataracts at this point.

Little Charles Herrera has only one useful eye because the other eye had a developmental abnormality and cataract and retinal detachment and a failed retinal detachment procedure. He has no vision in his left eye at all. It's small, it's turned in, and it's sightless. But he sees 20/40 with his right eye, even with a little bit of a face turn for nystagmus. I'm trying not to operate on his good right eye.

Then I saw Dr. Sudarsky's great-nephew. I've seen every relative of Dr. David Sudarsky known to mankind. Dr. Sudarsky is one of my best friends and he taught me so much when I was a resident, and even after. He was the first one to bring the scleral buckle procedure for retinal detachment from Boston to New York, and he is one of our greatest ophthalmologists at Manhattan Eye, Ear and Throat Hospital. He's the former president of the board of surgeon directors and former head of the retinal service. David has been a great mentor and friend to me. I see all his assorted nieces and nephews when he asks me to.

We then drove up after the office hours on Thursday. Usually we stay overnight Thursday night and drive up in the morning, but we drove up Thursday night to get to the house so we could have the evening there.

Friday, June 4

Northeast Eye Care is getting to be more and more oppressive for me. I think my relationship with Hal is getting worse and worse, or at least certainly colder and colder. I think he knows I'm getting ready to leave and not much chitchat goes on between us at this point.

I saw the patients there by myself, too, because my orthoptist, Ricki, also went to the Eastern Regional Orthoptic meeting. I got through all the kids and the few adults by 12:30 pm. We had operated on a few of those patients. Because Ricki wasn't there, the schedule was arranged so that I didn't have to see anybody new. A lot of follow-ups were scheduled, including the one who didn't show up the week before that Hal wanted me to see, who was my patient anyway. I don't think there's too much wrong with her eyes, but we'll just have to observe her symptoms.

Margaret Cloak came in. She's 75 years old. I had operated on her for a very complicated condition—convergence insufficiency in adulthood, which borders on convergence paralysis. She's one of the few people who still need some prisms for distance vision because of a small secondary esotropia. But at near, she's just fine. And she has to wear glasses anyway, so to wear a little bit of prism is no big deal for her, although she considers it a gymnastic exercise to try to get rid of her prisms.

Then I went to Centennial and hit a couple of buckets of balls and then played nine holes before having my massage with Lori at 5:30 pm. It was a beautiful weekend, mostly playing golf and spending time at the lake.

Monday, June 7

My associate Steven Greenberg and I did three operations, which is a lot to do at Putnam Hospital. One was his little patient on whom we did four muscles.

The second was Brady Rawlinson, who's four-and-a-half years old—a patient I've been taking care of since he was maybe six months old. He was one-and-a-half pounds at birth and spent his first 100 days of life in the hospital. He's a miracle child. It's a miracle he's alive. It's a miracle he can breathe and a miracle he can see anything at all. His mother's always asking me about his vision, as if she expects him to see like a major league baseball player. Anyway, we operated on Brady and did three muscles in one eye. I'm not touching the other eye because he had retinopathy of prematurity and I don't want to risk both eyes for a retinal detachment.

And then we did an exotropia operation on little Paige Moran. That's the same operation I did on her brother two years ago.

Steven and I then went across the street to the Barns Office Complex and checked out an office. We're thinking of starting a pediatric ophthalmology group with Michelle McLeod, our graduating Fellow, and we're looking at a few offices for rent.

I drove to Centennial, but it was so hot I couldn't even hit any balls. I got dizzy and had to lie down on the grass because it was 100 degrees. When I got up off my rear end I drove home and took the two dogs down to the lake and stayed in the lake for an hour. It was just wonderful.

Tuesday, June 8

I stayed at the house last night and drove into the city this morning at 6:00 am, ahead of the White Plainsers. The White Plainsers all get on the highway from Dutchess County at about 6:00 and they reach Putnam County at about 6:30 am, so if you can get ahead of the White Plainsers you can make it to the office by 8:00 am. I got to the office at 7:45 am, in time to do a little dictating before I started my schedule at eight o'clock.

Today was a killer because we saw 22 patients. I could spend an hour with each of several patients, and it amazes me that some ophthalmologists see 90 patients a day. You just wonder how they're doing it. In my practice, I couldn't do that.

One of the patients, Judge David Wilner—80 years old, double vision, referred by his ophthalmologist and my close friend, Larry Parsont—took a full hour of examination to sleuth out his double vision. He doesn't really have a true vertical imbalance. He's got no significant astigmatism. He has a lot of debris in the vitreous of his eye. He's got scattered hemorrhages from his cardiovascular problems. All of this made him see double and made him aware of a second image, which was really coming from only one eye—monocular diplopia—and it took an hour to diagnose it.

Another patient, Farida Garouva, had double vision as well, and she had a combined horizontal-vertical misalignment that took a long time to diagnose and to figure out. Sometimes you get a couple of patients like that. Another one, Roberta Kahn, was a new patient with esotropia. It was sometimes present, sometimes not. When it was present, it was gigantic. It was related to her being 41 and not being able to focus too well anymore. It took a long time to examine her.

We're getting ready to operate on Casandra Riggis, the little daughter of an ophthalmologist, for bad nystagmus and bad spasmus nutans. She took a long time.

I was halfway through the schedule when I looked at the waiting room. It was mobbed. Seats were filled. People were standing. People waited outside in the street. I don't understand the schedule, but I've been through this before.

I saw Eileen and Sandra Reichert, both with congenital nystagmus, both with congenital cataracts, both with cataract extraction. The mother, Eileen, had only one eye. Sandra had

20/100 vision and a large amount of nystagmus. I had done a YAG laser on her years ago to try to open her posterior capsule. I operated on her muscles to lessen her nystagmus.

Among the wave of patients were the two post-ops, Alexander Liberatore—the young boy from Brazil whose eyes are now straight—and Menachim Rappaport.

Menachim made the day. We operated on him last week for a convergent strabismus. He came in today with his father and his father told me that on the day after the operation Menachim looked up at the sky and said, "Daddy, look. The clouds." He had never seen the clouds in depth before. He had seen true binocular single vision with depth, and it was a miracle for him. We could charge that miracle to the grand rabbi Menachim Schneerson, whose picture Menachim's father had pinned to his pajamas when he went under the anesthetic last week for his surgery. Now he sees the clouds in depth. I'm floating on those clouds.

I was tired after seeing so many patients, but I journeyed to Manhattan Eye and Ear and commiserated with the residents over the imminent closing of the hospital. We talked about graduation having been canceled and we talked about the residents still not knowing whether they're going to be moved to another building and be absorbed into part of the Cornell system, or whether they should apply and get positions in other hospitals. One of the residents has accepted a position at UCLA next year. Another will have an interview in Philadelphia tomorrow, and some of the others are trying to be part of this group that Dr. Guyer is putting together to keep our faculty but teach the residents in the building Cornell is allowing us to use. I'm not so sure how that's going to work. I think it's a pipe dream, but that's what David Guyer says is going to happen, and we shall see.

Then I went to the Manhattan Ophthalmological Society dinner at the Mark Hotel, where all the luminary ophthalmologists, so-called, in the city gather to have dinner and present cases to each other. We stand around for an hour having drinks and *hors d'oeuvres* and have a gourmet dinner and then, if we have a case, we present it with the projection of slides. We generally have an enjoyable time because we're all pretty good friends and are essentially the elite of ophthalmology in the city. We enjoy each other's company and presenting cases and discussing them and having dinner. It's nice, but I don't like to get home too late on a Tuesday night because I operate Wednesday. I had three difficult cases scheduled tomorrow, but if I get home at ten o'clock, that's okay.

Wednesday, June 9

The operating schedule is getting smaller and smaller at the hospital. Fewer cases are being scheduled, but we're still doing our three every Wednesday morning. This morning we operated on Diane Schur, whose father is an anesthesiologist, and he came into the operating room with her. Fortunately, everything went well anesthesia-wise. She's 11 years old with a history of prematurity. We operated on her eight years ago and had a little more to do for her eyes, now beginning to diverge. We did both lateral recti. She did very well.

The second case was an optometrist, Kirk Flynn, who needed surgery for a convergent deviation and waited until he was 31 years old to do it. He's had vision therapy and all kinds of other forms of treatment, but he really needed to have his medial recti corrected, which we did. He did well, too.

The most difficult case was Harry Sofer. He had been operated on five times by a general opthalmologist, who shouldn't have operated on him even the first time because he's not a strabismus specialist. I don't know why he did him even once, and God knows why he did him five times. It took me two hours to dissect through all the scar tissue and the fat and all the other tissue in his orbits to get at the muscles I had to operate on. Then I had to resect all the scar tissue and revise the conjunctiva and do the surgery on the eye muscles for a divergent deviation, and a vertical, as well. After two hours, I was satisfied I had him straight and I had gotten rid of as much scar tissue as was humanly possible. I was exhausted when I finished. It was the sixth operation this week and it was the most difficult because it took me two hours. I walked out of the operating room after one o'clock, wiped out.

I got in the car and drove up to the house and went over to the golf course and found my good friend, Rudy Mahacek. Just the two of us on the course, not too hot, perfect weather, nobody else there, and we played 18 holes and I didn't think about Harry Sofer, not once, for four hours.

I came home and had dinner and watched the ball game

and fell asleep, exhausted.

Thursday, June 10

I saw 17 patients, starting at noon. A few were new ones.

My friend, Tom Dee, who went to Horace Mann and to Yale with me, lives in the same weekend community up in Sedgewood as I do. I had found a malignant melanoma of the choroid in one eye on an incidental examination, just looking at him routinely a couple of years ago. It was an amazing find, because it was way, way out in the periphery, and I just caught sight of it as I was going around looking at his retina in all the quadrants of the clock-face dial. There it was. So I probably saved his life by finding this melanoma when it was in such an early stage, and he had a radioactive plaque put in in Philadelphia. He's done pretty well. It's not gone away completely, but it's not any larger, and he seems to be doing okay.

That was an amazing find. I almost wasn't going to dilate him that day, too. But I did, and there it was. I never thought I was going to see a melanoma in him. I was just looking at his periphery because he's nearsighted. I was looking to see if he had any weak spots in his retina or any breaks or any tears and, boom, there was melanoma like an iceberg looming up at you.

We ended the day with little Justin Bean, who's got such a big astigmatism in each eye he only sees 20/50, 20/40, but he functions okay. He's on Ritalin now, so that helps him behave a little better too. Justin always worries about the "drips" in his eyes. Often I tell him "no drips" if he reads the chart right. He always tries his best.

Friday, June 11

We started at the usual 8:30 am at Northeast Eye Care and saw many patients, several of them post-ops.

Brooke Donald, who's now 11 years old, had nystagmus, severe face turn, and strabismus, and we operated on her when she was little. We were about ready to operate on her again, but I decided her face turn wasn't bad enough for surgery. This morning she looked terrific. She hardly has any face turn at all. It would have been a mistake to operate on her again and would have run the risk of giving her a big divergent deviation. It's so important to know when to operate and when not to operate. (January 2020: I still see her and her mother up in my only remaining Yorktown Heights office. She is beautiful, a graduate in social work, straight eyes, and with 20/25 in her better eye.)

Little Paige Moran looked terrific. It looked like she had never been operated on, and we had just done her three days ago.

Olivia Torok is doing well and so is little Brady Rawlinson, the miracle child who weighed one-and-a-half pounds at birth. His eye is doing pretty well after Monday's operation. He has straight eyes, minimal inflammation, and he lets his mother put the drops in once in a while.

Nothing in the morning had been really exciting. We got ready to leave at 12:10 pm because the last patient hadn't shown up for her 11:45 am. I was on my way out the door when in walks the 11:45 am patient. I came back and we saw her, and then we had to dilate her pupil and so we ended up staying there 45 minutes more.

That's a drag when the last patient comes in a half hour late and then has to be dilated because it's a new patient. It's very inconsiderate. If the first patient of the day doesn't come or comes late, or if the last patient of the day comes late, that really screws up the doctor's schedule. So that was Friday morning.

Friday afternoon, I hit some golf balls and practiced and got all ready for our member/member tournament on Saturday. Then Kenny Piersa—the cookie man—and I almost won the member/member, but we didn't because we played a great front nine and were leading the field, and then we collapsed. Well, we didn't collapse, but we just didn't have a great back nine and another team won. Oh, well.

Wait till next year for the member/member.

It was the second straight year for the winning team—three years in a row, actually, because one of them has a handicap much higher than it really should be. Those two always come in with a low net score. Nobody seems to be bothered by it as much as I am, but I just don't think anything unfair should take place in a sporting event. Maybe it's my background.

Monday, June 14

The ophthalmology department is going to take Manhattan Eye and Ear residents to the St. Regis Hotel for a gala dinner because their graduation has been canceled. Another huge black mark against our lay board, which couldn't even see fit to give them a graduation. Amazing.

We're still trying to find places for them at other hospitals, but it's a problem of financing their salaries by the Health Care Finance Administration (HCFA) and the residency review board. Who's going to pay for these residents to be residents in other hospitals? The hospitals only have certain slots HCFA pays for, and none for additional residents who might come. And then there's a scheme by the lay board to transfer the existing residents over to Gracie Square Hospital, a defunct psych hospital on 72nd Street and York Avenue. I think that's a crazy scheme, but some of our leaders think they can manage having the residents see patients over there. I don't know where they're going to get the patients from. We have 85,000 clinic charts at Manhattan Eye and Ear. We're going to transfer all those charts over to Gracie Square? And the patients don't know to go to Gracie Square. They know to go to Manhattan Eye and Ear. When they hear it's closed, they're going to go to other existing hospitals, not the Gracie Square Hospital that nobody, not even I, knows is in existence.

Everyone asks me when the hospital is going to close, and

I can't tell them. Nobody knows except the administrator and the lay board. I think after June 30, when the residents leave, there will be no more clinics. Maybe the operating rooms will stay open for another month or so, but that's probably it.

Tomorrow night I have an interview with the credentials committee at the New York Eye and Ear.

Tuesday, June 15

We saw 22 patients, starting at eight o'clock, an exhausting schedule for the city. A couple of patients we operated on got beautiful results.

Rose Noble, 75, no longer has double vision after the cataract operation. I did her under an adjustable suture, which was no mean feat in Rose, who doesn't follow directions that well and keeps talking. It's very hard to communicate with her when she won't stop talking to you. I'm trying to get her to fixate on a target on the ceiling in the operating room and tell me which image I'm taking away, the higher one or the lower one, and she keeps talking to me and telling me different things unrelated to the object on the ceiling. I had no idea whether I had adjusted her to be perfectly straight or not, but it ended up that I did. She's fine and has no double vision.

Problems continue for Pamela Bishop. John Hermann operated on her four times, and I operated three times. She's always straight for a period of months after surgery, and then one eye goes right back out again. She's got a gigantic divergent deviation after those seven operations. I can't say she was in bad hands either time, but she just forms scar tissue and pulls that eye right back out again. I will not operate on her again. I'm afraid if I keep detaching her muscles and re-attaching them to the eye, I will get the worst complication possible—an anterior segment ischemia and possible loss of the eye. This is one of my failures and I feel sorry every time I see Pamela, but I'm not going to risk her eye to try to get it straight, and that's it for her.

Laura Campanis, the little girl with the brain tumor, is walking now and has regained the use of her right arm. Her eyes are straight. She doesn't require prisms anymore. She's undergoing rehab because of the residual problem with her gait. Considering she had a brain tumor operation within the past two months, she's doing quite well.

I saw Foti Zondiros, a young Greek man. I had to search for his lateral rectus and found it 19 mm back from the front of the eye. He has no more double vision. That was a remarkable case. I'm very proud of having gotten him straightened out.

Seth Tracy had a neglected Duane's syndrome with a gigantic face turn. I helped him, but I didn't make him as good as I could have because I couldn't move that muscle back any further. He can fuse with a face turn, not the face turn he had originally, but he can't fuse with his head straight, either.

Steven Hammon—the young man in the automobile accident—has eyes nice and straight after we operated on him. However, he has great difficulty getting out of his walker and walking any distance without support. He has to have someone on either side to help him.

My old friend Jerry Graham came in. His daughter Allison died of AIDS disease, and Jerry and his wife, Carol, have been very active in AIDS research and in supporting the fight against AIDS. The loss of their wonderful daughter affected their lives tremendously. She got AIDS from a boyfriend who did not tell her he had the AIDS disease.

Little Carol Hall, who's one year old, on whom we operated a few months ago, looks terrific. She's got straight eyes. She comes in walking now. She's just a wonderful, beautiful little girl and walks in barefoot, of course. She doesn't wear shoes, but she's growing up—and growing up with straight eyes.

It was an exhausting day, but a good day. I saw a lot of important patients, many very, very gratifying to me in their ophthalmologic condition. Sadly, Pamela is a failure.

I had to go down to New York Eye and Ear Infirmary for an interview. I've applied to get on the staff because of the possibility Manhattan Eye and Ear will close. Here I am at the age of 64 at an interview for appointment to a hospital to start doing surgery in a different place. I had been on the Infirmary staff years ago, but I gave it up because it was too much to be there and at Manhattan. Now here I am back amongst old friends, talking about coming down there to do my surgery. Among those friends was Donald Wood Smith, who helped me close up the chest on the young woman I did open cardiac massage on at Manhattan Eye and Ear when I was a resident. I was pleased to see again Joe Walsh, the head of the eye department, and Bob Rosenthal.

Wednesday, June 16

We operated on Ann Funk for residual lateral rectus palsy. John Hermann had operated on her in 1979, and she still has a residual right VIth nerve weakness. She's on Coumadin. She has valvular heart disease. We had to stop the Coumadin a week before surgery. There's always a risk of getting a stroke when you do that, but there's a terrible risk of bleeding of the eye if you don't do it when you operate. So we take the risk. We stop the Coumadin. We hope they don't get a stroke during the period we need them to be able to clot their blood. We operate and then we restart them on the Coumadin, which is what I did with Ann. Surgery wasn't difficult, even though one muscle was previously operated on. I got her straight, and she did very well on the operating table.

The other case was Stacey Silverstein, 37. I had seen Stacey when she was one year old, 36 years ago, and I told her mother then she didn't need surgery, we could wait. She evidently waited 36 years and then came to me this year. I had to operate because she's got a big, big esotropia. She did very well. It was a relatively easy procedure for a large deviation.

After surgery, I went outside and, on the steps of the hospital, joined a major news conference. Dozens of newspaper reporters hovered around us, and all the local television stations had lined up their cameras. Steve Fochios, the head of our medical board, and Norman Medow spoke, along with Paul Owens, the black ophthalmologist on our staff who has worked in our Harlem facility. Everybody was very emotional, very animated, talking about how the hospital, which is so important, was being readied to be dismantled. What's going to happen to the clinic patients? What's going to happen to the residents? What's going to happen to the people who work in the hospital? Dennis Rivera, the head of local union 1199, was there with all the hospital workers. He talked. Several reporters interviewed us.

I spoke to the reporter from the *Times* for some length, telling him about how long I'd been in the hospital and what I did at the hospital and how this was a voluntary hospital where the doctors come to supervise the training of the residents and to see clinic patients, and we do it for nothing. We don't get any compensation. We don't get any faculty appointments in medical schools for it or any positions. Many of those who do this are the world leaders in their specialized fields. Many voluntary hospitals still exist in large cities, but the HMOs are slowly taking over management of most of them. It's a unique situation in this day and age to have a voluntary teaching hospital like this where the teaching is done by a volunteer staff of experts for no financial or other compensation. I told the reporter I'm going to operate next week with a young resident, as I do every Wednesday, and I've done this for 40 years, and next week will probably be the last time at this hospital.

After the news conference, I drove up to the country and started whacking golf balls so I wouldn't get too depressed over what I had just been involved with on the steps of the hospital.

Thursday, June 17

I drove back in to see 20 more patients in the office, starting at noon.

I saw George Danielovich, on whom I had operated. He came from Moscow—he's 17 years old now—and his mother had told me he had had an operation by Federov on his cornea for radial keratotomy in Moscow. During my operation on him, I saw no evidence of any radial keratotomy scars—slits in either eye—and he was just as myopic as he was originally. I don't know what Federov had done to his eyes, but he certainly didn't do any radial keratotomy. We operated on him for his motility, and he looked straight when we saw him today.

Elizabeth Friedman, five, was remarkable. She'd had previous surgery. She was misaligned. We had to re-operate and got her absolutely, perfectly straight. A wonderful case.

Little Buzzy Rubenstein was supposed to be operated on for a superior oblique palsy, but he doesn't have a superior oblique palsy. He's got a Brown's syndrome of the other eye. It would not have been such a good idea to operate on him for a superior oblique palsy. Fortunately, his mother was smart enough to realize what I was telling her was correct, so we've just been following him, and he's not ready for any surgery.

Marlene Brunvasser is 16 years old and has nystagmus, cataracts, retinal hemorrhages, esotropia, high myopia,

albinism—you name it, she's got it. We operated on her to
get rid of her double vision, and we did, but she's still left
with nystagmus, albinism, high myopia, cataracts, and retinal
hemorrhages. She seems to be carrying on just fine.

Sarah Jacobs, on whom we operated last year, has multiple
medical problems. Her doctor wants her to be on Plaquenil
now. She doesn't have arthritis, she doesn't have malaria, and I
don't know why he wants her to be on Plaquenil. I operated on
Sarah and on her husband, Paul, who has Parkinson's disease.
(In fact, I still see them both in Yorktown Heights, and did so
in January 2020.)

A few new patients filled out the schedule. Little Molly Wilder
and little Benjamin Wilder came in with their two mothers,
who live together—at the turn of the century we began to see
more same-sex parents than in years past; never when I first
started to practice—so these children are growing up together
too. Little Molly has a lump on her eye. I don't know what it is.
It might be a dermoid. You never know until you take it off, and
it's small and not growing, so I'm just watching it. And the boy,
Benjamin, needs some surgery for his divergent deviation.

I operated on Andrew Lewis a few years ago, and he still
has a little bit of a residual right hyper. I had told him I would
again operate on him eventually. He's now 13 years old and
he's looking more and more like his father, Bert. I went to PS
3 in Forest Hills with his father in the third grade. His father
beat me in a checker tournament one year, so I know what his
father looked like when he was a little kid. (Update from 2020:
Andrew, age 32, was named Emergency Task Force Director

for the NIH [National Institutes of Health] in Washington, D.C., in March 2020).

Katherine Ochs, the daughter of one of our anesthesiologists, Mark Ochs, is 14 now, and I've avoided operating on her all these years for an esotropia and a superior oblique palsy. This time, I had to give her some glasses with prisms because it's hard for her to keep doing all the computer work kids do in school and still be comfortable binocularly.

So that was Thursday. It was a long day and, fortunately, it meant the end of the work week for me. I was taking Friday off so I could go up to Burt Berson's club in Connecticut and he and I could take on Dave Schachter and John Small, two retired doctors who play a lot of golf. Last year, we beat them. This year they ambushed us and they took 11 bucks each from us because they played well and we didn't and that's usually the reason when the money changes hands.

But it was enjoyable to be out there on the course with Burt, my best friend from medical school, the orthopedist to whom I send all my friends and all my professional athlete friends with problems, and he operates on a lot of them. He even operated on my son, Nick, when he broke his elbow in a motorcycle crash when he was a teenager. Burt has had a lot of problems in his life, and he makes my problems pale in comparison. But he keeps right on going, and he's still seeing all the challenging orthopedic cases in the city. He's probably taken care of more people in orthopedics in the city than I have in ophthalmology, but I think it's probably close.

We were roommates in medical school—Burt, me, Marv

Pomerantz, and Steve Trokel. We all ended up doing fairly significant things. Burt became the head of sports medicine at Mt. Sinai and a noted orthopedic surgeon. Steve became an ophthalmologist at Columbia, and he's the one who really did the original research on all this keratorefractive surgery (lasik). He's a millionaire for it now. And Marv went to Denver as a chest surgeon, and he's the one now doing all the chest surgery there and teaching it to everyone else in the country because he learned how to do it many, many years ago as a resident at Duke University. He became the president of the American Board of Chest Surgeons. Not bad for a kid from the "valley," as we used to say—Spring Valley, a small town in Rockland County, NY. It was an interesting group that rented that house on Mt. Hope Avenue in Rochester in 1955 to study medicine together—all coming from very, very different backgrounds and different academic institutions to study together.

Saturday, June 19

I went to Temple Rodof Shalom this morning to attend the bar mitzvah of my friend Richard Lewis's son Zachary, who is also a patient of mine in the city. Zachary did a wonderful job, and his speech was beautiful, as was his reading from the Torah and the Haftorah. He has a lovely singing voice. He spoke about his ancestor, Commodore Uriah Phillips Levy, a veteran of the War of 1812 and the first Jewish commodore in the U.S. Navy. Zachary's family has been in this country—

Sephardic Jews—for 500 years.

At the end of the day I drove up to Sedgewood to play a little twilight golf. I didn't want to miss the entire Saturday away from my true love of golf. I played again Sunday.

Sunday night, I got a telephone call from one of the Manhattan Eye residents, Lana Costello, who was crying on the phone because she's finishing her second year and ready to start her third year in July and she has no place to go. She can't leave New York City because her mother has just gotten a bad medical diagnosis. The deal Dave Guyer was trying to put together to preserve the residency at a hospital on the east side, connected with Cornell, is evidently falling through. She thought I was connected with the Manhattan Eye Foundation, which was possibly going to fund the residents being trained in a hospital on the east side. I'm not part of it, and they're not going to fund it anyway. That idea is going to fall through. David Guyer's plan of it even taking place was foolish from the start. Instead, he should have spent the last three months helping the residents find positions elsewhere. Now here we are, a week from the end of the month and he's finally told them his plan has failed to move to a hospital close to Cornell, and they have to find their own way. It will soon be July 1, and five of the six residents have no place to go.

It's a terrible situation. Dave Guyer should not have let the residents get to this point. It could have been predicted this thing was going to fail and we could have had them placed by now. Hard to believe for me, really. David Guyer is one of the smartest guys I know. He did some of the most important research on finding the treatment for macular degeneration and is probably responsible for preserving millions of eyes with the "wet" form of the disease. Go figure.

Monday, June 21

We started to see some patients in the city this afternoon to accommodate some of the children who can't come in the morning. We're switching the Thursday schedule to our summer time, which is mornings instead of afternoons. I drove in from the country in time to start at 2:30 pm and see a small schedule of follow-up patients.

The main focus of the day was trying to locate places for the residents. I began that struggle as soon as I finished with the last patient of the day. I put in calls to almost every chief of a department in New York City. I had a long discussion with Steve Podos, chief at Mt. Sinai. He's on top of it because he's part of the American University Professors of Ophthalmology. We discussed David Guyer's idea of transferring all the residents to an empty hospital near Cornell on the east side of 72nd Street. David thinks he can get all the hospital charts—85,000—sent over there. Each patient would have to request the administrator of Manhattan Eye and Ear to send his or her chart individually to this new place. Most patients who come to Manhattan Eye and Ear have enough trouble getting to our hospital, let alone obtaining their charts from the administrator and then finding their way to Gracie Square Hospital on 72nd Street.

It's a cuckoo idea—absolutely nuts. But David Guyer persists in trying to get the residents to be trained over there. I and a few others are trying to find places for them elsewhere, although we don't have the official capacity of a residency director (I had that job 25 years ago, but I don't have it now). And so we're calling all the chiefs to get positions for the residents, and we're kind of fighting what our existing residency director has been trying to do with them. We also have the Manhattan Eye Foundation—which has a lot of money—at our disposal from the years when we collected the fees for clinic visits supervised by the doctors until it was taken over by the hospital, when it stopped collecting the fees. We could support paying for these residents in many other hospitals, which gives us a little bit of clout.

Tuesday, June 22

We saw about 20 patients in the office, starting at eight o'clock. A new patient, Abraham Elman, is 75 years old and has a gigantic divergent deviation. He's had cataracts taken out of both eyes—one made to be focused for near and one for distance. When he focuses with the eye for near, the other eye is way out, and when he focuses with the eye for distance, the first eye is way out. He plays golf over at Alpine at the Montammy Golf Club, says he has trouble keeping his eye on the ball. I can understand why. We're going to have to operate on him.

And then Edith Gordon. She's the mother of George

Gordon, who has been one of the lawyers for the hospital and for Hal Farquhar upstate. Edith has an eye muscle problem, too. She needs her cataracts done and then to have her eye muscles taken care of. She's only 83 years old.

Ralph Roland, 80, has Parkinson's disease. We had operated on him. We were lucky to get away with it because we had to stop his Coumadin for a week before we did it, and he did not get a stroke during that time and we had no bleeding on the operating table. He's very, very appreciative. He understands the amount of work we put in to do him.

Then Jerome Manheim came in. He was kicked in the eye playing football at the age of 14 and he's now 66 and he's got a paralyzed inferior rectus muscle. So he's been walking around for about 50 years with his chin way down because that's the only position where he can use both eyes together.

"Why didn't you have this taken care of before now?" I asked.

"Well, I was told that I might die if I had it done."

"Well, I don't know why somebody told you that and made you walk around for 50 years with your chin way down into your neck, but we can fix it."

We saw a few others, including Ann Funk. She's back on her Coumadin, and her eye is nice and straight, and she doesn't see double anymore. That was very satisfying, too.

After work, I hit a few golf balls and then went down to pick up my son, Nicholas, at the job he's been working at on Wall Street, selling oil and gas deals. I don't know how much money he's going to make doing that, but it's a good entree into the world of sales and the world of Wall Street. We went out to dinner at a Chinese place in Rego Park, and I took him home and said hello to Grandpa. Grandpa had a little bit of a mini-stroke, and I've been kind of doing the medical advising on it. I put him on some aspirin, but I'm not going to put him on any Coumadin at his age. He seems to be okay. His speech is pretty good. I can detect a little bit of slurring, but not like when he got the episode two weeks ago. I just hope he makes it for six more months, so we can celebrate his hundredth birthday. I want him to win something. I want him to be number one in something, and if he gets to be a hundred that will be a victory.

Of course, I'm on the phone with my sister about how to take care of him. She's a retired physician, so she looked up in her practice guidelines book how to treat transient ischemic episodes.

"I agree that you shouldn't hospitalize him, but what about anticoagulating him?" she wondered.

"I'm not anticoagulating our ninety-nine-year-old father with Coumadin and then he has to take all the blood tests and he'll have to go to the doctor and he'll have to go to the hospital," I said. "Aspirin will thin out his blood just enough."

So that's the way I'm doing it.

Wednesday, June 23

We operated on Ruth Brandt, who is 75 years old and was told by Dr. Max Chamblin in 1950 that she could never have any more eye muscle operations because she had too much scar tissue. He was almost right. It took me an hour and a half to get through all that cement-like scar tissue to get to her lateral rectus. We got it done without too much bleeding. I didn't perforate the eye and didn't expose too much fat. I put it way, way back and I put her on an antibiotic because some sutures were exposed. We'll see now whether she gets an infection and how straight her eye is and how she survives that onslaught. It took two hours to do her.

In the second case, I helped Lisa Park, a first-year resident, do an exotropia operation on young Andrew McFarlane, a 16-year-old black boy with an intermittent exotropia. Everything went very well, and it's probably the last time a resident case will be done at Manhattan Eye, Ear and Throat Hospital because the residency is officially closing at the end of the week.

It marked my 40th year at Manhattan Eye and Ear helping a resident surgeon do surgery. I think I pinpointed or I punctuated the moment, because it will probably be the last time a resident surgery will be done at the hospital. It was appropriate I was the one who supervised the case since I've been doing that longer than anybody else at the hospital.

When the residency closes June 30, I'll have to follow that young man in my private office because there is no more clinic, but that's fine.

I drove up to the country and played golf and went home. I was on the phone for a good part of the rest of the evening with Ruth Brandt. She had a little trickle of blood and because she got a little bit sick from the antibiotic we put her on, I had to start worrying about Ruth. Frequently, that's what happens. The first few days when the patient is home and the surgeon is in the city, or at home too, there's more of a problem than when you're actually doing the case because you don't see the patient in front of you and you're dealing with it on the phone. She's in New York City, I'm upstate, or I'm in the city, the patient is home in New Jersey, or wherever.

A couple of weeks ago I spent the weekend on the phone with Kirk Flynn, on whom we did a beautiful operation. Three days after we did him, he was afraid he was getting an infection, and he was afraid not enough surgery was done, and he was afraid he had conjunctival chemosis (swelling). He's an optometrist, so he has a little bit of knowledge, but not that much of the medical end of things. And you do more worrying and more energy on the weekend, after the case has been done on Wednesday, than you do when you actually do the case.

Thursday, June 24

We started our summer schedule today, which meant I had to get up at 5:00 am and drive into the city to start seeing patients before 8:00 in the morning, because now Thursday's schedule is morning instead of the afternoon.

I saw little Anael Mermelstein, on whom I had operated. She was the first patient with a latex allergy done at Manhattan Eye and Ear. I had to turn the hospital upside-down to make everything latex-free for her operation. Everything has latex in it: the syringes, the bottles you take the medications out of, the tubing, the endotracheal tube, the IV tubing, everything on the cart, and the gloves. Every instrument has some coating with latex on it, but we now have a latex-free cart in the recovery room, in the operating room, and in the pre-admitting room. It cost thousands and thousands of dollars to make everything latex-free, but now we have it.

Anael was the stimulus for the first latex-free procedure we did at the hospital.

I saw Adele Lewis, the wife of Tommy Lewis with whom I played in the juniors. He used to be a very good player. He also was a good card player in those days. We operated on his son Fred as an adult too.

We saw several other patients, some of them new, some of them follow-ups, including Menachim Rappaport, who still sees in 3-D. He's the miracle from Chief Rabbi Schneerson. Maybe he's got something there.

When we finished, I drove up to the country so I could play golf in the afternoon and spend half the evening again calling all the different chiefs of departments to try to place our residents.

Friday, June 25

I saw 18 patients up at Northeast Eye, and then I had a conversation with Hal about my future at Northeast Eye. I've been there 15 years. I think I made no money at all during the first six months of this year. The reimbursement rate is so low. I give him 50 percent; I have to give him a third of the surgery; Steven comes up to help me and doesn't even get reimbursed anything because there are no more assistant fees in surgery. I have to pay my technician, Ricki, when she comes up, $40 an hour. I ended up, after six months of work, earning nothing, which is ridiculous. And Hal knows it.

"Hal," I told him, "I'm not coming up anymore except once a month to see the surgical consultations. And I'm going to get our graduating Fellow, Michelle McLeod, to come up and take my place on the other Fridays of the month, and she can stay and see many more patients than I would be willing to do. And you'll pay her the same amount, the 50 percent, and she and I will do the surgery, and you're not going to get a third anymore."

He's going to consider that, but I think it's a fair deal. It's a good deal for him. He shouldn't get a third of the surgery, anyway. He can continue to get his 50 percent on the office visits, and she'll see many more patients than I was willing to see because I only work a half a day a week. He'll make up the lost third on the number of patients she sees a week. So, it should work out. And then, she'll spend the rest of her time over in Steven's office in Harrison and work for him and his partner for the rest of her income. It's a good opportunity for her, it's a good thing for Hal, and it's wonderful for me. I can spend the time I was spending coming up there half a day a week in my office in Manhattan and make a decent income every time I see another 15 patients in the city. That's the way we'll probably work Northeast Eye.

I finished with Hal and saw about 15 patients in time to get out at one o'clock and be free for the weekend, except for my continued phone calls on behalf of the residents.

When I got home I was on the phone with two of the residents, one of them Melissa Leung, who has had an offer from the University of Pennsylvania. I encouraged her in the strongest terms to accept that position and not to try to hold out for David Guyer's phantom residency over at Gracie Square Hospital on the east side.

"You've got a chance to go to the University of Pennsylvania. Take it."

The problem is Julia Katz. She was offered a position

at the University of Kansas, and she just doesn't want to go to Kansas. Here she is, chief resident at Manhattan Eye and Ear, and all of a sudden she's being asked to finish her final year in Kansas, and that's a tough blow to take. But she's got her head in the sand if she thinks she's going to get the same kind of training at Gracie Square Hospital under David Guyer's direction.

So that started the weekend. Friday night I was on the phone, and I even got one call at eleven o'clock from one of the chiefs in the city who finally got back to me to tell me they didn't have a position for any of our residents. The key to it might be the Manhattan Eye Foundation, with all the money it has, where we could help support a resident if a position is available in one of these hospitals.

It was a nice weekend playing golf, swimming in the lake. The temperature was 90. And Saturday, we went to a nice dinner party at Pearl Meyer's house, just outside the club in a beautiful, beautiful home with a swimming pool and a tennis court and gorgeous landscaping.

Her husband, Ira Meyer, owns several McDonald's restaurants, and he's going to be our interim buyer to purchase the old golf club at Sedgewood so the owners can then get up the money to form a group to buy it from him. He's buying it from the existing owner, Larry Biafra. We have a deal with New York City to buy the rest of the land, so hopefully we'll own the club, and the rest of the land will be preserved forever because it's never going to be developed. New York City needs it for watershed for the reservoir. And

Ira Meyer's going to buy the club in the meantime, before we can all get our money up.

All the golf and tennis members came to Meyer's house for the dinner party.

Sunday, June 27

Kenny and Fran came over with their little puppy and we had a barbecue and that was fun too.

Monday, June 28

Now today, we're heading back to the city to see patients this afternoon in the city.

Tuesday, June 29

Starting at 8:00 in the morning, we saw 15 patients. A number of them were new, so it was a little bit more involved than usual.

In a motor vehicle accident several years ago Simon Cohn sustained a third nerve paralysis, with a droopy eyelid and an eye that drifted out and couldn't elevate or depress. We've had him in prisms. He's never really wanted surgery, but he does okay. He fuses with the prisms. He still has a little bit of a face turn, with his chin up, but he's happy.

He's 63, and we've followed him for about 10 years since his accident.

A number of follow-ups came in. One new patient proved most interesting. Gianna Forte, who has double vision and an esotropia following brain surgery a year ago for an ependymoma, a tumor of the third ventricle of her brain. She has a right superior oblique palsy, not the usual result from an ependymona, but anything can happen with surgery for a brain tumor. We probably will have to operate on her.

At the clinic, I saw a couple of patients with the residents. It was the last time the residents would be in the clinic at Manhattan Eye and Ear after 130 years because on July 1 the residency program ceases to exist. I was glad I was there on the final day of the clinic since I have been doing this for 40 years. I was happy to be able to come to the last day of the clinic and supervise the residents and to see the clinic patients with them.

Wednesday, June 30

We did three cases. Emily Dewhurst, nine, was the most difficult. She had a traumatic experience a couple of years ago in another hospital where the surgeon tried to do an adjustment on her the next day. She was held down and he pulled the strings of the adjustable suture and she was psychologically traumatized from that. We operated on her and did both inferior obliques and the recession of one inferior rectus, and I put a patch on the more involved eye. I will be anxious to see what she looks like Thursday.

Then I drove up to the country and played golf all afternoon. I went to the lake with the dogs and Arleen and got up Thursday morning at five o'clock to drive back into the city to see patients starting at eight o'clock in the morning.

July

Thursday, July 1

A busy and somewhat vexing day began easy enough with Dr. Robert Puchin, who came in for me to probe his tear duct, which I do periodically because it becomes obstructed.

Then we saw a new patient, Catherine Bagwell, 82, who lives in Sunnyside near where I grew up and has had double vision since a cataract operation. The double vision is not related to the anesthesia; it's just a previously existing exotropia she wasn't aware of until she got good vision when the cataract was taken out. We might have to operate on her for her neglected, long-standing deteriorated exotropia.

We saw another new patient, Hilda Middlebrook, 78, who is a textbook on eye problems. She has had corneal transplants in both eyes, cataract surgery in both eyes, exchange of her intraocular implant in one eye, a retinal detachment procedure in one eye, two operations for strabismus that didn't work secondary to her retinal detachment surgery, a contact lens on the one cornea which is decompensating, and she's up now for a repeat corneal graft in the same eye. She also has strabismus of large degree, secondary to the retinal detachment, which was not improved by the two operations she had for strabismus. This is a lady you could spend three hours studying, but, of course, she was seen in a schedule of many other patients with the same types of problems. I think we'll probably have to operate on her strabismus in the eye in which she's not having the repeat corneal transplant. That'll be a problem because it's had two strabismus operations, a retinal detachment surgery, and a corneal transplant, too.

Then came a problem case—Albert Bandman, a new patient with a large exotropia. He insulted Amy in the waiting room. He insulted Barbara during his orthoptic examination, and when he came in to me he was wearing short pants and he crossed his legs so that his foot was sticking right in my lap as I examined him. It was a very uncomfortable situation for all of us. He told us our office was shabby and it reflected on all of us. He told Barbara she wasn't doing a proper exam on him, and then he asked me to operate on him, saying he didn't like the previous doctor he went to. Well, I'm not particularly anxious to operate on him, and this might be a problem, but we'll try to figure out some way to not do surgery on this irritating person.

In addition to this man verbally trashing our office and insulting everybody and making everybody feel terrified, we also had a problem with the post-op from yesterday. Emily Dewhurst is the little child who wouldn't open her eyes. She was terrified because of the surgery and the attempted adjustment she had last year that she thought she was going to have the same kind of trauma this time. She sat in the office for two hours before we could coax her to open her eyes. I had to take a look at her because she was complicated and I had to see what her eyes looked like before the long weekend. After two hours, we finally got her to open her eyes.

Amy and Barbara and I were exhausted at the end of the session. We left the office at about three, and I went back upstate to unwind and go for a swim in the lake and then start seeing patients Friday morning.

A reflection from 2021:

Early this year I had to be in court to defend a colleague in a malpractice lawsuit. For a doctor, there is nothing to compare to a malpractice suit for anger, grief, empathy, trepidation. Trust me—a host of emotions flood over you. I have had enough crises in my life to know. I feel compelled to say something about the subject here.

I did the operation in 1998, not 1999, but since this is such an important subject, and only happened one year before the diary, I discuss it here. Malpractice is a dreaded word for a surgeon to hear. But as my one-time mentor Phil Knapp used to say, "Any surgeon who has never been sued has just not done enough surgery."

For the first 30 years of my time in the operating room, I thought he might be wrong, but he wasn't. There is hardly anything in a doctor's life that compares with getting that subpoena charging all the grievous things enumerated in the papers served and then having to prepare and ultimately take the stand. What could be worse? Death of a patient? Terrible result—either by commission or omission in the care of a patient. A blind eye at the hands of the surgeon? Blindness, period? Sure, I have experienced all of that.

But to be charged with deviating from the standard of medical care in the community, and to have to withstand the onslaught of plaintiff's counsel, the anger of the patient, the glare of the public eye in the press, and certainly in my case—especially me, the notorious Renée Richards—devastating. All the *NY Post* needs is to check the court calendar and without fail the headline will blare out my guilt. Regardless of the outcome of a trial— and who knows how a jury is going to decide with me on the stand—the memory of the association between Renée Richards and malpractice will stick.

I have written only one death certificate in my 60+ years in medicine. In fact, I chose a specialty that did not usually deal with life and death. That my specialty did deal with the most precious of our senses seemed fine to me, but neurosurgery, for example, was much too morbid for me. The one death for which I ever had to write a death certificate occurred shortly after I first started practice in NYC in 1967. I did a cataract operation on an 80-year-old retired Air Force colonel, on whom I had done his first eye for cataract extraction two years earlier when I was chief ophthalmologist at the Navy Hospital at St. Albans. The colonel sought me out when I returned to practice in NYC after my Fellowship out west. He wanted me to do his second eye.

The cataract operation went well. In those days patients stayed overnight in the hospital after surgery. He died the next morning before I even got to check his eye. He had suffered a massive myocardial infarction (fatal heart attack). His children were wonderful to me as I remember.

I remember blinding an eye once, too. One of my first cataract extractions, as a resident, 1962, a complicated case, too complicated for my then-level of experience, too complicated also for the skill of the supervising surgeon. The opaque lens was dislocated and had dropped into the vitreous jelly in the interior of the eye. We did not have the vitreoretinal techniques back then to save such a catastrophe. The result was a blind eye.

I have had bad surgical outcomes—bad results we say—and I have missed diagnoses—fortunately, not many—and I have enjoyed a reputation of excellence from colleagues and patients. But from the public? Not so sure. Most people probably don't even know I am a real doctor; that's how notorious I was for years. It's not that I am extra careful because I have been notorious, a public figure (not so much anymore, but I certainly was in the later years of the 20th century). It just happens that I am a compulsive detail-oriented surgeon (thank God) and my reputation for skill, care, judgment is warranted—if I do say so myself.

So... when I get served with a subpoena, I have the usual surgeon's response of anger, fear, anxiety, pain, guilt, suffering any doctor would have... PLUS.

The fact that the more years you are in practice, the more operations you do, the more chance you have of ending up in court... is no solace. And the fact I don't know anyone who has been operating for more than forty years who has not been sued... no solace there either.

A malpractice suit starts with that dreaded subpoena—the summons and complaint listing all the terrible things you did to the patient, including making him/her sick, sore, disabled, disfigured, etc. The next phase is discovery, amassing all the information about the case, then meetings with counsel, and ultimately the deposition before trial where the plaintiff's attorney gets to take your deposition—your testimony—in answer to his questions about the case. It takes hours. Your testimony is then admissible at the trial. Finally the trial—you take the stand in your own defense.

I have been named in a few suits that never got as far as the deposition. Many times a maloccurrence (that's what a case is called before it is a lawsuit) occurs and everyone involved gets named regardless of any shred of responsibility for what happened. Most of the time, the non-responsible parties' names are dropped from the action. I have had a few of those, and my name was taken off the suits. But I never had a malpractice action go as far as a deposition until... 1998. I had been operating on eyes for more than 30 years. In 1998, I was sued twice, and in both cases I had to give a deposition.

The first case involved a patient who came to me with an increasing divergent deviation of one eye, an inability to read without closing that eye to avoid seeing double. I remember he was nasty to me and even nastier to my staff (anger toward the staff is usually displaced from the surgeon). There was no history of any neurological problem, but on my examination I found a very subtle nystagmus (shaking of an eye back and forth), and my suspicion of multiple sclerosis was immediately aroused. The patient became even nastier when I said he had to see a neurologist before I would agree to operate on his eye, and nastier still when I said his internist had to go over him too. He went to a neurologist of his own choosing, not taking my advice to see the one at NYU close by my office. His neurologist got an MRI which did show lesions characteristic of MS but stated the patient had no signs of MS and the MRI findings were caused by hypertensive infarcts (from high blood pressure). The internist found coronary artery disease, and the patient had to have coronary bypass surgery right away. So I probably saved his life back then, of which he did not seem to be aware. He came back to me. I discussed his neurologist's opinion about no MS signs, and I operated on the drifting eye. He did well for about a year but then started to see double again and consulted another eye surgeon, who operated on him a second time. Still no signs of MS. Eventually he did begin to show neurologic signs of MS, and he sued me and the second eye surgeon for needless surgery and the neurologist for missing the diagnosis of MS. Well, I was the one who suspicioned the diagnosis of MS in the first place. And, even when known to exist, MS does not preclude eye muscle surgery for diplopia. I have done that several times.

At the deposition before trial, the plaintiff's lawyer asked me why I did not refute the first neurologist's opinion of no MS when I spoke to the patient after he had seen the neurologist. I answered that the diagnosis of MS was for the neurologist to make. My job had been to send the patient to the neurologist for his evaluation and opinion, not to dispute that opinion. I added I was certainly not going to hit the patient over the head with a dire diagnosis for which he had no signs (according to the neurologist), a diagnosis he was told he did not have by an expert, and who was pissed off at me for sending him to the neurologist in the first place. I guess

I got a little hot under the collar at the plaintiff's attorney. (One is supposed to be very calm at these depositions, but I do have my boiling point, especially under oath.)

The case was set to go to trial in Brooklyn, not a favorable site for me—bigs hot New York city slicker, notorious Manhattan surgeon. There is nothing like the anxiety of going into court to trial, period. And the specter of a patient—now seven years after my surgery—by then with evident clinical MS confronting the still notorious Dr. Renée Richards was foreboding. On the day of the trial, the action against the second surgeon, and me, was dropped. The suit was settled against the first neurologist.

The second case took years, as often happens, and like in the first one I proclaimed to one and all, "Not guilty." That seems not to matter. A young girl was brought to me several years after having had eye muscle surgery for esotropia (crossed eyes) by my former mentor, Dr. Philip Knapp, the dean of strabismus surgeons in NYC at the time. After being well-aligned for years, one eye began to drift out, and her parents brought her to me for surgery. I operated, and she did well until eight years later when one eye started to drift out again. I operated again. The surgery went well, and, as was the usual Renée Richards overkill, I accompanied her to the recovery room. I made sure she was stable—vital signs, including normal oxygen saturation and more. Before I did my next case in the operating room I went back to recovery, made sure she was still doing well, and then operated on the second patient. After that case I went back to the patient's room, found my first patient sitting up, drinking some tea, and feeling well. I left the hospital, went to lunch, and then to my office.

One of the nurses called me at 6:00 pm and said my first patient had had a convulsion as she was leaving the hospital at 5:00 pm and had been transferred to Lenox Hill Hospital—a general hospital. The story I was told—I got details later—was that at about noon my patient had begun to complain of nausea, and an anesthesiologist was called and gave a telephone order for anti-nausea medication. The patient remained nauseated, and orders were given by telephone for different meds. She was never seen by an anesthesiologist until much later when an anesthesiologist came to see her and discharged her. After she got dressed to go home, she had a seizure and lost consciousness. When I heard what happened I raced over to Lenox Hill. I am not on the staff there, but it happens to be the hospital where I interned in 1959. I saw my patient there and while I was there she woke up for the first time since losing consciousness and I told her what had happened. She made an uneventful recovery and was discharged in the morning.

It was a mystery why she had the seizure, but the behavior of the anesthesia department was not. Someone should have come to see her at some point during her six hours of complaining of nausea. The internist who is our consultant in medicine at the hospital, and the one who transferred her to Lenox Hill, where he is also on the staff, made the diagnosis. The lab tests revealed dilutional hyponatremia—low sodium—caused by the patient having had an intravenous drip of dextrose and water all that time instead of dextrose and salts (sodium chloride, potassium).

I spoke to the parents at length about what happened. They did not blame me but they were pretty upset with what had happened to their daughter at the hospital. When I was eventually named in a lawsuit along with the anesthesiologists, I was upset and angry, but I know the way these things work. I told my medical liability insurance company to separate any suit against me from any suit against the anesthesiologists—separate attorney, everything separate. I was granted a separate lawyer. I fully expected to be dropped from the suit. It never happened. An appeal was made to the judge for discontinuance. Again, no luck, it didn't happen. The family's lawyer must have been thinking that maybe something Dr. Richards will say at the trial will further implicate the anesthesiologists. Maybe the jury will find against her too. After all—the notorious Dr. Renée Richards.

I was being sued for not adhering to proper post-op care in monitoring the patient. The fact that I had seen her three times post-op (a few times more than most surgeons) before I left the hospital, with the patient doing well, seemed of no importance. I have written chapters about complications of eye muscle surgery, but so rare is dilutional hyponatremia that it is never included on the lists. Was I supposed to monitor the intravenous medications for the six-hour period the patient was in the ambulatory post-op unit? I guess so.

I was pretty mad. I was going to have to testify in court. And I thought, "What the hell do I care?" The patient is fine, even her eyes. I was mad at her parents. They were sophisticated New Yorkers. They would know what the *NY Post* would headline— *Notorious Dr. Richards puts patient in coma*. I can take it, I hoped. Months went by before the trial.

During that time, the suit against the anesthesiologists was settled. Ever since that date there has been an unwritten rule at the hospital—Sarah's rule: Anytime a patient calls more than once in discomfort in the recovery room, an anesthesiologist must come to the bedside. The suit against me was dropped.

It has been my good fortune never to have taken the stand to defend myself. The two cases that were against me were dropped at the eleventh hour.

I have been on the stand, however, as I mentioned at the beginning of this discussion, as an expert witness and then in the past year in defense of a colleague. It is not fun. I am not sure how I would react if I had to defend myself.

Oh well, back to my diary...

Friday, July 2

We started with Herman Stander, a post-op from two weeks ago whose big conjunctival scar protruded through his eyelid. He also had a very divergent eye done by a doctor in the city who probably shouldn't be doing strabismus, but who operated on him twice.

I said to Herman, "Why did you ever let him operate on you the second time?"

"Well, I heard he was such a good surgeon and he does cataracts, and I let him do it."

He knew it was a mistake, but he looks terrific now. He has an eye that doesn't feel like it has a mountain in it, and his eyes are straight.

The rest of the patients were fairly straightforward. Terry Raskyn, who's probably a distant cousin of mine, is the editor of *The Globe* newspaper. She's post-op a couple of years, and her eyes are nice and straight.

Shelley Borden has always had a problem with her esotropia and has now been diagnosed with fibromyalgia syndrome. She said she sued her employer over her eyes and, when her employer found out I was her eye doctor, they settled the case. Well, that's pretty good, Shelley, if you can do it.

We ended the day at one o'clock, ready to start our long July Fourth weekend, which turned out to be a real burner because we got into a hot spell and the temperature in New York reached 101. It was brutal, but we spent the whole weekend playing golf and sitting in the lake with the dogs. It seems we've taken on board another dog, Boats, a Springer spaniel who seems to have adopted us. So now we not only have little baby Airedales, Travis and Lily, we have Boats, to go along with the two cats and the six fish and the three birds.

I played a golf tournament Monday that was called a shoot-out because all the players start together and the highest score on each hole drops out. I outlasted all but one other player, and the two of us had to have a play-off. It went to the third play-off hole and I finally lost it to my opponent's birdie. But I was very excited because I played well and it was a really fun event. I went home and jumped into the lake.

I had to sleep on the porch outside Monday night because

the heat was so brutal. No way could I sleep upstairs in my bedroom. We still don't have an air conditioner in the house. But it was nice on the porch overlooking the lake. A little bit of a breeze made it very comfortable.

Tuesday, July 6

I got up at five in the morning to drive to the city to see patients. We scheduled little Casandra Riggis, and she's going to have surgery next week for her esotropia. She also has spasmus nutans with shaking of her eyes, a head tilt, and head bobbing.

Mary Lane came in with her daughter, Sophia. Sophia has cerebral palsy. She can't walk, she has difficulty breathing, she has a spastic component, and now she's not doing well. She might not make it through the summer. I had a long talk with Mary about her daughter, who's been a patient of mine for many years. Sophia is now 18. Her father is a famous artist, and they have devoted themselves to their daughter. Sophia has such a bad case of cerebral palsy she has to be on a respirator now. The prognosis is not good for her.

We saw two new patients and several follow-ups, among them Bernice Kinseth, who is such a problem—such an overwhelming problem. She exhausts the office whenever she comes in. She's a -8.00 myope, she has cataracts in each eye, she has maculopathy, she has ocular migraine, she has strabismus, and she wears prisms. It takes such a long time to evaluate her every time she comes in. One Bernice Kinseth a day could exhaust you, and we're still in a heat spell, which makes it even worse.

When we finished, Dr. Shashou picked me up in front of the office and we drove down to New York Eye & Ear in the heat to have a guided tour of the hospital. We checked out all the changes made in the operating room, the ambulatory unit, the recovery room, and picked up our IDs and parking permits because pretty soon we're going to start operating at New York Eye & Ear. Things are looking worse and worse at Manhattan Eye and Ear, and many staff members have applied for privileges at New York Eye & Ear. Probably more than 90 applications have been made to come to work there since the board announced Manhattan Eye and Ear was going to close and be sold to Memorial.

I saw so many people I knew from when I used to work at New York Eye. I was surprised how many of them remembered me—people in the operating room, people in ambulatory, people in administration, people in the record room, people in the clinic—but they all were very friendly and they all welcomed us. I saw Dan Cochi, the nurse anesthetist I liked so much. He came to New York Eye & Ear from Manhattan a few years ago, and he told me the operating rooms are wonderful and the anesthesia is great. He made me feel a lot more comfortable about what I was to encounter when I start operating there in a few weeks.

The feeling there is so different from Manhattan. Everybody is friendly, everybody is upbeat, everybody is enthusiastic. They're not angry, they're not apathetic, they're not unfriendly. And it was a good atmosphere to see.

The temperature is still 100, and I'm back upstairs in the apartment now. It's the first time I've really been cool in the past five days, except when I was in the lake.

My efforts for the residents are over. I tried as hard as I could to get them to accept positions in other hospitals rather than to go along with David Guyer's scheme of transferring the residency program over to an empty hospital near Cornell. I believe he's doing that because he wants to continue to have a connection with the residents in Manhattan Eye and Ear. And Larry Yannuzzi would like him to do it, and I don't know why Jack Dodick's going for it. It turns out that, of the six senior residents, Gupta is going to UCLA, Candice Moy is going to Cal Pacific, and Melissa Leung is going to the University of Pennsylvania. So three out of the six are going to other hospitals to finish their third year, and they're smart, and the other three are going over to this empty shell of a hospital on 72nd Street and Second Avenue to finish and be trained for their third year. I just don't see it happening. I think the three I encouraged and cajoled into taking positions elsewhere who are in bona fide residencies are going to come out a lot better than the three who have elected to stay here in New York under David Guyer's tutelage. I don't know where the clinic patients are going to come from. I don't know where their surgery's going to come from. I don't know where their supervision is going to come from.

I think it's just crazy. All second-year residents have been placed. They're going to good institutions and, of course, the first-year residents were notified there was no program anyway. There's a meeting tomorrow of the whole staff at six o'clock. I'm not going to be there. When I finish operating tomorrow, I'm going home.

Wednesday, July 7

This morning we operated on Teri Douglas, a formidable operation—both inferior obliques and both medial recti for a large convergent strabismus as well as an upshoot of each eye looking to the side. It takes a little longer to do that, but it's frequently indicated and sometimes allows for only one operation to have to be done for it, too. It went very well.

But the other case was a tear duct probing on one-year-old James Josephson, who's had discharge and obstruction of the tear duct on the right eye since birth. Usually, I can do these tear ducts very easily. My batting average is maybe 99 percent successful, but this one I could not get through. An obstruction in the nasal bone stopped me every time I got the probe down into the nasolacrimal canal. It was like hitting a brick wall of bone. I tried for a half hour to do it, and every time I tried to irrigate fluorescein dye through the tear duct it refluxed right back out again. I think I failed and he'll probably need a procedure to drill a hole in the bone. When I went out to speak to the parents to tell them everything was okay, I said the child was fine, but I thought the operation had failed. That's a terrible thing to have to go out and tell parents. The father almost passed out, and this is a family I've known for 10 years because I operated on their daughter for strabismus when she was one year old, and she's done fine ever since. Mr. Josephson looked pale and sweaty, and I almost had to do some CPR on him because he really became syncopal. I did everything I could, but the anatomy was such that the bone was obstructing the passage of the tear duct system. It's an anatomical abnormality.

Anyway, I drove up to the house and tried to forget about little James Josephson. I hit a few golf balls and went in the lake with the dogs.

Thursday, July 8

I drove back down to start at eight o'clock, getting up at five o'clock to beat the White Plainsers, who have to start out from Dutchess County at about 4:30 am in the morning. And they all have their coffee cups with the tops on them so they don't spill on the ride down the Taconic. I got there early enough to see all the patients Thursday morning.

Anna James is still controlling her vertical misalignment following the anesthetic injury to her inferior rectus during cataract surgery, but we'll have to operate on her one of these days.

Anita Ho, the artist, is 85 years old and doing very well after her operation.

And then, finally, Denise Sommer, a new patient with double vision. She's had radial keratotomy, among other things.

The eye I would have to operate on has had radial keratotomy, which makes it at risk for a rupture of the globe because of the weakened cornea of the eye. So, you're dammed if you do, and you're damned if you don't. If you leave her the way she is, she's got a disfiguring strabismus with double vision, and if you operate on her, you run the risk of rupturing the globe.

All the post-ops looked good, even Emily Dewhurst, who came in this time with her eyes open.

Friday, July 9

At 8:30 am, I met with Hal and with Michele McLeod, our former Fellow who just graduated last week. She's going to start coming up to Northeast Eye and see patients every week, the children I've been seeing. I'm only going to come up once a month to see the problem patients. We met with Hal to see if everything would be okay and to introduce her to him. It looks like it's going to work all right. She'll start in practice up there, and also with Steven Greenberg in Harrison. I'll see patients in the city on the days I used to go up there, and I'll only go up there now just once a month.

Michele stayed and saw the morning schedule with me. It was pretty routine, with nothing particularly exciting.

We were supposed to see Connor Reamsnider, who had the meningioma removed from his cavernous sinus, but he postponed his visit until next week. I am anxious to see how he's doing. He had a partial speech loss and a hemiplegia following the operation, and he's needed rehabilitation.

I had a nice weekend playing golf, swimming, going out in the boat trying to catch a fish—I didn't. Just as well because we always put them back when we catch them, anyway.

Monday, July 12

We saw patients in the afternoon starting at two o'clock. First in the door was Linton Baldwin, who had stories about his 50th reunion at Yale. He was at Yale in 1948 when George Bush was the captain of the baseball team and Linton captain of the cross-country team. They were good friends.

I saw Jennifer Klipstein, who's got a secondary exotropia, and she drove me absolutely nuts because she's farsighted and the more farsighted correction you give her, the more her eye drifts out. She's at the age when she needs her farsighted correction because she can't see properly without it. So she's between the devil and the deep blue sea. She doesn't want to have her eye point out, but she can't keep trying to focus without her farsighted correction. Focusing helps pull her eye in. She needs surgery, and I keep telling her that.

She's worried. "Well, it might not work," she told me. "It didn't work when I was one year old."

"Well, that was a different situation," I said, and we went back and forth and back and forth. Finally, I said, "I don't have any more time to do this." I gave her a prescription for a stronger farsighted correction. "Come back in six weeks.

We'll see how far out your eye is, and then we'll operate for that amount."

Another friend came in, Dick Savitt. I've known Dick for many years. He's the most famous tennis player in New York's history—along with John McEnroe—because Dick won Wimbledon in 1951. He had a retinal detachment this year, and I had to stand by while my friend Tom Poole reattached his retina, but he's doing pretty well. When he had his retinal detachment, he was on Florida's east coast playing with Irving Levine. He started having flashers and floaters and said to Irving, "I gotta go. I gotta go back to New York and see Renée. I gotta check my eye out. I'm seeing flashes and floaters."

Irving says, "You can't see Renée. She's over in Tampa playing with Chum Steele." Which was true. I was in Tampa playing with Chum. But Dick called the office and Arleen told him to come right up and set him up to see Tom Poole, our retinal specialist, and Tom fixed his retina.

When I saw him today, he was seeing 20/30 out of that eye, which is just wonderful for a retinal detachment procedure. So, he's doing okay. He's a wonderful man and the hero in New York City to most of the Jewish sports fans, the same way Hank Greenberg had been in baseball in Detroit in the 1930s and 1940s.

That evening I went to Manhattan Eye and Ear for a surgeon directors meeting. These painful meetings are getting to be more and more difficult because George Sarkar, the administrator, just keeps going back and forth, answering our questions—"I don't know"—like he's volleying with us and sending back attacks defending himself with one more ridiculous answer after another. We are angry with such a passion for what he's done to this hospital, and we have to sit through a surgeon directors meeting with him. We have to listen to him making these plans to sell the hospital out from under us and move on with the lay board and his huge salary to some other venue after he's destroyed Manhattan Eye and Ear. It was almost impossible to sit through the meeting. When it was over, we asked him if we could meet privately, and he left the room and then we talked about what's going on.

Steve Fochios brought us up to date on the latest situation with the hospital. He said the state attorney general, Eliot Spitzer, and his deputy, Bill Josephson, are very upset with the lay board's plans to dispose of the hospital, and the board of health has told the lay board it cannot dispose of the hospital without an actual plan to do so. So the clinics are being kept open. There are no more residents, but attendings are volunteering their time to keep the clinics running. The hospital operating rooms are still running, and we're encouraging everybody to continue to operate at the hospital as long as the operating rooms are open. The attorney general realizes the so-called clinics the lay board wants to set up on Harlem and Jamaica are really a sham without having the mother hospital in existence, and so he is beginning to try to force the lay board to listen to offers from Beth Israel and Lenox Hill to merge with the hospital and to preserve it as an eye hospital.

The attorney general is also interested in what's going to

happen to the money that will go to the lay board after the proposed sale to Memorial and to the real estate company, so it's a very, very complex situation. The attorney general also realizes the lay board is acting irresponsibly in just disposing of the hospital to a real estate company and to Memorial without trying to preserve it as an eye hospital, which is what the charter of the hospital was originally intended for. Our hopes are high that the attorney general's office might not approve of the hospital closing and being sold to Memorial to become a breast hospital.

The directors at Beth Israel are very interested in purchasing the whole hospital and will even help to pay the fees of the lawyers, but we have to sue our lay board to recover the cost of our lawyers. That'll take some time. The attorney general was trying to speak to our lay board, but the lay board did not get back to Spitzer. The attorney general is now suing the lay board and is trying to prevent the board from going ahead with the sale of the hospital to Memorial. As of late last night, it looks like there's a possibility Beth Israel might be able to step in and save the hospital from going to Memorial, with the co-operation of the board of health and the attorney general. Both are trying to prevent the sale from taking place.

The deal with Memorial is still in existence. Of course, the people from Memorial have friends in high places, even higher than the ones we know, so Memorial might prevail in the end.

It still costs a lot of money for the lawyers we've got representing us. We've already paid them $300,000. We need to pay them $150,000 more. Fochios is asking us to contribute more money and to ask our colleagues also to contribute more. I find it very difficult to do that. I called several of our colleagues the first time, and I'm just not going to call them now. In fact, I'm not even sure I'm going to contribute more money myself. We've paid $300,000. That's pretty good. The idea is also maybe we can have a suit against the lay board to pay our legal bills, but that wouldn't take place until well into the future. In the meantime, the lawyers are not going to continue unless we pay them. It's a very difficult situation.

At any rate, the battle is heating up. The board of health said George Sarkar could not close the hospital forthwith; he had to have a plan, which takes 90 days by order of the board of health. He has to keep the clinics open. We're staffing the clinics with per diem attendings since we have no more residents in the hospital. The operating room schedule has been decimated.

Many of us are already on the staff at New York Eye & Ear. We're being encouraged to operate down there by that administration, which has been so nice to us. And yet, now our board of surgeon directors is urging everybody not to go to the other hospitals, but to continue to operate at Manhattan Eye and Ear as long as we possibly can. To be continued.

Tuesday, July 13

The first patient was referred by Sid Mandelbaum. Whenever you get a Sid Mandelbaum patient, you know it's going to be a complicated problem because he only sends patients who are elderly, have had cataracts, have macular problems, wear prisms, and have various unusual complaints about their eyes. This man happened to have excellent vision (Lester Rutner—he used to be in the Israeli army). He has excellent vision in each eye, but he complains of blurry vision, with difficulty especially in bright surroundings and with colors. I found very little wrong with him except he was sensitive to light and he didn't do that well up close. I gave him some glasses with a little bit of a tint and a little bit of a prism, and I hope he'll be okay.

Monroe Seligman is 78 years old. He recently had a coronary. He's got a regrowth of a lesion on the surface of his left eye I'll have to take care of. An hour after he left the office, some beautiful flowers arrived for me with a note that said, "Summertime is the time for flowers." It was very sweet.

Ginelle Barrett came in. She's the little girl on whom I operated for the same condition for which I operated on her mother 30 years ago. She's okay.

Shirley Booth, on whom I made the diagnosis of lateral rectus palsy due to blood pressure and not due to myasthenia gravis, is doing just fine now, having stopped her myasthenia gravis medication, which was bothering her anyway.

Gabrielle Bluestone came in for evaluation of her anisometropia, a big farsightedness and astigmatism in one eye and nothing in the other eye. She doesn't want to wear glasses, but she should wear them for near because she has better depth perception when she wears them.

And finally, Eileen Bannerman, who has nystagmus, doesn't wear glasses, and has a slight face turn, but I'm not going to operate on her for the face turn. It's too mild. And, besides, she has other considerations, such as oppositional defiance disorder.

Wednesday, July 14

This morning we operated on Casandra Riggis. Casandra has a very large convergent strabismus as well as spasmus nutans, which is a triad of head tilt, head bobbing, and nystagmus. We did a big procedure on her, putting each medial rectus back six mm. The procedure went very well, although it was a tiny eye. She's only one year old and it's always difficult to operate on such a small eye. When I went to the waiting room, the whole family was there, the mother (the ophthalmologist), the sister (also an ophthalmologist), the husband, and three grandparents, all hovering over this little one-year-old child.

The operating room schedule has been decimated. When I operated Wednesday, there were only five other cases. Scott

Greenbaum did four cataracts, and three of those were my patients. So I was responsible for four of the six patients on the entire day's schedule Wednesday. We're being beseeched to continue to operate at the hospital and to maintain the clinics because we must prove we can keep this hospital open. Otherwise, Dr. Sarkar will jump at any chance he can to close it.

Then I had my hair cut by my special hairdresser, Mai Tai, a little Filipino lady who gave me a layered cut without telling me.

"I did a layered cut but didn't tell you until I did it," she confessed when she had finished.

Anyway, it looks very good. Then I went to the house, played a little golf, and then went into the lake. We're suffering through a heat spell. It's 100 degrees in New York, and we have no air conditioning in the country.

Thursday, July 15

We started the morning with Jerome Percus. His family is one of the last from Ben Friedman's practice. Ben was my father's best friend, and, when he had a serious stroke, I took over his practice and his wife, Bessami, was my secretary. This was in the early days of my own practice. I worked three days a week in my office and two days a week in his office. And she kept bringing in one patient after another. Even on Saturday afternoons we worked until five o'clock because, whenever a patient called, she told them just to come right over, no matter what time it was.

Jerome and his wife Ora and their son Alan are patients of mine. As I said, the last remnants of the old Ben Friedman practice. I took off a squamous cell carcinoma from Ora's eyelid and did a transposition of half of her upper eyelid to the lower eyelid, a graft. Alan is a physicist who works at Los Alamos, and Jerome, whom I saw today, is a professor at NYU. They're remnants of the Upper Westside intelligentsia, second-generation Jewish families Ben Friedman took care of when he was alive.

Roberta Kahn has an eye that goes in only when she focuses, but she's 42 years old now and she's losing her power of focusing. She is a college administrator. She hates it when her eye goes in. So we're thinking about doing a small procedure on her, in spite of knowing that eventually she's going to need to wear reading glasses. When she does, her eye is not going to go in, and we might be dealing with a secondary divergent deviation years from now. That's the risk we take.

Teri Douglas is two years old. We operated on her last week on four muscles, and she looks absolutely wonderful.

Molly Hall came in with little Carol on her lap. It was Molly's turn to be examined. Carol was the one-year-old child we operated on a few months ago, and she's terrific.

Laura Campanis, who had a brain tumor removed from her posterior fossa, a cerebellar tumor, is now beginning to walk better. She has no more eye muscle problems. She doesn't need prisms and hardly needs to wear her glasses. She's making a very nice recovery. Her speech is better as well as her gait.

Ruth Brandt, another post-op, is doing well. She's 75 years old. She can keep her eyes straight now, even though Max Chamblin told her 40 years ago she could never have any more eye muscle surgery because of too much scar tissue. Well, she had a lot, but we managed to do it. Now she's playing golf, but she says she doesn't know which eye to use when she focuses on the ball. I told her to use just one.

Janice Danby has such a rare condition—a hemifacial atrophy with half of the tissues of one side of her face atrophying, including the eyeball itself, as well as the eyelid and the muscles of the eye. I operated on her on the other eye to normalize her muscle balance. She's done fine since that time.

Kim Vanorman works for Janice Danby at a major American tobacco company and is married to a friend of mine who just won the Westchester Open golf championship, so we were all excited.

We saw 20 patients, and then I drove up to play golf with Larry Levine, and, of course, that's even more exhausting. We played 18 holes, and I finally got home at nine o'clock. That was a long day.

Friday, July 16

I saw 15 patients at Northeast Eye Care and gave them instructions as to what the new plan is going to be—that I'm only going to come one day a month to see problem cases, and that our graduating Fellow, Michele McLeod, is going to come the four other days of the month to see the children in the community. Whenever she sees someone with a problem, she and I will see the child together and, if the child needs surgery, the two of us will do it together. So it should work out. The new arrangement means I can spend a little more time in the office in the city because I just can't make a living seeing patients up at Northeast Eye Care. I don't make any money there at all.

A lot of those 15 patients were post-ops. One was a consultation, a woman who's 69 years old and has had so many things done including cataract surgery, and retinal detachment surgery. She has a very large vertical misalignment of her eye, a droopy eyelid on the same side. She's got bad diabetes. She gets intraocular hemorrhages, as well as hemorrhages on the surface of the eye.

She wants me to operate on her to make her eyes straight so she doesn't see double. As I was looking at her, she was bleeding from the external surface of her eye. It takes little imagination to see what would happen if I operated on her and tried to get the eye muscle that's enmeshed in scar tissue from the silicone implants of her retinal detachment surgery. She's going to bleed externally, she's going to bleed internally, and she might risk detaching her retina. It's a terrible prognosis. She only sees 20/400 in that eye. She's had laser treatment all over the retina for diabetic retinopathy. And yet, in spite of seeing only 20/400, she still sees this blurry second image and she wants me to straighten her eye and get rid of the double vision. It's one of the worst prognoses I've ever encountered. Just looking at her, she was bleeding from the surface of her eye from all the conjunctival scarring and fragile tissue from her previous operations. I'm not sure I'm going to operate on her, but I probably will.

It was a big weekend, starting Friday afternoon and extending all the way through Sunday night, because it was our member-guest golf event at the club. I brought my friend—my best friend from medical school, Burt Berson, an orthopedist who is the head of sports medicine at Mt. Sinai and a very good golfer. I brought him up to be my guest and he brought his lady friend, who's also an avid golfer. They came Friday night for dinner and we had the golf tournament Saturday and a big dinner and entertainment at the lake Saturday night. It was a big event. Then we went over to Centennial and played Sunday. It was an exhausting weekend. It was lots and lots of fun, and it was especially more fun because Burt and I won the member-guest golf tournament at the club. It's terrific, because everybody always expects me to perform so well. I'm not that good a golfer, but because I have been a good athlete and a professional tennis player, they always expect me to do well in golf too. It was nice that, this time, we actually did well, and we won the tournament.

Note: Burt Berson, top sports medicine orthopedist at Mt. Sinai Hospital in NYC, who took care of as many of my friends and family's orthopedic problems in NYC as I did their eyes, even operating on my son Nick's broken elbow, died a few years after that member-guest tournament. A few years later I invited Dr.

Richard Gibralter, known as "rock doc," to be my guest. We didn't win the tournament, but at lunch after the golf he performed the Heimlich maneuver on the guest of a friend from the club, saving him from choking to death. Kind of made up for us not winning the tournament.

Monday, July 19

I'm back in the office again this afternoon, and I just finished seeing Ellen Janis, who has had pale optic nerves for years. I've been telling her I wanted an MRI for years. Finally, last week, she agreed to get the MRI. It shows severe chronic multiple sclerosis. There are lesions in the white matter and all over the MRI. She's going to have to start interferon, a very potent and experimental drug, and we'll see what happens. It took so long to get her to finally see a neurologist and to get this MRI.

I also saw Edna Wong, who is now a few months after the eye surgery I did on her for her bilateral VIth nerve paralysis, and she's doing amazingly well. She has a very famous Chinese restaurant here in New York City, and I want to go there soon.

Tuesday, July 20

We started the day seeing Cindy Polansky, 27, on whom we operated for a bilateral Duane's syndrome, and she looks very good. Her eyes are straight, and she doesn't have any face turn. She's quite happy.

One little boy came up from Florida, a 2½-year-old child with a coloboma of his left upper eyelid, which means there's no tissue there at all. You can look directly at his eye because he has no eyelid. He also has an adhesion from some eyelid tissue that's abnormal, an adhesion that goes right to the eyeball itself. He's going to need surgery for his coloboma and the adhesion to the eye. I'll collaborate with Dr. Richard Lisman on that. He's a top ophthalmic plastic surgeon. Sadly, Richard's wife died yesterday of kidney disease. He was very devoted to her.

Mona Wetmore, a 65-year-old lady, has a large convergent strabismus. How do some people wait until they're 65 before coming for surgery for a large, disfiguring deviation? She said it wasn't as bad years ago as it is now. We're going to operate on her.

And we saw little Richard Neckterloff, a Russian émigré by way of Israel. He's seven years old and has Duane's syndrome. He needs surgery for his face turn. His family lives in Forest Hills—the same route to America my father took 100 years ago.

The problem case for the day was George Rosen, referred by my associate, Dr. Steven Greenberg. I wonder if he had it in for me to send Mr. Rosen and his many complaints today. He took an hour and a half in the office. Arleen finally had to come in and say I had a long-distance phone call to tear me away from his repeated questions about his vertical deviation and his fluctuating vision, and the swelling under his eyelids, and the film over his eye, and the fact the vertical double vision came and went and he's not sure if it was after he was hit in the back of the head or after the pacemaker was installed, or the aortic valve was replaced, or the cataract surgery was done on each eye. It just took so much time going over all these questions and answering them. No matter how I tried, I could not give Mr. Rosen any satisfaction with any of the answers.

He will need surgery, but he's on Coumadin and, if you stop his Coumadin, he runs the risk of getting a stroke and, if you don't stop the Coumadin for a week, he's going to bleed when you operate on him. You're between the devil and the deep blue sea in a situation like that.

And then we saw Emily Dewhurst, the little girl who sat in the office for two hours a couple of weeks ago before she would open her eyes after we operated on her because she'd had a traumatic experience the year before. Today she came in absolutely perfect. I dismissed her until after the summer. That's a success story.

Also significant today was the fact I canceled surgery for tomorrow on Ramona Vincent because her eyes are really in such good position she only sees a misalignment when she switches fixation to her non-preferred eye and looks off to the right. And even then it's very, very small. I just couldn't see my way to doing something on her that might undo the good position she achieved by the last surgery we did on her.

I called her up today and I said, "I'm sorry, but I'm canceling the surgery."

I don't often do that. If I get to the point that it's time

to schedule and have measurements done, I'm pretty convinced the patient needs surgery. But after looking at her measurements and realizing this only occurs when she switches fixation to the left eye, and only rarely, I couldn't see myself clear to do something that might make her worse and give her no improvement, or very little. Canceling surgery is sometimes what you have to do. With no surgery tomorrow, maybe we'll go up to the country today and enjoy a couple of days of relaxation.

Thursday, July 22

We saw several patients in the city. India Weston, two years old, had surgery done elsewhere for exotropia. She's in pretty good shape, although her parents felt they needed reassurance the child was doing okay. Frequently, that's the case with the second opinions—the treatment of the doctor taking care of the patient was not inappropriate, but the communication was.

And then I saw Anita and Jack Reiner, my best friend, Leslie Pollack's son-in-law's parents. I've known them for many, many years anyway. They just needed ordinary examinations, but of course, it takes a long time to examine friends.

And then we saw Erin Creamer, the daughter of Marcia Creamer. Erin is 54 years old with severe diabetes. She doesn't see very well, but the organic basis for her poor vision is unclear. Yes, she does have diabetes and, yes, she does have a few tiny microaneurysms in her retina, but not near the important part, the fovea, and yes, she has some optic atrophy, on what basis I don't know.

She's a problem because she comes in seeing only 20/200 with minimal diabetic changes and optic nerves that look pretty good. And yet I could coax her into reading the 20/40 line. So you know something is going on in addition to the optic neuropathy and the diabetic retinopathy, which are both very, very subtle.

I also saw Anthony Risotto, who's now 15 years old. I operated on him when he was younger, and he's now writing a mass. He's a brilliant composer. He gave me a tape of one of his compositions a few years ago when he wasn't even 11 years old, and it was beautiful music.

Donald Coster has a significant blood-borne disease, and I didn't want to operate on him at first. Eventually, I did operate on him, and he got a perfect result. He told me that, when he's lying upside-down on the couch trying to watch television, he might see double.

"Don't lie upside down on the couch watching television," I advised him.

It's annoying when you have such perfect results and a patient says, "Well, when I'm in a crazy position and I look out of the corner of my eye, I can see two images."

And I saw Chloe Friedman at the request of my good friend, Steve Levy. Chloe is three years old, and she has significant astigmatism and wouldn't wear the glasses prescribed for her on Long Island. The glasses were correct. The question again was communication and just how severely she needed to wear her astigmatic correction.

"Don't make a federal case out of it and just get her to play with the glasses," I told her parents, "because she sees quite well without them anyway, and I don't think she's going to become a bilateral amblyope if her astigmatism isn't corrected."

That's always the issue. You're afraid that, if you don't correct the astigmatism, the child doesn't have a clear image on the retina and will become amblyopic, but not in this particular case.

Then I saw Chin-Sun Lee, a little Korean girl on whom I operated at the age of three. She's got nystagmus, overwhelming astigmatism, esotropia, and bilateral inferior oblique dysfunction. However, she had a very good result from surgery. She sees fairly well in spite of her nystagmus. Her father brought her in because he had taken her to the doctor around the corner from where they live in New Jersey.

"I have no confidence in that doctor," he said.

"Mr. Lee, you shouldn't have taken her there in the first place," I said. "She's a very complicated case. You can take your son there. He's got simple nearsightedness, but you can't expect a general ophthalmologist to deal with the problems of Chin-Sun Lee. You have to understand that. If you have to take a half day off to come into the city for her visit, well, then you must do that."

I think he got the message.

A fax from Dr. Steve Fochios upset me. He's the president of our medical board at Manhattan, and he's been working day and night to try to help our lawyers appeal to the attorney general to keep the hospital open and to make the lay board sell the hospital to another hospital that will keep it as an eye hospital rather than to Memorial. At our surgeon directors meeting July 12, we were all asked to get our colleagues to contribute more money.

Now, Steve sends a fax to the entire staff of the hospital listing who has contributed to the lawyers, how much they've contributed, and who has not contributed at all. I think it was just a terrible thing to do. I'm very upset about it because he has no business making that public information, even if it's just meant for the other surgeon directors. I'm not going to call anybody and ask them to give more money. We've given the lawyers $300,000, and now they want us to raise another $150,000 or they won't continue work. I think it is just awful.

Friday, July 23

We saw 15 patients—all children—at Northeast Eye Care up in Putnam, and it went very well. No significant problems, which makes it easy. No adults of the age of 80 with five pairs of glasses and macular degeneration and cataracts and double vision and prisms and all the rest of it. Just nice, simple children's ophthalmology.

One patient was Melody Masterson, who lost her father and her two siblings in an automobile accident, and she was injured severely, with neurological damage. But she's doing very well. I operated on her after the accident. Her eyes are straight. She doesn't have much fusion—I think she lost that from the head injury—but she walks, she talks, she's in full active life again. She just has to do it without her father and her two sisters.

The rest of the schedule was routine. As usual, I walked out on the dot at 12:30 pm.

The weekend was not too hectic this time. We did go to dinner at Geoffrey and Joan Bell's house across the lake, which was nice because their house is air conditioned, besides the fact they're good friends and we enjoy their company.

Geoffrey is British, and a famous economist. One time when we were golfing, he could only play nine holes. He abruptly packed up his car. "Renée, gotta go, having lunch with Tony Blair in the city."

"Okay, Geoffrey, go."

And on Sunday night, we went to dinner with Leslie, my best friend, and his wife, Yvonne, up in Pawling in a very nice restaurant.

Monday afternoon I'll be back in the city seeing patients. I have two gigantic trees in my car that I bought to bring to Grandpa's house to put in his driveway. For some crazy reason, Arleen had him chop down the trees in his driveway. She said they were dead, but they weren't. I'm going to take enough trees out to Forest Hills so I don't have to look at the fence and the neighbor's brick wall when I walk out of the house. Those trees had been there for 25 years and they were beautiful— and they weren't dead.

Monday, July 26

We saw eight patients in the office this afternoon, nothing special because Barbara, the orthoptist, doesn't come on Mondays. So we try to keep it just for follow-ups.

Erin Roach, who's now 20 years old, came in with a picture of her and me when she was four years old. She's a young lady I kept in glasses and bifocals rather than operating on her because she had a purely accommodative esotropia. Some other people probably would have operated on her somewhere along the line, but we got her to make it with just glasses, and now she wears contact lenses. She's happy and so is her mother because she never had to have surgery. Some cases are strictly accommodative and really only need to wear their glasses and eventually they straighten out.

Dr. Walton Simpson, a dentist, has multiple sclerosis. We had operated on him for an exotropia in addition to his internuclear ophthalmoplegia, which is a tricky situation. He had an exotropia all his life, then he gets multiple sclerosis and gets an internuclear ophthalmoplegia, which aggravates his exotropia and confuses the picture. But he did well with surgery, and he's in a fairly good state of remission with his multiple sclerosis. He doesn't practice as much dentistry as he did when he was totally free of the ravages of multiple sclerosis. He was on some drugs for MS, but he stopped them on his own and he's in remission. Multiple sclerosis can affect so many different parts of the body. We had a mnemonic in medical school to help us with all the different ramifications of multiple sclerosis. The mnemonic was INSULAR. Each letter stood for one of the ravages of multiple sclerosis: Intention tremor, nystagmus, scanning speech, urogenital disorder, locomotor ataxia, areflexia, and retrobulbar neuritis. At present, he has very little of any of that.

We were supposed to see my friend, George Segal, the famous actor who went to camp with me when I was a little child and on whom I operated several years ago for a droopy eyelid. Evidently, it was not an emergency and he was okay, so he canceled the appointment. He comes in about every 15 years with a problem and we renew our acquaintance from childhood and then I don't see him for another 15 years.

Another famous actor showed up in my office about twenty years ago with herniated orbital fat–that's bags under his eyes. I had not seen him since I had taken care of his then-wife's cornea problem in the 1980s. He wanted me to get rid of the luggage under his eyes. He was still getting leading roles and did not want to look like an old-timer. I told him I can fix the problem but I won't do it myself. I said I will have my good friend and colleague Richard Lisman, ace oculoplastic surgeon—and one of the leaders at MEETH in the hospital controversy—do it.

He said, "No, I want you to do it."

I shook my head. "Listen, Dr. Lisman is a specialist in this kind of surgery. He will do a good job."

"No, you do it."

"Okay, but I am going to have Richard there to make sure I

don't make any wrong mistakes."

"Okay, as long as you do it."

So that's what we did. Richard stood by while I did it. I took the right amount of fat pockets out, sewed it up so his eyelid position was not disturbed, and prolonged his career by several years, I suppose.

Tuesday, July 27

This was a busy morning because we saw several new patients. Every time we see a new patient, it takes longer and is, of course, more of a challenge for the whole staff.

A new patient was Leslie Allen, who played on the pro tennis tour with me many years ago. She's a beautiful, tall, brilliant, black woman—a true pioneer, one of the first African-Americans to be on the tour in the old days. Occasionally, she had some grief thrown her way by jerks in the organizations and in the stands, but she was smarter than they and is now doing very well. She's not in tennis anymore. She's working for the Jackie Robinson Foundation, and she's married and has a child.

Little Casandra Riggis, the daughter of the ophthalmologist on whom we operated last month, has made rapid strides since surgery. She's stopped nodding her head, her eyes are straight, and she's walking. Of course, she was destined to walk at that time anyway. She's making much more rapid progress since her eyes have been straightened.

We saw Jane Converse and her daughter. Jane is the wife of an ophthalmologist, and she has multiple sclerosis, but she's in remission. She's doing very well, with no lateral rectus palsy and no retrobulbar neuritis and no nystagmus. Her daughter was brought in just for a regular examination, and she's fine.

Elroy Shopauer was a new patient, age 46. He came in with nystagmus as well as a large divergent deviation of one eye. We spent an hour with him going over his nystagmus, his face turn, and his exotropia. I then told him I would perform surgery for his exotropia.

He pulled out a long consultation letter from another ophthalmologist, Dr. Marshall Parks in Washington, the old dean of all our strabismus brethren. The letter was written to an ophthalmologist in New York whom I had trained originally. The letter of consultation on Mr. Shopauer described and analyzed his problems and made recommendations. He presented this letter to us after we're all finished examining him and telling him what he needs. And, of course, the recommendation is different from what I suggested to him.

"Why are you giving this to me after we're all finished examining you and spending an hour with you?" I asked. "Now you pull out this letter of consultation."

Well, that's just how patients do it. You just have to accept that.

"They made a very nice analysis, but I don't agree with the recommendation," I said after I read the letter. "If you want me to operate on you, I will do what I recommend to have done."

He agreed, and we scheduled him for surgery.

We saw another little boy, also an orthodox Jewish child from Brooklyn, Meir Rechhafer. Meir is 11 years old and has needed surgery since he was about two. His parents put it off and put it off and finally have decided they want to have their child's eyes straightened. We're going to operate on him too.

Sean Dougherty was in. He's the prizefighter who has a superior oblique palsy, a very bright young black man.

"No more fighting, Sean," I told him.

"I don't want to fight anymore anyway. I'm going to go to college."

He's scheduled for surgery next week. We'll get rid of his double vision and get rid of his getting bopped on the head all the time, too.

Wednesday, July 28

For the second consecutive Wednesday, no surgery was scheduled. Very unusual, but we're in the midst of this transition between New York Eye and Ear and Manhattan Eye and Ear, and we don't know whether Manhattan Eye and Ear is staying open too much longer. We haven't scheduled patients yet at New York Eye and Ear, so with all the confusion we didn't schedule any surgery for today. That meant I had the day off, and I came home upstate and played golf and went to the lake and did a little fishing and a little swimming with the dogs and with Arleen, and it was a nice day.

Of course, it always makes me nervous and upset when I don't have any surgery because I wonder how we're going to pay the bills. I still have to keep operating in order to pay the mortgage and pay the taxes. I would have thought that by this stage of my life I could take as much time off as I wished and not have to worry about the tax bill or the mortgage payment. But things haven't worked out that way for me and, I think, for a lot of other doctors too because of the problems with the financial aspects of medicine.

A reflection from 2021:

In 2020, MDs practice medicine in many different forms, most but not all so vastly different from when my parents started to practice in the 1930s, and in different forms as well from my practice in the year 1999. Still, the basic models have changed only a little in the past 100 years. The basic models are:

Full time academic career—teaching, caring for patients, operating, and research in a medical school. Any fees collected by the institution for patients seen in the offices at the medical school hospital or operations done by the staff MDs are divided between MD staff and institution as per prior arrangement.

Part-time medical school teaching and research in a hospital and part-time private practice outside the medical school hospital.

Private practice, with appointment on the staff of a teaching hospital—medical school or private hospital—for teaching duties, including clinic, supervising resident surgery, lectures, and rounds.

Private practice—not connected to a teaching institution—on the staff of a private hospital, for admission of patients for care and operating room privileges.

Surgery by private surgeons performed at certified hospitals, and within the past 20 years since 1999, at private ambulatory surgery centers—surgicenters—owned and operated by private practicing surgeons certified by state medical boards.

Managed care in various forms—in existence since the 1930s as an alternative to private practice—is discussed in more detail in my reflection after the March 10 diary entry. Some MDs are in managed care groups only, some in combination with private practice.

In the 21st century, private organizations, some hospitals, and even some medical schools have formed large groups combining teaching, research, and medical practice.

When my father graduated from Yale Medical School in 1924, there was no managed care. The choices were private practice or full-time teaching staff at the medical school. His best friend there—David Davidson—was an expert biochemist. He chose academic medicine and spent his career on the staff of one of the medical schools in NYC doing research and teaching. My father chose to pursue private practice. His decision in 1930 not to take a residency in orthopedics so that my mother could take one in psychiatry at Columbia University Medical School in

NYC drastically affected his professional career ever after. With two young children to support, both parents could not afford to give up private income (they both had early jobs with insurance companies doing examinations for a fee), but if one continued to earn some money in insurance jobs or starting to see private patients, the other could pursue specialty training (three years). My father chose to have my mother take her residency, and he would continue to earn some money. The result is my mother became the first woman resident in neurology and psychiatry at Columbia, became board-certified, an assistant professor at Columbia, and assistant attending psychiatrist at the Psychiatric Institute there. She started private practice in our home first in Sunnyside, then in Forest Hills, in Queens NY, and was attending psychiatrist at Creedmore State Mental Hospital in Queens, where she went to supervise young psychiatrists in training. She also served as attending psychiatrist at Queens General Hospital, a NYC hospital in Queens not far from our home. She continued to attend psychiatric clinic at Columbia for her lifetime. She took care of many of the families in Queens as private patients in her office at home (her foxhole, as she called it) as one of the first psychiatrists, certainly female ones, in Queens.

My father opened an office in Long Island City in an industrial area, took care of many of the trauma cases in the factories close by, and gradually built a practice in orthopedics, albeit without formal residency training and therefore without board certification. Because he was never board-certified, he never achieved promotions on hospital staffs that having his "boards" would have led to. He attended clinic at the Hospital for Joint

Diseases in NYC—forerunner to NY Orthopedic Hospital—never being promoted beyond assistant attending. He also attended Queens General Hospital and its orthopedic clinic. His practice grew. He took care of most of the trauma cases in the industrial area in Queens and learned his orthopedics by attending the clinic at Joint Disease Hospital weekly in upper Manhattan and from his own practice. He went to all the meetings of the American Academy of Orthopedics despite no formal board certification. In order to take care of more orthopedic cases, he joined one of the first managed care plans in the USA—the Hospital Insurance Plan of NYC—as a staff orthopedist. HIP was an organization that contracted with NYC to take care of its city workers—teachers, policemen, firemen. It paid specialists a salary apart from whatever private practice they had in their own offices to see patients in one of their private clinics scattered about NYC. My father was in two HIP groups, actually, one in Flushing, Queens and one in Long Island City. He received a salary from each in return for his care of patients in their office settings and his operations in hospital. This association enabled him to take care of orthopedic patients who otherwise would not be referred to him by private physicians in the community.

Because he was in the HIP, he was semi-ostracized by some of his colleagues in the community. Once an active member of the Queens County Medical Society, and slated to be its president, he was never elected to that post—largely ceremonial but of some importance to the large group of private physicians in the county.

He stayed in HIP throughout his career and received a modest pension from each of the two groups he was in when he retired.

The HIP continues today as one of the many managed care plans in NYC, and, interestingly, it is one of the plans whose patients I accept in my private office.

My father was a good orthopedic surgeon. I know; I observed him in action in his office. I saw him stick a needle the size of a horse into my thumb when I fractured it punching a locker door in high school instead of Freddy Zuckerman, who ducked. Eluding my punch was not the only quickness Freddy showed. He grew up to become treasurer of the Chrysler Corporation. I fractured my thumb so the bone was pushing thru the skin. My father reduced the fracture with his hands and put my thumb in a splint for three weeks. Another time, I saw him put back together little Sissy Van Den Bosch's leg, crushed by a truck in front of the old Sunrise Tennis Club—the clay courts on which I first played, in Sunnyside, Queens. HIP was good for him; it was his avenue to practice the specialty in which formal training had been denied to him.

All his other friends in Queens in those days were in private practice. Most of them were board-certified specialists with no wives to abdicate their training for. However, for some reason they all thought my father was the rich one of their social group. Besides his own practice, he was part-owner of a private hospital—Horace Harding Hospital, now St. John's Hospital in Queens, where I mentioned earlier that my sister and I both had summer jobs a long time ago. They all thought he made a lot of money from that endeavor. I don't think so.

One of his friends, Ben Friedman, was professor of ophthalmology at the old NY Medical College at Flower and

Fifth Avenue Hospital in NYC and had a private office on 74th Street off Fifth Avenue. I spent a summer following Ben around at the eye clinic at Metropolitan Hospital (the NYC equivalent of Bellevue uptown at 96th Street—the only totally free clinics in NYC) where he was the chief. I remember that summer well— no air conditioning, and we worked on a new device for the old monocular ophthalmoscope to visualize retinal tears. Ben thought my father was rich. Ben was also cognizant that he was the only one of their group who went to the war—World War II. Like me years later he was LCDR (lieutenant commander) in the Navy. He thought all his friends were making a fortune in private practice while he was serving his country. I took over his private practice when he had a stroke in 1968. His wife, Bassami, was the secretary. She would never tell the patients they weren't going to see Ben and then surprise them with me there instead. I was developing my own practice at the time in my own office on 68th Street. I saw his patients three days a week in his office and mine three days a week in my office. Bassami never turned a patient away. Even on Saturdays, if someone called at four o'clock in the afternoon, she would tell them to come right over.

My father's other friends were mostly specialty-trained and had good careers in private practice. Some had academic appointments as well.

Al Fisher—my father called him "the skin man"—had a very busy private practice in Sunnyside in dermatology. He would have the patients all lined up in a row and go from one to another, telling his assistant what to prescribe for each. In dermatology, all you have to do is look. He was one of the first to have the patients stay put while the doctor went from one to another—modern-day medicine in 1940. He was also professor at NYU Medical School, then at the old Bellevue Hospital. He was chief at the skin and cancer clinic there.

I remember once my tennis student, champion Martina Navratilova, developed a rash on her chest. I wanted her to see Al Fisher but he was at his clinic that day.

He said, "Send her down here to the clinic."

When she came back, she said, "The doctor made me strip to my waist in front of 500 medical students."

That was in the old amphitheater semicircle of desks, each one a little higher up than the first, like the old lecture halls at Oxford.

Not much on formality, Al Fisher did love tennis and was a good player himself. He was also a world authority—he wrote the book—on contact dermatitis, which by the way is what Martina had.

My father's other friends mostly all did well—Bill Filler, the ob-gyn; Dave Warshaw, general surgeon who owned the old Jamaica Hospital (his son Andrew opted for an academic career and is still professor of surgery at Harvard Medical School); Dr. Arthur Fischl, cardiologist, with a private office in his home in Astoria, and professor of medicine (part time) at NYU Medical School. He was chief of cardiology at Queens County Hospital, and one summer I made rounds with him at 7:00 am every day at the medical clinic there while I was in college. Rounds were at 7:00 because his private office hours were nine o'clock to noon, and then he had a tee time every day at one. His son, Alan, was on the tennis team at Yale and was instrumental in my decision to go there to college—another story for another day.

My father's roommate at Yale medical school, Mike Sallick, became a general surgeon on the staff of Mt. Sinai Hospital in NYC. He had a private office in Manhattan. Mt. Sinai at that time was not connected to a medical school. In order to increase his surgical practice, my memory says, Mike was also in a HIP group in Manhattan. So he had both his private office and a managed care plan, and this was in the 1940s.

In my father's time and into the '50s, in order to develop private practice, MDs attended specialty clinics, attended weekly presentations at grand rounds, went to conferences in their specialties associations and in the general staffs of their hospitals. Word of mouth was the source of referrals. Advertising was just not forbidden; it was just unheard of. I remember one doctor in Queens, a colleague of my father, who was an allergist. On the shingle with his name on the wooden post in front of his office was another shingle attached underneath his name that said "Allergist." He was ostracized by the Queens County Medical Society for advertising. In this century, advertising is common on the radio, TV, and in print. The managed care groups and conglomerates, besides private MDs, spend millions on advertising.

There are many different models for the practice of medicine. I have described only a few on the spectrum from total individual private practice on one end to salaried position at an institution, private or public, teaching or medical care, on the other. I don't have experience with most beyond my own career—for example, about the Veterans Administration with clinics and hospitals that employ MDs all over the USA, I know very little.

I was, however, in the USNMC (United States Navy Medical Corps) and I recall very well what that experience was like. It could be called a form of socialized medicine, started many years before I served in the Navy, and present to this day.

In the early '60s, MDs were being called to active military duty as part of the draft. The country was getting over Korea and getting ready for Vietnam. The Berry Plan was in full effect. It was named after Dr. Frank B. Berry, who served as the assistant secretary of defense for health and medical affairs from 1954 to 1961. The plan allowed a young MD graduate to sign up for the military instead of being drafted, and he—very few women joined the plan—would be given a deferment for three years to take a residency in a specialty of his choice and then serve two years of active duty. This plan allowed a young MD to continue education, including specialty residency training, before going on active duty. It also gave the military knowledge of how many MDs in each specialty would be available at any given time to staff the military hospitals. I joined the Berry Plan, opted for the Navy, and deferred my active duty until my residency was completed in 1963. It was great. I knew I could complete my residency uninterrupted. The Navy knew I would be available and ready July 1, 1963, to serve as a trained naval ophthalmologist. Ingenious. The Navy knew exactly how many MDs of each specialty it would have available to be on staff at any time.

My time in the Navy is well documented in my two autobiographies, but in this setting I only want to describe the format of naval medical practice at that time—as I said, probably little different from the way it is now, despite the fact my Navy hospital—U.S. Navy Hospital No. 59, St. Albans, NY—has been closed for many years.

One of several Navy hospitals in the USA and around the world, it was the only one serving the NYC area—it took care of Army, Navy, Air Force, and Marine personnel on active duty as well as 500,000 dependents (family), both outpatient clinics, and in-patient beds for treatment, including surgery. An injured active-duty soldier or sailor could choose whichever Navy hospital he wished for care in the USA. Frequently, St. Albans was chosen. Our outpatient clinic for ophthalmology was busy, our surgery schedule as well—trauma cases for the active duty, as well as cataracts, eye muscle problems (strabismus), glaucoma, retinal detachment, cornea for the dependents. We took care of everything ophthalmological. The hospital was large, the adjacent outpatient clinics were in free-standing old Quonset hut-type structures, ground level. In the clinic were two ophthalmologists—me and my partner—one optometrist, four corpsmen (three enlisted men, one woman). Once a month, the civilian consultant, a professor from one of the medical schools in NYC, would come out to St. Albans and we would present problem cases to him at conference. Rarely would he then assist us at needed surgery, usually saying to me, "You know how to do this." I remember well a patient with a retinal detachment in his only remaining eye. After my tour of active duty, I became the civilian consultant there myself, having finished my Fellowship year in 1966 and just starting my own private practice in NYC as well as being the resident instructor at MEETH.

The medical care at St. Albans was first-rate—and of course 100 percent socialized medicine. I received my paycheck, according to my rank, as did all corpsmen on the staff. The care to the patients was free, including the dependents.

After my two years of active duty, I chose to leave for private practice. I did remain, however, on active reserve, *gratis*, for six years and as civilian consultant, *gratis*, for two. Had I elected to stay in active duty, I would have been eligible after 20 years of active duty for a pension. Some MDs, especially those whose residency training had been while they were already in the Navy and therefore had a number of years already served, opted to stay for the full 20 and then go into private practice—receiving full pension. I also know of one pediatric ophthalmologist, still very active, who elected to stay on active duty for a career, has not retired even after 20 years, and is now a captain in the USN (and might someday become admiral).

The stories of my active duty naval career could make a book and are not the purpose of this writing. The differences between the enlisted personnel and the officers, between the two-year active duty MDs and the Navy career MDs, my own personal saga of joining up, playing some tennis for the Navy, my own personal Navy pilot, helicopters, Navy airplanes, experience on the submarine the *USS Sarda*—all are well-documented elsewhere.

Oh well, back to my diary...

Thursday, July 29

We started at eight o'clock this morning and our new pediatric Fellow—a little Vietnamese doctor named Lan Nguyen— came to observe. I don't know why Norman Medow decided to have a Fellow for this year because we don't have a hospital anymore and we don't have a residency program. Why he's persisted in hanging onto the Fellowship, I don't know. But he hopes to train Nguyen partially at the New York Eye & Ear and partially at Cornell and partially in my office and partially watching me or helping me operate. I don't think it's a good idea, but she showed up in the office and I tried to teach her as much as I could with all the patients we saw for the morning schedule. Of course, it slows things down when you're examining a patient and then teaching the Fellow at the same time, but I've been doing that all my life, so it's nothing new for me.

We saw a few new patients, two new little children with strabismus, one who was doing very well just with glasses and the other one might need surgery. And we saw the little girl who was visiting from California, who I thought might have an epidemic keratoconjunctivitis, but her eye looked pretty clear and I sent her back to California after her New York visit with an eye free of infection. I recommended that one of my colleagues in California follow up with her for her unrelated myopia.

We saw a young lady from Egypt, Fariba Deruvar, who had a motor vehicle accident and has a significant vertical misalignment as a result with a paralyzed superior oblique. She needs surgery, so she brought her husband in this time for a consultation before we scheduled her. I went over with them all the things that can happen if you do surgery, and what the problems would be if we didn't do surgery. In other words, it was a surgical consultation all over again for the benefit of her husband. We went through anesthetic problems with respiratory, cardiac arrest, laryngospasm, malignant hyperthermia, oculocardiac reflex, slowing of the heart, and all the problems with anesthesia. And then we went through all the other problems with the eye itself, over-correcting and under-correcting, and the need for more surgery and limited rotations and problems with double vision way off in one field of gaze, even if we corrected in another field of gaze for infection and allergy, and slipped muscle and perforation and intraocular infection and hemorrhage.

When you get all finished, you wonder that anybody is agreeable to have an operation done on them. You have to put it in perspective and you have to say these things are rare, most of them we talk about. There might be double vision, and there might be a need for a second operation, both less rare. Risks are associated with eye surgery. She is scheduled for surgery in a few weeks.

And then we saw Masako Jacobson, a Japanese lady married to a Jewish man, and she has had surgery by me on her muscles and on her pterygium with conjunctival grafts. She seems to be doing just fine. I don't think I went through quite as big a list of the risks with her before we operated.

With each patient, it's different. Some patients, you have to go through the whole list of things that might go wrong and mention potential accidents and catastrophes. Other patients, you simply say, "We need to operate and we're going to schedule surgery," and they say, "Okay." So I don't do exactly the same thing for every single patient. For some patients, it's different than for others, and I have to size each patient up to determine how much they want to know and how much they need to know and how much they insist on knowing before we operate on them.

Ruth Brandt is 75 years old. We operated on her in spite of the fact Max Chamblin told her 30 years ago she could never be operated on again because she had so much scar tissue. Well, he was right in one respect. She had a lot of scar tissue, but we did manage to get to the muscle, and she's delighted because she's got straight eyes, finally, after three-quarters of a century.

And then Morton Palfrey came in. Morton is 67. We had operated on him. Every time we see him, he comes in with a list of all the things that have happened to his eyes in the preceding few months. I mean, it's a most obsessive-compulsive thing, all in perfect lined paper with lines underneath it so everything stays straight on the paper, describing every little detail of his vision—seeing blurry when driving for five minutes two weeks ago, or seeing double when he's lying on the couch on his back with his head cocked way off to the side, or seeing funny scintillating brightness for three seconds yesterday. We have to go over all the things on his list and explain each one of these symptoms to him. It takes a long time.

We saw 20 patients and, of course, it did take five hours. But then, being the summer, I hopped in the car and drove up to the country to spend a pleasant afternoon at the lake and hitting some golf balls.

Friday, July 30

It was the last day my orthoptist, Ricki, was going to be with me at Northeast Eye Care. She's been there for 10 years. She's a terrific orthoptic technician and she's helped me a lot. But we're going to start a new schedule at Northeast Eye Care where I come up only once a month and our graduated pediatric Fellow is going to come up the other three Fridays of the month. And so Ricki is no longer going to come up, and I can't afford her on the one day I come, anyway. We gave her a very beautiful gold key chain that said "Ricki" on one side and "Renée Richards, MD 7/31/99" on the other side, and thanked her for the 10 good years she's put in as my orthoptist up there. She's a wonderful orthoptist and she helps me so much. She's so quick and so efficient and so organized. I really can't afford her anymore, and she was getting tired of her trip up from Long Island, anyway. She works full-time for Maury Marmor in Port Jefferson. I found that job for her, so I feel pretty good about that. She's going to work just as much but won't have to make the trip, and I can save the money I had to spend to pay her when she came up to see the patients with me. I just can't afford her anymore. So this was her last day with us.

We saw a full schedule, 15 patients, at Northeast Eye.

Several were new, but no one needed any surgery. They were mostly routine pediatric ophthalmology visits.

Little Jules Wasserman came in for a check-up. He's got ocular albinism. Little Jules sees only 20/100 with best correction, but he seems to be getting along fine, and his parents have enrolled him in the services for the blind and for low vision that help children with various problems of low vision, like albinism. There's a network, and they have a lot of good tips on computer aids for the visually disabled and educational devices and interaction to help kids who have various low-vision problems get every advantage they can possibly get. With increased information on the computer, there's so much more information that gets to families of kids with all kinds of low-vision problems.

And then little Paige Moran came in. We operated on her for exotropia, and now her parents periodically insist she has an intermittent convergent strabismus. She's only four years old. It was the most perfect operation you could imagine. The day after surgery, she looked like she hadn't been touched and her eyes were perfectly straight. But it's two months now, and, intermittently, she can go from being perfectly straight to a gigantic esotropia. I put her in a bifocal this time and I'm going to make her wear a bifocal for a few months to relax her accommodative convergence and, hopefully, keep her straight 100 percent of the time.

That was it for Northeast Eye Care, and that left the weekend to start without too many appointments to annoy us. We had to go to one party Saturday night at Tom Dee's house. Tom had a new house built on China Lake after having lived on Barrett Lake for so many years. In fact, the year we came to Sedgewood, we rented his house on Barrett Lake before we built our own house there. Tom and I have an old history because he was the editor of the yearbook at Horace Mann when I was a junior, and I had to be his slave because I wanted to be the editor the next year and he was one of those who chose who would be the editor. I had to do all his errands for a year so I could get to be the editor the next year. Then, of course, I ran into him at college at Yale, and then I rented his house when I came up to Sedgewood. And then he became a patient, and I found a malignant tumor in his eye, just by chance, because I'm so obsessive-compulsive. So, I probably saved his life. And then we always go to his party in August, once a year. We always get invited when all the old-timers are invited too, which annoys me to no end, but I do it. He's a wonderful guy and he's a brilliant guy and he's one of the princes of Sedgewood. Even though I don't like the company at his party all that much, we do go, of course.

That was the weekend. We're still in our heat spell. We still haven't had the air conditioner installed, so it's quite oppressive, and we spend as much time at the lake as we possibly can. I even went fishing Sunday and caught three big bass, which is unusual for me. Monday morning I have to go to New Jersey to play in a celebrity golf event hosted by Dick Schaap of ABC for the Crohn's Foundation and Ulcerative Colitis. Dick was a patient of ours at Manhattan Eye and Ear. He had a very bad eye injury and a resultant hemorrhage from being hit with a tennis ball last year. He almost lost his eye. He was given very good care under our resident instructor, Amelia Shrier, who, essentially, saved his eye. I consulted with her a little bit, but she's the one who really saved his eye. He's hosting the Ulcerative Colitis Crohn's disease golf event, and I'm going there Monday morning.

August

Tuesday, August 3

Larry Yannuzzi called first thing to say a small group of the core faculty from Manhattan Eye and Ear is being invited to join the staff of Cornell at New York Hospital. We will be given an operating room, but the hitch is we have to go to grand rounds every Thursday and participate in the teaching activities of the department at Cornell. He wants me to do it, but I'm not sure I want to. It's taking on an additional academic obligation, and I'm a little bit burned out at this stage with what's going on at Manhattan Eye and Ear. I'm going to think it over for 24 hours before I say yes or no. Besides, I already did that years ago—in 1967 when I was on the staff at Cornell before I left for my five-year sabbatical from medicine.

We saw 16 patients this morning, and it was difficult because they were mostly older people with refraction and medical ophthalmology problems, and no one with a nice strabismus for us to get our teeth into.

Another doctor recommended surgery for Lily, a little Chinese girl adopted by a Jewish family. She's 19 months old, and her mother doesn't know why the surgery was recommended. There doesn't seem to be much wrong with the child's eyes, except she's 19 months old and doesn't co-operate very well. I can't imagine what this doctor wants to operate for, and the mother doesn't have any idea.

"How do you anticipate getting the child operated on if you don't know what the child's being operated on for?" I asked.

The mother had no answer, and I suggested she do nothing at the moment. We'll take a look at this child again in three months.

Tomorrow, we have to operate on Sean Dougherty, the 29-year-old black man who got hit on the head in one of his professional fights and started seeing double. He's got a paralyzed superior oblique. We're going to do him under the adjustable technique. I hope he's a good candidate for it. I also hope he stops fighting. I always recommend these prizefighters give up the sweet science. Sometimes they're smart enough to give it up, and sometimes they aren't.

Wednesday, August 4

This morning, we operated on Sean Dougherty for his vertical double vision, which he incurred getting hit in the head while fighting as a professional boxer. I told him to quit, and I hope, after we get his eyes straightened out, he will. I think he's smart enough to do that.

The operating room at Manhattan Eye and Ear is like a morgue now because the operating rooms have hardly any patients. Only a few of us hangers-on are still bringing some patients to the hospital to be operated on. Everybody else has jumped the ship for Lenox Hill or New York Eye & Ear or New

York Hospital or private ambulatory centers. Some of us are still scheduling patients at the hospital. Instead of having 25 or 30 patients for the day, the operating schedule has maybe five or six. It looks so eerie in the operating theater, walking down the halls that used to be so busy with patients coming in and out of operating rooms and equipment and the nurses and the techs, and now it's just a few people here and there.

I did Sean under the adjustable technique, which meant he was awake while I was working on the muscle. I put the muscle in the position I wanted it and just tied the knot in a slipknot instead of a complete knot. He looked at the target on the ceiling and, if he still saw double, I would undo the slipknot and move the muscle into a different position, over-correcting or under-correcting his vertical misalignment until we got it exactly where it should be so the target on the ceiling appeared single instead of double.

In the beginning, he was a little bit unruly because we gave him some tranquilizers to calm him down and he fell asleep from the sedative. He woke up with a start, and it was a little bit tricky for a few minutes until we got him completely awake. Once he was completely awake, he was quite co-operative. He was able to tell us which image of the target on the ceiling was higher and which was lower, and he was a good case to do the adjustable technique on. He was a little bit uncomfortable because we did him with practically no anesthesia, just the anesthetic drops and a tiny bit of tranquilizer from the anesthetist.

I kept saying, "Sean, how are you doing? Does it hurt?"

Sean kept saying, "I'm a soldier. I'm a soldier."

Indeed he was a soldier, and we got through it. It's a tricky operation because he didn't see double looking straight ahead, only looking down and to the left. To try to improve his muscle balance down and to the left, you don't want to disturb his good muscle balance straight ahead. You don't want to trade double vision in down gaze for double vision straight ahead. Double vision straight ahead is the most important position, obviously.

Anyway, the operation went well, and I left the operating room to drive out to Long Island to play golf with my friend Steve Levy, Alan King, the famous raconteur, and my good friend Larry Parsont. We had a wonderful time at Fresh Meadows and then had lunch afterward, talking about the world of medicine and managed care. Steve Levy, who's a very wealthy man, can't understand why we don't just stop accepting managed care at all because our reputations—Larry's and mine—are good enough that the patients would come to us even if we didn't have managed care plans. The fact is, in my field, which includes operating on so many little kids, I find parents really can't afford a private fee, so they have to go to the doctors on their managed care plan. Those of us who are still doing this have to be on some of the managed care plans. I'm on only five of them. Some doctors are on 50 of them.

Thursday, August 5

Starting at eight o'clock, we saw about 20 patients. Robyn Hammerfeld has a vertical misalignment and now dry-eye syndrome and a few other assorted problems, including arthritis. I'm trying to help her, not only with her vertical double vision, but also with some of these conditions not really connected to her eye muscles.

A new patient, Adam Service, is eight-and-a-half months old and has significant nystagmus (shaking of his eyes). He's already had an MRI, he's already had an electroretinogram, and his parents brought him for a third or fourth opinion, which is frequent. He's a cute little boy, and his eyes do jump up and down. He can see some things, but he doesn't have very sharp focus. His electroretinogram suggests he has achromatopsia, which is an absence of cones in the retina, which means he can't see color and doesn't have the sharp vision that only the cones in the retina can provide. He's also very farsighted, and his parents asked me many, many questions. I spent about an hour with them. That's the other thing—managed care's going to pay me a $90 fee for that consultation. I spent more than an hour with the parents and, before managed care that would be a $300 or $350 appointment. We talked about genetics and genetic counseling because the mother is pregnant and there's a situation with a donor involved here, and it's going to be the same donor again, and what are the chances of getting another child with achromatopsia or nystagmus. So we talked about ocular genetics, about having a specialist in genetics (a pediatrician here in the city) look at the child and go over the family tree. We talked about going down to the Wilmer Institute at Johns Hopkins in Baltimore to Irene Maumenee, a world authority on ocular genetics. A lot of issues came up apart from just examining this little child with nystagmus and farsightedness.

I did a tear duct probing on my old friend, Linton Baldwin, who was captain of the Yale cross-country team when George Bush was the captain of the Yale baseball team. That was a few years before I was captain of the tennis team. Linton is an old friend, a very, very wise gentle man on whom we've done cataract surgery and several other things. I probed his tear ducts with no problem in the back room.

Howard Millman, a psychiatrist who's had convergent strabismus his whole life and is now 54, wants to have his eyes straightened. He does work for major league baseball on drug counseling and drug testing. He's seen a few other ophthalmologists now that he's finally decided he wants to have his convergent strabismus fixed. We're going to schedule him and get him straightened out.

Little Diane Shur, the daughter of an anesthesiologist, on whom we operated a few months ago for the second time, came in. Diane is doing well.

Stanley Goldstein, 81, had a childhood amblyopia in one eye so he could only see 20/200 out of that eye. Then he got optic neuritis and optic atrophy in his good eye, so he ended up with only finger-counting vision in that eye and had to depend for most of his life on the vision from the amblyopic, 20/200 eye. And that's the eye he essentially uses. He comes in every six months because he's got cataracts now and I'm trying to decide whether, at some point, the cataracts are enough to cause him decreased vision below the 20/200 he has had all these years from his amblyopia.

It was international day because we saw Natasha Stern, a beautiful little girl who came from Russia last year for me to operate on for her convergent strabismus. Her mother is Russian and her father is an American who's posted in Moscow. We operated on her, and I follow up on her when they make their yearly visit to the States. The father is one of the most obsessive-compulsive people I've ever met (Harvard-trained, naturally), and he's a pip—the questions he asks, the letters he writes. I wonder if he ever got his face smashed in when he was a little kid with that kind of personality. How has he survived so many years? His wife is almost as compulsive as he is, but the little girl is fine. She's got straight eyes.

And then we saw Gregory Chang and his family. Gregory is the grandson of Chang Kai-shek, the premier of China during the Second World War. Gregory lives in Taiwan. He came with his wife and his two kids for their yearly visit, mostly just for refraction and to check on the health of their eyes.

We finished the day with little Joseph Ida, who screams on sight. He's two years old and impossible. You can't examine him. He walks into the room screaming and he walks out of the room screaming. You just do the best you can. You hold him down for the important things you absolutely must do, and for the rest of it you just do observation. Someday he'll co-operate, but it would be nice if he would co-operate a little bit better at the age of two than he does.

I drove up to the country in the afternoon to get ready to see patients at Northeast Eye Care on Friday.

Friday, August 6

This is the first time at Northeast Eye Care that I was to see patients without my orthoptist, Ricki, who is no longer coming because we're changing our schedule. I'm going to come infrequently, and our newly-graduated pediatric Fellow, Michelle McLeod, is going to come on the Fridays I used to come. We really can't afford Ricki because we don't get enough from the fee with managed care to justify paying her what I have to pay her. I've been doing it out of my own pocket for the past 10 years. So, no more Ricki, and now I see the patients by myself, which means I have to do the measurements, I have to do the history, I have to do the visions, I have to put the drops in, I have to do the recording on the chart, I have to do all those things Ricki used to do for me. Ricki and I could see a schedule of 20 patients and be guaranteed to walk out the door at 12:30 pm.

I tried to do it myself and I actually did pretty well. Michelle came up to observe because she's going to start seeing the patients herself pretty soon. Even though she was with me, I essentially did the whole thing myself. I saw a full schedule of

15 patients starting at 8:30 am and we walked out at a quarter to twelve. If those were 15 patients in the city, we'd walk out at a quarter to two.

Anyway, we saw a full complement of patients. One was a dentist's little child, a twin whose parents and grandparents swear is cross-eyed. She really isn't. She's got straight eyes. She just has a broad bridge of her nose, which we call the epicanthal fold, and it makes it look like she's got a strabismus. When she looks to the side, the eye looking in that direction looks like it's closer to the nose than it should be, making it look like a crossed eye. If you look at her straight-on the eyes are perfect. It's called pseudostrabismus. You have to be careful you don't confuse pseudostrabismus with real strabismus and dismiss someone as having a pseudo when they actually have a real one. Nor can you say they have a pseudo that can't develop into a real one three months later. It's a tricky diagnosis to make and you can't make it forever. You've got to observe the child several times after that. That was the case with Dr. Vasco's little daughter.

Then we saw a few other patients: The Werners came in—Christy Werner, whom I operated on when she was two years old, and now she's in high school and she's 5'10"—and little Robert Werner, who had eyelid surgery for his droopy eyelids when he was two because they were hanging over his eyes, and now he's 11 years old. I've known the Werners a long time, like I've known several of the families up at Northeast Eye who are part of our community in the country.

It's such a nice difference: the practice in the city, which is a very city kind of practice, and the practice in the country, which is a community-based practice. The city is all referral, second and third opinions, consultations, complicated cases, and, of course, a lot of old friends and old acquaintances and people who have known me in the city for a half a century. The population in the country is younger families and kids I've watched grow up in the past 15 years. Two different populations.

From now on I'm only going to come once a month, and I'll see more of the complications and more of the surgical problems and less of the routine children's ophthalmology than when I was coming once a week.

We finished at a 11:45 am, and I took Michelle out for lunch over at the Centennial Golf Club. It was nice sitting outside on the terrace at Centennial, which is only five minutes from the office. We had lunch and talked about her coming into the practice with me up at Northeast Eye Care and also joining Steven Greenberg in his practice in Rye. She's going to work in both offices. It's a great opportunity for her, and it'll be good for Steven to have her in his office in Rye, and it'll be good for me to have her here so I can spend a few more of those days I used to come up here in the city instead, where I'll make much more of an income because I don't make anything up here. It should work out for everyone concerned.

Now, my other decision is whether I want to go on the staff at New York Hospital. Larry Yannuzzi says the chief doctor, Jack Coleman, wants 12 of us from Manhattan Eye and Ear, the so-called core faculty, to come over and go on the staff at

New York Hospital. I'm not sure just what's in it for me. I have the operating facility now at New York Eye & Ear, so when Manhattan Eye and Ear closes I can do my cases at New York Eye & Ear. So what do I need New York Hospital for? It would mean I'd have to go to grand rounds there every Thursday. I don't know what else Coleman might want me to do. I've had enough of New York Hospital. I used to be on the staff there. I used to run the clinic there years ago and was associate professor of ophthalmology there. I'm not sure I want to go back to New York Hospital. I turn 65 in a few weeks. Why should I need to go on the staff of yet another hospital at this stage of my life?

The latest with Manhattan Eye and Ear is that Attorney General Eliot Spitzer insists the lay board entertain offers from Beth Israel to buy the hospital and keep it an eye hospital. If the lay board doesn't do that, the attorney general is threatening to fire the board. Wouldn't that be great, if the attorney general fired the lay board of the hospital and then made a conservator take it over until a new board could be formed? I think its wishful thinking, though, because, from the look of that operating room Wednesday, I think it's not going to be long before the doors are closed forever. A lot of the OR personnel have already been given pink slips, so the end is not far away.

Meanwhile, I must be under a lot of tension with all of this because my right arm was so painful over the weekend and I almost lost the feeling in it. It was almost like it was dead because my neck is so tight and I'm getting some axillary compression of my neck. My masseuse, Lori Jorgensen, worked on me for an hour last night, Sunday night, and got it a little bit loosened up, so at least I'm pain-free. I must be under a lot of tension, with all that's going on between the hospital, New York Eye & Ear, New York Hospital, the office in the city, the office up here, and then being upset with Arleen because the trees were chopped down in Grandpa's driveway. The trees are really not an important issue, but I just centered on it for a while—maybe as a displacement from the things that were important. And then my sister Josephine called me last night. She's going to be 70 as I turn 65—and she's just retired from her practice of psychiatry in Oregon after many, many years. I think she has to think up things to do now, although she certainly has a lot of activities she can do. She does so many things. But it's not the same as working, and I don't really look forward to retiring, but I would like things to be less hectic and less up in the air. I certainly would like to sell this house because it's killing me that we can't pay the taxes and the mortgage on the income we're making in 1999.

Tuesday, August 24

We saw 25 patients from eight until one o'clock, and that's a lot of patients for me to see. I hope in the near future I can cut down the schedule a little bit because at my age it's pretty exhausting to see 25 patients, especially the kind of patients we have—they require a lot of time and energy and consultation.

The first patient was Millard Boston, a very up-tight middle-aged man. He's very precise about everything and very concerned about his eyes. He was referred by Dr. Luntz for a muscle problem, but he really had minimal in the way of a muscle problem. He was more concerned because he thought he was going the same direction as his father, who had to have an eye operation suddenly at an advanced age. He needed more reassurance than anything else.

And then we saw Constantinis Navritos, the 16-year-old Greek boy who had a brain tumor. He was operated on a few years ago and then his eyes went astray and he developed a divergent deviation, as well as a paralysis of upward gaze. We operated on him last year and haven't seen him until today. He had been fine when he left for home, but now he has a residual divergent deviation and needs more surgery.

"Can you do it while he's here?" his father asked. "He'll be here for two weeks."

"Well, maybe we can get it on for next week."

"What about this week?"

I gave that a quick thought. Manhattan Eye and Ear is now getting closer and closer to closing, and I know the OR schedule is wide open there.

"Sure, maybe we can do it tomorrow."

We put him on the schedule for Manhattan for tomorrow. He comes from Greece on Tuesday and gets scheduled for surgery Wednesday. Amazing. But now the problem is we have to find an assistant because my usual assistant, Dr. Shashou, is in Hawaii on vacation. We weren't planning to do any surgery tomorrow. That's Amy's problem now, to find an assistant.

Lastly, we saw a bunch of kids who are getting ready to go back to school. That's why we're so busy at the end of August, as are all pediatric ophthalmologists. All the kids are coming for their check-ups before they go back to school—kids we operated on, kids we've never seen. We saw a whole bunch of them, including Jackie Garren, who's 13 and needs more surgery. She's adamant she never wants any more eye muscle surgery, a wish I am acceding to and not operating on her until the day comes when she says she wants me to do it.

Wednesday, August 25

This morning, I operated on Constantinis Navritos, and, all of a sudden, I had two assistants. Norman Medow showed up to assist me because he heard I didn't have an assistant. Our pediatric Fellow, a little Vietnamese girl, Lon Nyugen, also showed up, and the two of them helped me, which was very nice. I did a big procedure on Constantinis and, hopefully, will send him back to Greece fully cured this time.

Thursday, August 26

Again, 24 patients filled the morning schedule, mostly the kids who are getting ready to go back to school next week.

I saw a little five-year-old girl whose mother is a pulmonary specialist and whose uncle is my friend Simon Parisier, the number one ear surgeon in the city, who went to Horace Mann School, the same place I did. The child, Elisabeth Sanz, goes to Horace Mann School too. I told her I went there a little bit before she did, because I graduated from there in 1951. Anyway, she was fine. She didn't have any problems.

I saw Sean Dougherty, who is now an ex-professional prizefighter, because—with our suggestion and his own good brains—he has decided not to be a boxer anymore after having eye muscle surgery because of getting hit in his orbit.

Friday, August 27

I took Friday off from Northeast Eye Care and stayed home and practiced for a golf tournament over the weekend. Practice paid off because I won two matches and a play-off on the nineteenth hole, which was amazing for me. It put me in the semi-finals of the club championships for the first time, and I felt very good about it, especially the way I won the two matches. So it was a very hectic weekend.

Monday, August 30

We were in the office in the afternoon only and saw 12 patients, a relatively easy day.

I don't know how many times I've operated on David Carr.

I did eye muscle surgery after a retinal detachment with a scleral buckle, eye muscle surgery for a residual deviation, and then eye muscle surgery because he developed a VIth nerve paralysis. David is a wonderful 62-year-old black man from Bridgeport, Connecticut, where my father grew up, and he knows some of the old-timers. He's been a patient for about 30 years. I was happy to see him today and even happier he is doing amazingly well.

I brought John Hyler down to the office with me from the club upstate. John works around the club just to help out. He's retired from the telephone company, and I know him well because he's very good to me at the club. He takes good care of me. He took a bad fall while working on the course. He hit his head and started seeing double, so I brought him down to the city and took him over to the radiologist's office for an MRI to make sure he didn't have a subdural hematoma. I'll follow him to see whether he gets better from his lateral rectus paralysis. I have to worry there might be something else because he's got all kinds of other medical diseases and it might be just a hooker that he fell down and cracked his head. I'm not doing anything heroic on him at the moment, except I do have to watch him carefully.

Tuesday, August 31

Twenty-two patients today. Again, a lot of them are the children going back to school, but some of them were problems.

Luke Focuccio's mother is worried about her young son. We operated on Luke last year because he had had a procedure done the year before with a very poor result that left a tremendous amount of scar tissue in his eye. We took out the scar tissue when we operated, and we also did one eye muscle procedure on him. He's doing very well, actually, but his mother's very nervous. She's already taken him to someone else for a third opinion, but she's sticking with us because she knows we did such a good job on him to rectify what had previously been done. She's very concerned about him, to be sure.

Rita Ho is 85. She's the artist we operated on and got her eyes perfectly straight. She had a gigantic deviation. I was amazed. She can even fuse. She brought me a beautiful book of her paintings, which are just wonderful, with dazzling colors. She's from the Philippines, and all the figures in her paintings are people who look very, very gentle and serene in their native forest. It's a gorgeous book.

And then the Eidlers—Callie and Karen and Max. Max, a wonderful little boy, has nystagmus. He turns his face to the side. We had the puppy tied to a desk outside my office watching me eat my lunch when we finished, and little Max said, "Do you want me to bring the puppy in so she can be with you while you eat your lunch?" It was so thoughtful of him to think of that.

September

Wednesday, September 1

We operated again at New York Eye & Ear. Now we're hop scotching back and forth between Manhattan one week and New York Eye & Ear the next week. We did two cases. Little Meyer Reckshaufer is an 11-year-old Hasidic child on whom we did a bimedial recession for an esotropia since early childhood. So gratifying to see how delighted he was having his eyes straight. It was just a pleasure to do him. His parents kept saying, "God thank you for giving our son straight eyes now."

He looked terrific. He looked almost like he hadn't been touched an hour after the surgery, sitting up with his eyes wide open and no discomfort and straight eyes.

The other case was 25-year-old Elena Bassler, who had surgery in early childhood for esotropia, and then her eyes drifted apart and we did a recess/resect on the deviating eye, and she did well too.

I raced out of the operating room to get home in time to be picked up by Rick Gibralter for our golf outing sponsored by the Merck Company, the drug company in New Jersey. We were taken to a beautiful golf course about an hour out in the hill country in Far Hills, New Jersey, to Fiddler's Elbow. We had a nice round of golf and then enjoyed cocktails with the representatives of Merck. Then Rick drove me back to the city.

Thursday, September 2

We saw 24 patients, starting at 8:00 am in the morning and finishing at 1:00. One patient grew up where I live in Carmel. Her father used to be the principal of the local high school. She's a young adult and lives in the city now and she needs eye muscle surgery. I'm going to have to do her, probably in the city.

Another patient, little Aviva, was one of the most difficult children we've taken care of in years. I used to give an award for the most difficult child of the year. Aviva won it this year, but now she's a well-behaved young lady, so these kids do go through phases. Her mother's a psychologist. Aviva is no longer hostile and no longer resistant, so we're getting along a little bit better these days. She's actually quite a pleasure.

I saw Lennie Bryant, who was in a terrible automobile accident and had all kinds of facial trauma. We operated on him two weeks ago. His eye is in good position, but he still has facial scarring and still has ptosis of his upper eyelid. He wears a black patch, which he will continue to do until his eyelid is elevated again and until some of the facial scars are dealt with to make him more comfortable with his appearance.

Ora Perkus is one of the last remaining patients from Ben Friedman's practice. All the Upper Westside intelligentsia Jewish people were in Ben's practice in the old days, but very few of them are left. Ora and her family are some of the survivors of that practice I still take care of. I had to do a cancer operation on Ora's lower eyelid for a squamous cell carcinoma many years ago, and she's been fine, with no recurrence since that time. I watch her carefully. Her son, Alan Perkus, is a physicist at Los Alamos.

Little Adam Reifsnyder, on whom I did a wonderful superior oblique tuck, only to have his head tilt return a few weeks later, came in. Maybe it wasn't so wonderful. I'm going to have to operate on him again.

Friday, September 3

I was hoping not to have to work at Northeast Eye today, the start of the Labor Day weekend, and before I played my semi-final club championship golf tournament Saturday. For some reason, 15 patients were scheduled for me to see. It was the usual schedule at Northeast Eye, from 8:30 am until noon.

They were all there: Staunton Young, on whom I've operated three times and his eyes are still divergent; Paige Moran, who's doing well following surgery; and little Jeremy Calvin, two years old with nystagmus, and we're going to have to get an electroretinogram.

Little children with nystagmus and poor vision are such a problem because they can't give you subjective answers very well at that age, and you have to diagnose why they have poor vision and nystagmus. You have to do an electroretinogram and a visually evoked potential, a special study done by a retinal physiologist. Sometimes you have to get an MRI to check for any midline brain developmental disorders. It's a tough situation to deal with.

Saturday, September 4

I played my semi-final golf match against the club champion, Marty Connolly, and although I played the very best I've played all year long, it wasn't quite good enough. Marty is almost a professional. It was a lot of fun, but he won it on the sixteenth hole, and I can't say I felt bad because I played as well as I could under the pressure of playing such a good player in the semis of the club championship. But being as driven as I am, of course, I wanted to win, and I wanted to win the whole thing. But that was a little bit unrealistic, considering my level of golfing ability.

The rest of the weekend was a little more relaxed. I played golf again Sunday, and Monday, Labor Day, I went to the U.S. Open tennis tournament. I took my son Nicholas and his girlfriend Oxana, and we saw some good tennis matches with my friend John Poster. I took them home and visited with Grandpa, and there I was, on September 6, 1999, having gone to the tennis matches, visiting with my father, age 99+, and my son, age 27, and his girlfriend Oxana. It was pretty nice. I considered myself very lucky at that particular point in time.

Tuesday, September 7

Twenty-two patients were scheduled, but I ended up seeing 24 because of two emergencies.

We saw Douglas Carter, on whom we operated twice for a Brown's syndrome. He's now 12 years old. He's not such a little boy anymore. Niles Anderson has a very weird genetic defect. Like Douglas, he's a pre-teenager now. As is Jesse Caranella. We operated on him for a face turn. They're all 11 to 12 and they're all growing up and they all had serious eye disorders when they were little. They seem to be coming out of it now and growing into young men.

Zachary Lewis is the son of my friend Richard, with whom I play golf every weekend. Zachary has an intestinal disorder, and we have to keep an eye on his eyes because we might make some connection between the two. We check him periodically. Of course, he just got hit by a tennis ball last week, which he didn't tell me about over the weekend when I saw him with his father several times. Just typical of a 13-year-old kid.

Stacy Lester has had all kinds of things. She had cleft lip and palate; she had scoliosis; she has had all kinds of congenital abnormalities. She's eight years old now, status post-surgery for scoliosis and cleft lip and cleft palate. She's getting there. She can co-operate. She can read the chart, with all her handicaps.

Susan Trent is seven, with multiple congenital problems and developmental delay.

You have to give the mothers credit with some of these

little kids who have such serious problems. The mothers just keep after them and take them from one specialist to another and attend to all the different problems and deal with the children at home, and then deal with the other children in the family who don't have these problems. That's some job.

Wednesday, September 8

We did surgery again at New York Eye & Ear, three operations.

The first was little Brian Pingeron, a one-year-old with a superior oblique palsy, on whom we did an inferior oblique recession.

Douglas McCohen, 47, had an exotropia. I operated on him 15 years ago, and he came back recently and I did the other eye.

Helen Galbraith has had thyroid myopathy. She had surgery by me, then had surgery up in Westchester a few years ago, then lost the vision in one eye, then the vision came back, and then the right eye went in until we operated on her for the convergent deviation. It's a little bit tricky because she's 77 and we did her under general anesthesia.

Today we did a one-year-old, a 47-year-old, and a 77-year-old. I'm eager to see what they look like tomorrow.

After I finished operating, I went out to the U.S. Open and joined my friends Les Pollack and John Poster in their box and watched some great tennis. We saw a couple of hard-fought matches, including a terrific match between Mary Pierce and Lindsay Davenport. You expect great tennis at the U.S. Open, and we certainly got it today. After the matches, I drove back into the city to get ready for Thursday morning in the office.

Arleen went up to the country. She drove up to take care of some business and then drove right back again Wednesday afternoon. We're in the process of selling the house, finally. It looks like it's going to take place. We have a nice couple this time who want to buy it, and we've agreed on the price. Now we have to go through the details of the inspection and the septic system and the oil tank and all the other things that have to be attended to in order to get the house appropriate for the sale. It's a big deal to sell a house after finding a buyer and agreeing on a price. Arleen is handling most of it, along with Reba, our real estate agent, and if we are able to consummate the deal, we have to find a place to live, either build or find an existing house. I'd like to stay in the community in Sedgewood, because I'm comfortable there and I'm too old to look for a new community to become a part of. I don't know if anything's available and whether we can find some land to build on, and we'll just have to take it one step at a time.

But here we are now, at the beginning of September. We had the problem of selling the house, finding a new place to live. We thought about leaving the office up there and finding a new place. We thought about leaving the old office in the city and finding a new office in the city. We were at one hospital that was going defunct, and another hospital we had to find to operate in. Then we had to decide about New York Hospital because the hospital administrators want me to go over and be on the staff there too. So here we are in September with all these problems—the office in the city, the office upstate, the apartment in the city, the house upstate, the different hospitals—and things are beginning to resolve themselves a little bit. The attorney general is still working on trying to get the lay board to sell Manhattan to a place where it will continue as an eye hospital. The attorney general is very angry at the lay board, so that issue is not completely resolved yet, but in the meantime we are operating at New York Eye & Ear.

I decided I am not going to go on the staff at New York Hospital. I simply don't want to. We got a new lease on the office in the city. We are staying at Northeast Eye Care and bringing up Michelle McLeod, our former Fellow, to work in addition to me up there and also with Steven Greenberg in Rye. We are selling the house and will find another place to live. And Grandpa is four months away from his 100th birthday.

Thursday, September 9

Amy had scheduled the patients to start in the afternoon this Thursday because that's our winter schedule, but she was premature because the U.S. Open is still going on and it's still beautiful outside. So, we re-arranged the schedule to see patients in the morning for one more week, and not in the afternoon. We started at eight o'clock and finished at 12:30 pm so I could get out with my friend John and go to the

U.S. Open for the afternoon.

It was a fairly unremarkable schedule. Little Jordyn Hanratty has already seen three ophthalmologists and she's only five months old. She has a congenital esotropia that needs surgery. I implored her parents not to keep trotting her around for more dilated examinations but to choose a surgeon and to have the surgery she needs for her esotropia.

I also saw John Hyler, whose bilateral VIth nerve paresis is getting better. He's the man who works up at the golf club and fell down while working on the course and cracked his head. He's better, and his MRI was negative.

Gloria Gold is 75 years old and has esotropia. I think she got double vision from switching her fixation from one eye to the other, as the one eye developed a cataract. I wrote a paper on that a couple of years ago. I'll send Sid Mandelbaum a copy of it, along with my consultation letter.

We raced out with our lunch boxes at 12:30 pm to go to the U.S. Open and spent a wonderful day at the matches.

Friday, September 10

I was supposed to play golf with Billy van Orman and a patient of ours, Janice Danby, an executive at a major American tobacco company. Janice has a very unusual condition I operated on—hemifacial atrophy—and Billy had to cancel because he had a conflict. With the day free, I went home and played golf at our home course. Turned out to be a wonderful day.

Monday, September 13

It was a nice weekend—beautiful weather—and I came to the city today for the surgeon directors' meeting. This might be a watershed for us because it turns out the attorney general, Eliot Spitzer, and his associate attorney general, Bill Josephson, have laid it on the line to the lay board. Either the board enters into good faith negotiations with Lenox Hill or Beth Israel to keep Manhattan Eye and Ear as an eye hospital or Spitzer is going to serve papers on them. The possibility he might ask the board to be disbanded would be absolutely wonderful.

He hates the board and is going to make sure it is either disintegrated or does the right thing by the hospital and does not allow it to close. That news couldn't be better. We're all very excited about it, even though some of us are beginning to operate at New York Eye & Ear.

Interestingly, I am doing two procedures at Manhattan Eye and Ear on Wednesday, and we are encouraging all our colleagues to do as many cases there as they can in order to keep the hospital open. These surgeon directors' meetings are still a charade because the executive director (not an MD)—a man hated by all of us—sits at the head of the table during our meetings. He has been the instrument of the destruction of the hospital, along with the lay board.

But we have to go through this sham until we can eventually

disband the board and get rid of the executive director. Hopefully, that will come to pass. The situation is full of a lot of "ifs" until that point is reached.

Tuesday, September 14

This morning we saw several patients—22 to be exact— and I have told Amy I only want to see a maximum of 20 patients because it's really too much for me to see more.

The first patient, Katie Kain, 20, had multiple surgeries in Denver with my friend Bob Sargent and had another procedure in Utah. Even so, her eyes eventually turned in and she sees double. It looks like we're going to have to do a re-operation on her because she's had a secondary convergent strabismus.

We saw a young lady, Paula Frade, who had surgery as a child in her native Colombia. She doesn't need any more surgery, but she's very, very farsighted and needs to wear correction for her farsightedness.

Laura Campanis is recovering beautifully from her brain surgery. Her eyes are straight. She has no lateral rectus palsy. She's still going to rehab for her gait and balance, but she's doing wonderfully.

Samantha Udal, 6, is straight now after surgery. Also straight after surgery is Ralph Roland, 80. So is Brian Pingeron, on whom we operated last week for his vertical. He's doing well. Corby Simpson, with her amblyopia, is doing well with her patching. She's the granddaughter of my friend Paul and the great-granddaughter of my friend Herman Goldring.

We saw 21 patients and finished at one o'clock.

We had a meeting of the New York Society of Pediatric Ophthalmologists at the Lotus Club. My friend, Scott Brodie, gave a lecture, and then we had cocktails and dinner. We meet about four times a year, and it's always a nice event.

There's a lot going on. It looks like we have sold the house. The inspection Saturday seemed to have gone well. We've agreed on a price of $725,000. Barring any shenanigans after the inspection, it should go through, and then we have to look for a new place to live. All the problems during the early part of the year are beginning to resolve themselves—the lease on the office in the city, the apartment in the city, the problems with Northeast Eye Care upstate and staying at Northeast Eye Care upstate, the selling of the house, the problem with Manhattan Eye and Ear going under. All are slowly getting resolved—not completely yet, in the middle of September, but slowly and, it seems, surely.

We have two cases tomorrow at Manhattan Eye and Ear, which is good because the more cases we do there the better it is to show the hospital is still viable. After those operations, I'm taking my friends Steve Levy and Larry Parsont upstate, and they'll be my guests to play at Centennial Club on Thursday afternoon.

Wednesday, September 15

I operated at Manhattan Eye and Ear and Dr. Shashou, and the little Fellow from Vietnam, Lan Nyugen, helped me. We did two cases. Only seven operations were scheduled for the whole day, so it's a pretty small schedule because of so many defections from our ranks. The two cases turned out to be very interesting, to say the least.

I had operated on the first little girl, Susan Trent, years ago and was doing the other eye this time. It should have been a very uneventful operation with no problem. All of a sudden, a tremendous hemorrhage erupted from one of the blood vessels in the medial rectus muscle, developing a very large hematoma. I did all the things I've been trained to do with the crisis of a hemorrhage in front of me. I had no time for thinking; it was purely reflex. I got wider exposure, I put two hooks under the muscle to stretch it out, I located the area of the bleeding, I cauterized it and then I put a suture ligature in it, all within the space of about 30 seconds. The hematoma was contained and the bleeding stopped. It was the kind of thing you do as a reflex when you've been in that emergency before and you call on a memory not totally consciously but a little bit subcortical. Anyway, that was interesting for the young Fellow to see.

The second case was Andrea Foster, 44, who has had five operations on her left eye, and the eye is still quite divergent. We attempted to make her straight. I had never operated on her before, and, when I exposed the lateral rectus muscle, the choroid was visible right through the sclera. The choroid is the layer underneath the sclera and, if the sclera is not a healthy, hard shell, the layer underneath it can be visible. If the layer underneath it becomes exteriorized, the eye can have an expulsive hemorrhage and the interior of the eye can be extruded. It's a terrible catastrophe and one an ophthalmologist dreads. There I was, staring at the choroid, with no scleral shell overlying it. I had to be very, very careful with tugging or pulling or doing anything on the eye that created any pressure for fear of the interior of the eye coming through the thin scleral shell and becoming an expulsive hemorrhage with the contents of the eye coming from the inside to the outside.

Anyway, we managed to be very, very careful with it and not put any sutures near it and not put any traction on the eye and ended up doing just that one muscle. I didn't dare do the muscle on the other side, which could have required a lot of traction. It was a case of choosing between getting perfect alignment by doing both muscles but risking the possibility of rupturing the globe or having less of a perfect alignment result, even though she's been done five times and was very anxious finally to have her eye straight. Still, the risk of a ruptured globe was not worth trying for perfect alignment.

That was the decision I made on the spot, and it's the right decision—because why risk rupturing the globe just to get better alignment? There's no difficulty in making that choice. We did one muscle, kept the eye intact, and whatever improvement she gets, fine; and if it's not perfect, then that's all right too.

So, those were the two cases in the operating room Wednesday.

Friday, September 17

I should remember today, because September 17 is my son's mother's birthday. Anyway, that's beside the point. Other things happened that kept my mind focused.

I was supposed to take Larry Parsont and my friend Steve Levy up to Centennial to play golf Thursday, but the beginning of Hurricane Floyd caused a torrential downpour that afternoon, and we canceled the golf. I came up to the house, which is not far from Centennial Golf Club. I was up in the country when the hurricane began to show its rain and beginning winds. Amy canceled the patients for Thursday, and that meant the two patients we operated on Wednesday would not be seen Thursday. I would have to take care of them over the phone. Then we canceled the patients at the Northeast Eye Care for Friday morning, too, because this hurricane had been forecast as gigantic and no way could the patients get to the office in the city on Thursday with transportation being knocked out in the city. No way could patients up in the country come to Northeast Eye Care on Friday morning, either.

So, Thursday we stayed at home up in the country, and Arleen and I spent a good part of the time battening down the hatches, hammering plywood into the floor to keep the French doors from flying open, getting all moveable things off the porches, sandwiching the Corvette between the two trucks so that, if a tree fell down, it would hit the trucks instead of the antique Corvette, and buying supplies, including flashlights and candles and everything we could think of, in case the power were to go out. We had all these preparations for the onslaught of Hurricane Floyd. As it turned out, Brewster and Carmel got the most rain of any towns in the metropolitan area—15 inches. All the roads became flooded. A fallen tree closed the road out of Sedgewood we use to get out of the club, and I had to call the highway department to tell them to come and remove it. I don't even know if they've done it yet. There was no way in and no way out because of the tree over the road, so we were stuck in the house. I couldn't have gotten to Northeast Eye Care on Friday morning, anyway. We just stayed in and weathered the hurricane. No trees fell on our house or on our cars, fortunately, and none of the doors blew open. We felt pretty fortunate because things could have been a lot worse. All roads in the town flooded out. The Bronx River Parkway was closed, Sprain Brook Parkway was closed, and Sawmill Parkway was closed. It was quite a storm.

In the midst of it all, Jack Dodick called me Thursday night to tell me he had spoken to the attorney general. Eliot Spitzer was ready to serve papers on the lay board to sue it for being irresponsible in its custodianship of Manhattan Eye and Ear and in breaching its fiduciary responsibility to the hospital and to the charter of the hospital. If the suit is successful, the board will be thrown out, along with the executive director, and a conservator will be appointed to take over the running of the hospital until either Beth Israel or Lenox Hill—both are happy to take it over and run it as an eye hospital—comes in to do so.

Jack also said the attorney general wants to speak to Richard Troutman, the only MD on the lay board until they kicked him off the board a few years ago. Jack said Dr. Troutman is incensed over what is going on and is going to tell the attorney general exactly what this lay board is all about.

So things look promising for the saving of Manhattan Eye and Ear, and now we've tried to get some of the doctors to come back and operate there again to show the hospital is still viable during this time of litigation. In the meantime, I'm still writing letters of recommendation for some of our residents who, because of the closing of the residency program, have no place to go. I just wrote a letter for Lisa Park, who finished her first year with us and is doing nothing at the moment because she didn't get a position as a second-year resident in any of the other hospitals. Five of the six did, but she decided not to do anything yet. The three senior residents who were supposedly at the Manhattan Eye and Ear program affiliated with Cornell are not having a particularly good experience. Hopefully, if all this comes to pass, we will re-institute the residency program at Manhattan Eye and Ear. But, that's in the future and probably won't take place until the end of the year and the beginning of the new millennium.

So, to recapitulate, as we approach the end of the Jewish New Year, not the end of the millennium yet, but Yom Kippur was Monday, and, as of today, Friday, many of the issues...

I was just interrupted by Manuel, who takes care of the landscaping and the grounds for us, and he said the tree is still across the road so we can't get in or out of our home. I called the highway supervisor again. He's got 16 families who can't get out of their homes because of closed roads, and he's been up all night working on it. He's going to get a crew out here as soon as he can to get the tree off the road and fix the washout so we can get in and out, but it's not going to be within the next few minutes.

Here I am Friday morning, with a beautiful sunny day, although it's still windy—the aftermath of the hurricane—and I'm sitting here contemplating the developments of the year. So many things that were in a state of change and upheaval are gradually beginning to resolve themselves.

To begin with, the lease on the office in the city became resolved when Mr. Steinman at Rudin Management agreed to reduce our rent and we signed a four-year lease. That was nice, so we didn't have to uproot our office in the city and move somewhere else.

Monday, September 20

It's Yom Kippur, so the office is closed today and I'm not working. I'm also not in Temple because I'm not that observant. However, I'm also not supposed to be playing golf, but I might sneak out onto the course anyway as long as nobody sees me there except Clarence, the pro. And he won't tell anybody I'm there.

It was an interesting weekend because of the aftermath of Hurricane Floyd, the hurricane of the century. New York and New Jersey were declared disaster areas, and 15 inches of rain pounded Brewster. We're the next town to Brewster, and all the roads in Sedgewood flooded and downed trees blocked several roads. The electric company had to come and get trees off the roads. The day after the hurricane, Friday, the road to my house is still out. The road around the lake completely caved in and became a rock pile because the stream underneath the road erupted and water gushed out and lifted the road. For a section of about 100 feet, the road is nothing but rocks. We couldn't get beyond where the road gave way. I had to walk with our two Airedales through the woods and across to the road on the other side and to the house. It's about a half a mile walk.

It's the same area where several years ago I cracked my face on the ice in the winter and broke my nose and reset it myself. That spill gashed my eyebrow open and I had to go to the hospital and get my friend Hal to sew me up. Nicky trudged through the ice in the blackness of night—all power went out—to get a four-wheel-drive Jeep to pick me up because I was in shock. But that's another story. It was many winters ago. This was this weekend and the aftermath of the hurricane of the century.

Anyway, the road gave out and the prospective buyer came yesterday to look at the house again, mainly to survey any damage from the hurricane. We had to get the road temporarily fixed before the buyer came because if he saw he couldn't even get to the house I'm sure the deal would have been screwed. We got a private guy to temporarily patch the road so at least we could get through. The highway supervisor says he'll come this week and take care of the road.

So that was the excitement this weekend—to get the road patched so the buyer could come Sunday (yesterday). The buyer and his wife spent a couple of hours here, looking at all the things in the basement. He was instructed by his father-in-law, an engineer, to look for water in the basement. He looked. The basement was dry. I showed him the tennis court and the lakefront, and it looks like the deal is going to go through.

Arleen and I then went down and took a look at Ned Dorsey's house, which is a little bit in disrepair. The good news is it's inside Sedgewood, it's only on an acre, the taxes are low, it's on one level, and we could do a lot to fix that house up and make it very livable for us and not incur the yearly expenses we've had to run the house we're trying to sell. Ned's house looks promising, and I hope somebody doesn't buy it first. We're already thinking about what kind of additions and renovations we would do to make it work for us.

Of course, we got a flat tire in the Jeep from going back and forth over those weathered rocks that make up our road. Now we have to go down and get the tire fixed, and then I'm going to take the Jeep into the city and leave it off at the Jeep place to get it fixed because it's in a terrible state of repair. And then I start work in the office tomorrow, and maybe I can come back up after I operate Wednesday to sign the contract if our attorney, John Porco, has it in his hands.

A reflection from 2021:

If I may, I'd like to mention one of the nicest things to ever happen to me. My life was immeasurably brightened a little more than a year ago—November 30, 2017—when the Horace Mann School Alumni Association thrilled me with its highest honor, the Award for Distinguished Achievement. The same award was given to our Attorney General Elliot Spitzer and a few other notables, such as Attorney General William Barr years ago. A portion of my remarks that wonderful evening follow:

"Thank you... to the wonderful surviving segment of Renée's Army, that loyal band of friends and family who are here today, who stuck by me during those tumultuous years when I was struggling with the whole world watching my every move. Thomas Wolfe reminded me so many times, 'You can't go home again.' Well, here I am, again.

"When one of my dearest friends died a few years ago, he left instructions for his memorial service: 'Renée to speak, but not long winded.' He knew me well. So I asked my son Nicholas to write something for me. He did, and I delivered it—five minutes. I don't promise that today, but I wrote down a few notes so I won't have to pause and think and take forever talking. I have been known to ramble some.

"I am truly humbled to be on the list of former recipients of this award—authors, scientists, philanthropists, heroes in medicine, sports, human rights. I know I have had multiple careers in some of these arenas, but none so accomplished as are those on that list. In fact, I really had just one career—for which I was destined from birth, my parents and only sister physicians before me—and I still practice ophthalmology more than half a century since medical school. I guess that might be of some significance—thousands of eyes operated on, hundreds of residents and Fellows taught and counseled—but I still think of Einstein's remark on winning one of his many awards: 'I don't really know what all the fuss is about, I wrote about six papers that only half of which were read, and only half of those were understood.'

"One might say I had three careers—medicine, tennis, and human rights pioneer—the last for which I had no ambition, never trained for, never planned, almost didn't do, and didn't understand its significance for many years. My personal struggle with gender dysphoria and its ultimate resolution was private, and hardly humanitarian. My decision to become a professional women's tennis player was at first selfish, and only eventually after I started that struggle did I realize the effect it was going to have on disparate disenfranchised groups of many kinds. I remember receiving hundreds of letters cheering me on. When I quoted Robert Frost in my book, *No Way Renée*: 'Two roads diverged in a wood and I took the one less traveled on,' I was referring not just to my own personal life decision but also to the legal and social fight that I embarked on after I was outed in that famous tennis match at La Jolla which suddenly thrust me onto a world stage. It was fortuitous, maybe serendipitous, that my own private personal struggle would eventuate in my becoming an unwitting advocate for people without the voice or resources that I had. Achievement can be providential. I still wonder how it all came about.

"I wonder why I was able to have a larger-than-personal effect. I was never a recluse, but I was a private person, and with no experience on the public stage. Maybe because I was fortunate to be successful in my private life I became a role model by leading by example, not by promulgation. I am not given much to introspection, but as I think about it on this occasion, I think part of what helped me was the trait of concentration, not even seeing opposition or even danger sometimes. I just forged forward, happily unaware. Or so it seems. However it came to pass, I am happy I was able to help some people less fortunate than me.

"I first read *The Scarlet Letter* in Alfred Baruth's English class as an HM junior in Fifth Form. Maybe this quotation was in my mind during some of my odyssey in the world's eye—

"'No man for any considerable period can wear one face to himself, and another to the multitude, without finally getting bewildered as to which may be the true.' Was Hawthorne writing that for me?

"I think I tried to make the multitude understand. I hope so. But I am well aware that there is still much work to be done in human rights, especially for so many of the socially oppressed. I applaud the efforts of current activists in our country. I was perhaps too selfish, too private, actually, to be one. Social activism is fighting for the rights of disadvantaged human beings—there are many ways to do it.

"And I want to make note too of a few of the stalwart friends in my life who made it possible for me to have the success I have had. First in the world of tennis—for sticking up for my rights—

Billie Jean King, and some of the other women players on the pro tour who embraced me for sticking up for my rights, and some of the men players who were outspoken in their support too. Names that might surprise you: Rod Laver, Don Budge, John McEnroe, Dick Savitt, among others. I played a tennis exhibition in Boynton Beach, Florida, one time in the late Seventies, having just started on my time in women's pro tennis. And in that small group of onlookers, who was there to cheer me on? My old baseball coach from HM—Moose Miller and his wife Mary. They had never met me as Renée before. And second—in the lesser-known struggle I waged to return to the practice of medicine—the battle to be the first to do that publicly with a new name in a different sex. I had been away from medicine for five years, I was infamous, I had no idea whether I could even learn all the new advances in my specialty, let alone take care of and operate on the eyes of children. The chiefs of my hospital had been my students years before. I no longer had a practice of my own. Some of the surgeon directors of my hospital were not in favor of my returning to the staff. The chief, my former resident Jack Dodick, simply said, 'Dr. Richards is back.' That was it. If not for the support of my colleagues, and even some patients, I don't think I could have made it back. The dean of all the eye muscle specialists in the country, white-haired, conservative, imposing, invited me to spend the winter months in his office in Washington, D.C., gently reintroducing me to the language of my specialty. Then a colleague at my hospital said, 'Renée can come work in my office in Jackson Heights until she feels ready to open her own.' I did that, and when the opportunity came in the spring of 1982, the right practice was held open for me until I returned from coaching Martina at Wimbledon. I have been there ever since. I have indeed been fortunate.

"Finally, I want to congratulate the Horace Mann School for selecting me for this award. Our school should be proud for having the courage to choose Renée Richards this year. I know full well the grief and bitter times that went on at the time of the scandals years ago; good for HM.

"In closing, I would like to say that the five years that I spent on the hill—from Second Form through senior year—were probably the most important formative years of my life. I came to the then Horace Mann School for Boys 70 years ago in the winter of the school year. I had told my mother I wanted to go there. My parents, who were not native New Yorkers—Mother had never heard of the school. She arranged a meeting with the headmaster. I suspect my reputation as a young lefty pitching prospect had something to do with Dr. Charles Tillinghast agreeing to have me start classes the very next Monday—in the middle of Second Form. I have been the most fortunate recipient of the best education that this country can offer—special class in public grammar school in Queens, HM, Yale, the University of Rochester School of Medicine, ophthalmology training at the Manhattan Eye and Ear, then post-graduate Fellowships at Columbia, Iowa, and Oregon. It was at the Horace Mann School where I learned how to behave as a good citizen—combining my own personal agenda for education while learning how to connect with my Fellow students and teachers...

"And all the while preparing us for college. When I got to Yale, I was as prepared for higher education as any student in the class.

I was indeed privileged to be a Horace Manner. It was a second home where we studied, played, and dreamed with optimism and the zest of youth. I am indeed so grateful to stand here today. Thank you."

Oh, well, back to my diary...

Tuesday, September 21

This morning we saw 22 patients, a very busy schedule, including the two post-ops from Wednesday we hadn't seen because of the long weekend, Hurricane Floyd, and Yom Kippur on Monday. We saw them for the first time post-op today.

One was Andrea Foster, on whom I had found a weak wall of the eye and could only do one muscle because I didn't want to risk rupturing the globe. I explained that to her when she came in today. She looked pretty good. She wasn't perfect because I couldn't do two muscles. The eye looked healthy, and I told her what the risk would have been if I had tried to do the second muscle. She was appreciative, and she's healing up pretty well.

The other was little Susan Trent, who had a hemorrhage in her medial rectus muscle. She looked very good. She wouldn't let her mother put any drops in during the weekend, so I gave her some ointment and she opened her eye for me to put the ointment in herself, which was very good for Susan to do.

And then we saw several patients, a few of them new. Randy Gibson has a convergence insufficiency and needs exercises. Another had a terrible accident with a fracture of his orbit and communication between the para nasal sinuses and the orbit so that every time he breathes he feels air above his eye.

And then there was Gloria Gold, who's 75 years old and on Coumadin, so I don't want to operate on her eye muscles. I think we'll let her have her cataract done first.

Gustavo Velez had strabismus surgery in Ecuador and now has a pterygium and very uncomfortable eyes. I think his problem is primarily one of dry eyes.

We saw several other follow-ups, including Robin Wright, who had a brain hemorrhage, and we operated on her for her vertical misalignment. She does very well. However, if you look at her on the microscope, you can see the rapid oscillations of her eyes in a rotary fashion. It's amazing she doesn't have her entire environment visually rocking back and forth. She says she is aware of some oscillopsia (images moving back and forth).

Tomorrow, we operate on Joey Shaffer and Benjamin Weiser, two young boys who have almost the same condition, an intermittent exotropia, which requires surgery on one eye only. We're going to be back at New York Eye & Ear. We've been going back and forth for the past several weeks between the two hospitals.

Wednesday, September 22

Joey Shaffer and Benjamin Weiser underwent uneventful surgery this morning. We did one muscle for intermittent exotropia on Joey and two muscles on Benjamin because he had a more significant problem at near range and required surgery on the medial rectus as well as the lateral rectus. They are so efficient at the Infirmary that, even though we did two cases, we were out of the operating room by ten in the morning.

My associate Dovelet Shashou drove me over to Chelsea Piers so I could hit some golf balls and then back to the office to do some paperwork before the pediatric ophthalmology meeting at Mt. Sinai. The meeting is part of the Greater New York Ophthalmologic Society Resident Series, the same series in which I gave a lecture earlier in the year.

As I was hitting some golf balls, I remarked to myself how much of a New Yorker I truly am—operating in the morning, then hitting golf balls at Chelsea Piers in the afternoon, going to a meeting at Mt. Sinai in the evening. My son lives in the city, my father is still in his old house where I grew up in Queens, and although I'm very worldly and I have lived in many different cities in the country and spent a lot of time in Europe as well, I'm basically a New Yorker. I enjoy living in New York, both in the city during the week and in my country home on the weekend. I have the best of both worlds, with New York at my fingertips. I can go to a ball game at Yankee Stadium to watch the Yankees or to an affair in the city, perhaps a reception for someone being celebrated, like Henry

Kissinger's reception earlier in the year, or to Lincoln Center for an opera or to a theater on Broadway. I do none of these things often, but I do them occasionally, when they come up. River Dance, the Irish dancing group at Radio City, a play with Sam Levine on Broadway, *The Sunshine Boys*, a revival of a musical. Whatever it is, the city is here, and I live here, and it's available to me when I want it. It's just great. And then I live in the country on the weekends and can fish in my lake and hike in the woods and play golf to my heart's content. Traffic is horrendous in the city. The people are sometimes short and abrupt, but basically everyone is friendly and, in my particular world, which is comfortable and relatively free from crime, it is indeed a very nice place to live. The climate is good; we have four seasons, we're relatively free of great natural disasters like hurricanes and earthquakes, and there is no place to live like New York—that is, for a New Yorker. I understand people from other cities who have a difficult time here, even when they visit, but for a born-and-bred New Yorker there's no place like it.

Of course, it took me 40 minutes in the taxi to get from 36th Street to 100th Street and Madison Avenue to the meeting at Mt. Sinai, but that's just one of the things you accept. If you go at rush hour at five o'clock, you're going to be sitting in traffic until you get almost out of the city.

The meeting at Mt. Sinai was good. Residents from New York Hospital and New York Eye & Ear and other residency programs in the city presented pediatric ophthalmology cases. Many of the better-known pediatric ophthalmologists in the audience offered comments. And then, of course, all the residents in training from all over the city were in the audience as well. The cases were interesting. My young associate Steven Greenberg was there, as was the present pediatric Fellow Lan Nguyen and some of my older colleagues, like Norman Medow and Ed Raab. Norman cochaired the event with Lisa Hall, one of our residents a few years ago at Manhattan Eye and Ear. Unfortunately, there were no Manhattan Eye and Ear residents there because we no longer have a residency program. This is part of the general winding down of Manhattan Eye and Ear engineered by the lay board of the hospital. I hope that board is being sued by the attorney general. I haven't heard anything further on the subject.

Thursday, September 23

I did some paperwork at my desk, and Arleen showed up from the country to run the office for the afternoon because Amy had a family funeral. Arleen brought our Bernese mountain dog little Midget, the little bear cub of a puppy, who is now sitting underneath my feet, beneath my desk, while I do some paperwork and dictate this note, waiting for the afternoon schedule to begin. We will see about 25 patients and then, if we're not exhausted, drive up to the country tonight to see patients early in the morning at Northeast Eye Care. If we're too tired, we'll stay overnight and drive up Friday morning.

We started seeing patients at 12:30 pm, and we finished after five. Arleen hasn't done this for some time, but, of course, this was her job before Amy. Midget stayed underneath the desk for most of the time while Arleen did her work in the front office and I saw the patients in mine. We saw 25 patients even though we had the pediatric Fellow, Dr. Nyugen, visiting. I had to go over each patient with her. She stands behind me and looks over my shoulder as I see them. I have to go over the findings of each patient with her, which usually slows us down, but we managed to get through the schedule remarkably well.

The first patient was a semi-emergency, the son of my old friend, Poncho Segura, the great tennis pro. His son has a pterygium which is kind of active now, and his father had had one too. Of course, the family comes from Ecuador, and pterygia are common in people close to the equator because of the breakdown of the external (outer) tissues from the ultraviolet exposure.He also has an eye muscle problem—he sees double at distance—and I think he's got a long-standing superior oblique palsy from childhood which he was never really aware of. Anyway, we'll have to keep an eye on his vertical, and he might need surgery for his pterygium.

We saw several patients we've seen for many years, including Brittany Herman, on whom we operated, and her twin sister, on whom we are going to have to operate.

We saw Andrew Fennerman, who has a very large astigmatism and amblyopia in his one eye and nystagmus and wears contacts. He carries on pretty well.

Carol Little was a new patient, a woman about 30 years

old who was operated on elsewhere for a large convergent strabismus and didn't get any improvement. She can't even move the eye past the midline, and so we're going to have to re-operate on her and explore the muscles. It's a complicated situation. She had Lyme disease, which she felt made her eye muscles worse, and she had scarlet fever in childhood, which caused the problem to begin with. You never know how much of which contributes to a present condition. She's got a very disfiguring esotropia and she has to turn her face way over to the right in order to use her right eye at all.

Bonnie Schneider is 76 and, for the first time now, her diabetes is having some effect on her eyes. She's got background retinopathy with some microaneurysms close to the macula. We're going to have to keep an eye on her because she might need some laser therapy.

Zoe Rowe is three years old, Oriental, and adopted. She looks like she has strabismus, but she doesn't. Her eyes are perfectly straight to the cover test. It's just a pseudostrabismus (prominent epicanthal folds that won't be so prominent as she grows).

Arthur Lustberg, a 74-year-old speech teacher, had a retinal detachment and a scleral buckle, a cataract extraction, and then he saw double. We're managing him with prisms rather than with surgery.

And then all the little Walden kids came in. Samantha had a capillary hemangioma I diagnosed at the age of six weeks. Several consultants wanted to operate on her, which would have been unfortunate if they cut into a capillary hemangioma, which could cause a tremendous amount of hemorrhage. I talked everybody out of it and insisted on watching her, and here she is at the age of 11 and the hemangioma has practically resorbed into non-existence. If I didn't know where it was originally; I wouldn't even be able to palpate it. That's a good lesson in being conservative, although sometimes you have to be bold. In her case, I took the road of just watching her because I felt sure she had a capillary hemangioma and not a very bad malignant tumor. Fortunately, I turned out to be right.

Little Meyer Rubin was in for a post-op visit. He's so delighted his eyes are straight now. His parents waited until he was 11 years old to have surgery, and we did him a few weeks ago, and he's just fine.

Jeannette Konstanty is two years old and complains of not seeing in the dark. Does she have congenital stationary night blindness or some retinal dystrophy, or is she just afraid of the dark? I turned out all the lights. I made her pick things up off the floor. I made her read the chart. She does just fine.

The next-to-last patient was Louisa Moreland, who has a well-controlled esotropia. Her parents had a million questions about how long she's going to need to wear glasses and when she should wear them and is her esotropia better—just one question after another. I said she was a garden variety case of esotropia needing glasses—accommodative esotropia. Of course, to them she's not garden variety, and so I have to give the parents equal time and make all the explanations to them. After seeing patients for five hours, I'm probably not as patient as I should be.

The last patient was Emily Dewhurst. We operated on her for vertical strabismus, which was very complicated because she's been operated on elsewhere and had been very badly charged emotionally during an attempt to do adjustable sutures on her the next day. She remembers being held down while she was adjusted. When we operated on her, she wouldn't open her eyes for two hours in the office the next day, until we finally convinced her we weren't going to be pulling on any strings on her eyes. We got her to open them, and she seemed fine. She's fusing, using both eyes together. She can lapse into a turn when she gets very tired, but all things considered she did very, very well. So that was it for today, and tomorrow we start all over again up at Northeast Eye.

Friday, September 24

I saw 16 patients at Northeast Eye Care, and I see them by myself now because Ricki isn't there. I miss her, but I'm still able to do it. I get through the schedule and seem to still walk out about 12:30 pm.

The first patient was Nadine Sonnenberg, on whom I operated for a complicated strabismus after three years of watchful observation. She had a bilateral Duane's syndrome, which is unusual, and I got rid of her face turn and straightened her eyes. Her parents, like the last patient from yesterday in the city, still have a million questions about her. I dutifully answered them, as I usually try to do.

We saw several follow-ups on children I've operated on and Ann Rosenberg, who's going to need some surgery.

The most complicated case was poor little Jason Knox, who's six years old. He doesn't walk, he doesn't talk. It's hard to tell whether he sees anything. His grandmother feeds him from a baby bottle. He's had all kinds of examinations, including MRIs and genetic testing and metabolic tests, and nobody's come up with a diagnosis on him. From my standpoint, I know he's got small optic nerves, and I think he's showing some optic atrophy now, which means his optic nerves are degenerating. I don't know whether he's got a degenerative neurologic disease, like congenital Leber's amaurosis, which is a terrible condition, and the patients go blind in early childhood, or some other degenerative disease. I'm really not sure whether he sees anything. His pupils do react, and he makes random eye movements, but he certainly doesn't fix and follow on objects. I spoke to the neurologist to tell him I think the optic nerves are now worse than what they looked like two years ago when they were just small. Now they're showing atrophy or degeneration and loss of the pink color the optic nerves are supposed to have. So, they might have to do another MRI, and maybe we have to do electroretinograms on him. He's continually being studied. He doesn't have much brain function and continues to be a diagnostic problem.

The rest of the patients were fairly routine, including Steven Marcello, on whom I operated twice—once for convergent strabismus, and then for a secondary divergent strabismus. He's okay now.

One patient like Jason Knox can throw me for a loop because it's such a sad case. His function in life is so handicapped, and his grandmother and mother shower such love upon him. His mother is pregnant again now, and it will be interesting to see, when she has a hopefully normal child, how Jason is going to fit in with this young family.

The weekend was wonderful. The weather was clear and perfect for golf. Arleen and I looked at some land with the thought we might want to build a log cabin again on a smaller scale than we did the first time, but the land is very scarce in Sedgewood. I'm not sure we're going to find anything reasonable enough for us to buy and have enough money left over to put a log home on it.

Monday, September 27

Back in the city this morning, with 13 patients on the afternoon schedule.

Andrea Foster is pretty upset. She had high hopes I was finally going to be the one who could straighten her eye when I operated on her last week. I disappointed her because I didn't get much of a result. The wall of the sclera was so thin I couldn't do as much as I wanted. I explained the problem to her today in great detail. I told her I chose to be safer with her eye than to get good alignment.

"Yeah, but I don't see very well out of that eye anyway," she complained.

"You see something," I said, "and something is worth preserving at the expense of getting perfect alignment."

I promised her I would go back when she's healed up and try to do the one muscle I couldn't do last week.

Chandler Casenova is 68. He has Parkinson's disease, and he's got cataracts. I've operated on him for his muscles. At one point, one doctor thought he might have myasthenia gravis because he had a variable deviation. He doesn't have myasthenia, he's got Parkinson's, and the Parkinson's impacts his eye muscles. After he gets his cataracts done, maybe we'll go back and do some more eye muscle surgery on him.

Two cases like Chandler and Andrea keep me humble and make me realize that, even though I do pretty good eye muscle surgery, I'm not infallible. Some things, even with my skill and experience, I just am unable to do in order to get a perfect result.

I saw Caitlin and Matthew Anthony, three-year-old twins, and they're just fine. Little Matthew even does the stereo test for 3-D stereopsis at his tender age, which is amazing.

I saw two patients on whom I operated more than 25 years ago: Mary Catherine Parr and Louie Ferrara. Louie, now an emergency medical technician, always used to come in with his grandmother. I said to him, "Louie, is your grandmother still alive?" I was nervous about asking him because I thought his grandmother would probably be dead by now.

He said, "Sure. She's sitting out there in the waiting room."

I went out and said hello to Mrs. Ferrara, who still comes

in with Louie just like she did 20 years ago.

Tuesday, September 28

We saw 22 patients this morning, starting at eight o'clock. It was a lousy morning because they were all follow-ups and most of them older people with general ophthalmology problems and very few strabismus problems. In fact, there were no new patients. The new one didn't show up, a retinopathy of prematurity baby.

The only kids we saw were the two Zacharys: Miller and Katz. One mother prosecutes and the other one psychoanalyzes. Two Zacharys, both we operated on.

And then we saw Ann Guisseppe, whom I've taken care of for 30 years, and Joey Shaffer, on whom we operated last week. Then we saw the three little Norton kids—Adam, Jennifer, and Matthew—who are really Avi, Esty, and Moshe. Little Moshe is doing well, and Avi has a nevus of ota, a pigmentation all over his eye and on his iris. He has to be watched very carefully

Patricia Lane is now 43, and I operated on her 27 years ago. She has been a patient of mine for more than 30 years. Now I just watch her for her high myopia and her retina.

And then we saw Ruth Brandt, who is 74. We operated on her eyes and she is thrilled that we got her using her eyes together again.

Wednesday, September 29

This morning we operated at the NYE+E and did a bilateral recession for esotropia on little Charlie Roger, four. We did a recession of the left inferior oblique for a vertical misalignment on Avalon Goebel. For some reason, I was nervous about the anesthesia for both kids, and sometimes I don't sleep well the night before surgery. It's almost always in relation to being nervous about anesthesia. For today's cases, when I saw my favorite and trusted anesthetist Dan Kochi getting my room ready, I immediately felt a lot better, and surgery went well.

Then I went upstate because I had to meet with my attorney John Porco to sign the contract to sell my house. I started getting messages at every stop I went to—at the golf club, at the house—that Amy was trying to reach me from the office. All I could think of was that something had happened to the kids we operated on in the morning. I tried to call her and she was out to lunch and I got more and more nervous. When I finally did get a hold of her, I learned it was related to a nonsense call about a patient from North Carolina calling about an itching burning eye.

I was absolutely livid. I said, "Don't ever call me and track me down all over Westchester and Putnam County if you can't be available for me to answer the call. I've been worried about this ever since I got the message to call the office." Anyway, so much for that.

Thursday, September 30

We saw 19 patients. The two post-ops from yesterday looked terrific.

One patient had such a large convergence misalignment he had to turn his face way to the right to see with the left eye and way to the left to see with the right eye. He had a bilateral complete VIth nerve paralysis from an automobile accident three months ago, when he fell asleep at the wheel and hit a tree. He's in for a lot of surgery to try to get him lined up so he doesn't have to turn his face to a particular side to see with that eye. Hopefully, we can get him to use both eyes together again, but I don't know if that is at all possible. He's going to need major surgery, but it's too soon to do it now because it's only three months since his accident. His measurement is 90 prism diopters of turning in. That's huge. He can't even get either eye anywhere near the center position, let alone move it out toward his ear. Completely paralyzed lateral rectus muscles. He also has paralyzed superior oblique muscles, but that's not such a big problem.

We saw another patient, 72-year-old Lloyd Tompkins, who has had a blow-out fracture of the floor of the orbit and now has a residual limitation of elevation of that eye as well as a small convergent deviation. We're managing him with some prisms in his glasses.

Arthur Hausman came in with double vision after a retinal

detachment operation. We're going to manage him with prisms, too, because I don't want to operate on his muscles if I can avoid it, at the age of 85 status post cataract extraction and retinal detachment surgery. We'll see what prisms can do.

Cameron Stoltz is the son of my friend Dr. David Stoltz. He came in because the union told him he needed a glaucoma evaluation. His optic nerves do look a little bit cupped, but his pressure is normal, and we'll just follow him with the visual field. He also has an eye muscle problem we might operate on.

Jason Domenico has an intermittent exotropia. He's seen four other ophthalmologists. All he needed was a slight change in his prescription. He might need some surgery eventually for his exotropia.

The remainder of the patients was fairly routine follow-ups, including Manuela Arias from Venezuela. She's two years old, status post-surgery for a very large convergent strabismus, and she also has a large amount of farsightedness. With her glasses, she's perfectly straight.

Tomorrow is Northeast Eye Care, but I'm tired and we've seen a lot of patients and it's now almost six o'clock, so I think I'll stay in the city tonight and drive up in the morning.

October

Thursday, October 7

I missed a few days, but I'll try to catch up as best I can. This has been an extremely busy week, although I ate well. I went to the Manhattan Ophthalmological Society dinner and the American Jewish Historical Society dinner, and I went out to Forest Hills to visit Nicky and take him out to dinner. I also worked on completing the sale of the house and finding a new house. It's been a very, very hectic time, but not as interesting to anyone else, so I didn't bother to write about any of it.

Today, we saw 15 patients, five of them new. As I've said, new patients take more time, and five new patients fill up a day.

One family of orthodox children—Meyer Abelson, Lottie Abelson, and Albert Abelson—all came in with unusual strabismus problems. It's hard to tell how much of those problems are inherited, and just how much are a recessive inheritance because of the small community many of the orthodox Jews in Brooklyn hail from. One child has Brown's syndrome and can't elevate the eye. The other child has Duane's syndrome and can't abduct the eye. The mother has a long-standing strabismus from childhood, which is where the children may have gotten this in the first place.

Poor little Careen Calvetti has cerebral palsy from a birth injury. She's 13 and she's in a wheelchair and she doesn't talk and she has to be cared for. Her mother does such a great job taking care of this child who's now becoming not a child anymore. It's an intensifying problem as she comes into the teenage years.

In the afternoon, I saw Dick Schaap, the famous sportscaster. He'd gotten hit in the eye a year ago by a tennis ball and had a terrible hyphema, with blood in his eye that took weeks and weeks to clear. At one point, I thought he might even lose his eye, but now he's okay and that eye sees pretty well. Today, he revealed unusually distributed opacities on the surface of the cornea of each eye which I had not seen when I saw him last year. It turns out he's on a very potent anti-arrhythmic heart medication called Cardurone. The opacities in his corneas are from Cardurone. He needs this medication to regulate his heart, but he doesn't need to have his corneas become cloudy because of a side-effect of the medication. I spoke to his cardiologist, and it's a very tough call. He desperately needs to stay on this medicine, but we can't watch his corneas become opaque either. It's going to be a problem in management.

Friday, October 8

I saw 15 patients again at Northeast Eye. Remember—I'm now seeing them alone, without my helper, Ricki, and I managed to get through them from 8:30 am to 12:30 pm—all 15.

The weekend was relaxing. At the annual golf club cocktail party Saturday afternoon, those of us who had won some tournaments during the season received our prizes. I got a nice silver dish for the one event I was part winner in. That was fun.

Tuesday, October 12

Back in the city, we saw 20 patients. Two members of the Ordierno family—Bianca and William—have very weak eyes. Both children have tremendous astigmatism, and the best they can see is 20/40, 20/30, and even that is difficult for them. Now the older child, William, wants contact lenses. He's 17, and we'll see if we can get him fitted with contacts.

Little Adam Reifsnyder, with head tilt and post op superior oblique tuck, is doing pretty well. I'll eventually do more surgery on him, but I'm going to hold off for a while.

Shirley Bart came in. Other doctors thought she had myasthenia gravis, but I knew she didn't. Her eyes are perfectly straight. She was a recovered VIth nerve palsy, not a myasthenic.

Dr. Howard Millman's eyes were straight following the surgery last week. I was happy to see that.

Fannie Bartolomo, whose file is about an inch thick, has thyroid myopathy, and that's one of the most difficult conditions we deal with. Now she's seeing a little bit double in a vertical direction again, so I had to give her some prisms.

Tuesday night, I had to go to the Hank Greenberg dinner at Lincoln Center. I hate to stay out late the night before I operate, but I was committed to this party and dinner. I'm on the committee for the American Jewish Historical Society, Sports

Division, because my best friend, Les Pollack, is the head of it. He put me on it, and I had to go to the party and the movie. The movie was interesting. I knew Hank Greenberg, so it was nice for me to see the movie celebrating his life and his life in baseball and his life as a Jewish athlete.

Wednesday, October 13

We did three operations. Michael Rivera, a clinic patient, I did privately because the clinic is no longer in existence and there are no more residents to take care of the clinic patients. We had followed him in the clinic because he needed surgery for his exotropia, and it seemed prudent to do him privately.

And then I did Xander Nieman for an inferior oblique recession for superior oblique palsy following an automobile accident.

And then we did a very interesting thing. Paul Owens and I injected botulinum toxin into the medial rectus of both of Jerry Willander's eyes because he has a complete VIth nerve paralysis with a gigantic inward turn of each eye, unable to get either eye even near the midline. We couldn't inject him with the botulinum without surgically exposing the medial rectus and then putting the needle directly into the muscle. We injected the Botox® into each medial rectus and, within a couple of days, his medial recti will become paralyzed and his eyes will become straight. It should last 4 to 6 weeks. I'm waiting for him to show some signs of recovery from his paralysis. If he doesn't, I'll have to do a muscle transposition on him on each side. He has to turn his face way over to the side to use each eye because he can't get either eye anywhere near the midline. It's almost grotesque. To look with his right eye, he has to turn his face way over to the right. To look with the left eye, he has to turn his face way over to the left. Following the Botox® injections, he should be able to use his eyes straight ahead, at least for 4 to 6 weeks until the injection wears off.

Thursday, October 14

We saw 15 patients in the office, a few post-ops and a few new patients.

Pam Maura cried, and I smiled. We had done an inferior oblique on one side and an inferior rectus on the other side two weeks ago. Today, she sat in the chair and started crying because she was so happy her head was straight now and her eyes were in perfect alignment and she didn't have to tip her head over to one shoulder in order to avoid seeing double. She was so emotional. She said her whole life she's wanted to do this, and now she feels so wonderful.

The little boy, Michael Rivera, whom we did even though he was a clinic patient, came in with a dozen red roses for me. How lovely.

Friday, October 15

I saw 15 patients again at Northeast Eye Care. June Gilchrist has had cerebral palsy her whole life. Her father, Thomas Gilchrist, was a famous prosecutor who was a patient of mine. He was one of the prosecutors against the communists just after the Second World War in the Red Hunt days of Joe McCarthy and Richard Nixon. Gilchrist was instrumental in bringing the charges against Alger Hiss, the Soviet spy. Thomas Gilchrist is long since dead. He was my patient many, many years ago. His daughter came in by herself, and she manages to do pretty well considering she doesn't have the ability to be totally independent. I find it terrific she's had some independence.

Jessica Healy, now 12 years old and on whom I operated when she was a baby, came in. It's so nice to see these kids growing up and to know I had something to do with making their eyes okay when they were one year old.

Saturday, October 16

We gave a party at the house, the annual golf club lobster bake. We served lobster dinners to 55 people—on the deck, on the pool table, on the dining table, all over the house. It was a wonderful event, as it is every year.

Sunday, October 17

We looked at some land we were thinking of buying to build our house on, since we just sold ours. We decided we liked the land, so we made an offer and we're going to buy it. Then we went over to see Vince Gizzi's house that we were considering renting while we're building our new house. We liked his house so much we decided to buy it. Even if we buy Vince's house over on the reservoir, we still think we're going to buy the land we want to build our house on. We don't have to build right away; we'll just buy it. We'll take the money out of my retirement account and buy the land, and the money we get for selling this house we'll use to buy the house we were going to rent. In the space of two days, we end up owning a new house, still occupying the house we just sold, and buying land to eventually build a mountain house on—all with no money at all since we're in financial straits. If we take the money out of the retirement account, we can buy the land and, with the money we're going to get from the sale of this house, minus paying off the mortgage, we'll be able to buy the house we were going to rent.

Arleen and I are feeling rather giddy at the moment, with all these gigantic transactions taking place.

In the meantime, I'm getting ready to go to Florida to the Academy meeting. Arleen's getting ready for the onslaught of having my sister come from Oregon to visit Grandpa. That's always a *tour de force*. And Nicky is bracing himself for

Josephine's visit as well.

We renewed our lease on the apartment in the city at the same rent, and that was good.

Northeast Eye Care is quite a saga. I'll discuss that in a few moments, but suffice it to say that for the time being we have decided to stay at Northeast Eye Care, and I don't have to look for a new office to start a new practice upstate in Putnam, which would have been quite a chore.

I think we have finally gotten the house sold. The inspection was last week. We haven't heard anything bad, and it looks like the prospective buyers are truly going to go ahead with the deal.

The Manhattan Eye and Ear problem is ongoing, as I have been discussing.

So I sit here in our home we have just hopefully successfully sold, and I don't have to work this morning, so I can begin to look over some of the literature I'm supposed to read every month. I must say I've been delinquent in my reading because it has been such a hectic year.

Let me enumerate some of the things I am supposed to read monthly. The refereed journals in ophthalmology are my primary responsibility to read. A refereed journal is a journal in which the articles are gone over by referees of peers— colleagues in the same field—and one member of the editorial board goes over each submitted article and writes a review to the editor. The editor then decides whether to publish the article with revision, without revision, or to reject it. In fact, I'm on the editorial board of one of the journals I'm supposed to read every month, *The Journal of Pediatric Ophthalmology and Strabismus*. Frequently, I have to review articles submitted to that journal. Here are the refereed journals I'm supposed to read every month:

The blue journal called *Ophthalmology*, a journal of the American Academy of Ophthalmology. It features major articles on different subjects.

The white journal, *The Archives of Ophthalmology*, has smaller articles and also many research articles.

The yellow journal is *The American Journal of Ophthalmology*, a combination of clinical articles and research articles.

The British Journal of Ophthalmology, the British equivalent of *The American Journal of Ophthalmology*.

The Journal of Investigative Ophthalmology, the journal of the Association for Research in Vision and Ophthalmology. It is all research articles.

These are the major refereed journals in ophthalmology an up-to-date ophthalmologist has to read every month. If he or she doesn't read the full journal every month, which of course is impossible, the abstracts of the articles printed at the beginning of each article must at least be read. If the abstract shows something of interest to the reader, then the whole article should be read. So we have, in general ophthalmology, the yellow journal, the white journal, the blue journal, the British journal, and the green journal, which is the research investigative journal.

Then we have the refereed journals in my particular

subspecialty of strabismus. We have *The Journal of Pediatric Ophthalmology and Strabismus*. It is the original journal of pediatric ophthalmology, and I am on its editorial board. We also have *The Journal of the Association of Pediatric Ophthalmology and Strabismus*. We have *The Journal of Binocular Vision and Strabismus,* a very specialized journal with articles of interest just in strabismus, not in pediatric ophthalmology too. Then, of course, there are journals in all the other subspecialties of ophthalmology, which I do not subscribe to. These include *The Journal of Glaucoma, The Journal of Plastic and Reconstructive Surgery of the Eye and Orbit,* and *The Journal of Neuro-ophthalmology,* which is related to neurologic diseases. There are other subspecialty journals in ophthalmology for each subspecialty.

The ones I am responsible for reading—and I should read—are the journals in my subspecialty and the general journals of ophthalmology. When I used to be the director of residency training at Manhattan Eye and Ear in my younger days, I read all these journals very, very carefully. I would have all current articles at my fingertips so when I went on rounds with the residents I could pronounce the article and the year of the journal and I would have a comment about any subject in ophthalmology. The residents would play a game. They would fool around and mention something and then wink to each other as the trigger was turned on and I would spew forth the journal article and the journal of the pertinent subject, while they would kind of laugh at me behind my back.

Of course, I can't do that now. I don't have that kind of

memory anymore, and I don't read each journal religiously like I did in those days when I was the director of the residency and felt I had to be current on every single subject.

Besides all the refereed journals I mentioned, I also get so-called non-refereed journals every month—*The Review of Ophthalmology, Ophthalmology Management,* and *Eye Net,* which feature articles of interest to practicing ophthalmologists that are not exactly scientific articles but are more of general interest and mostly to do with the private practice of ophthalmology.

For example, in the current *Review of Ophthalmology,* the subtitle is *How Five Top Surgeons Maximize Efficiency.* Everything in the practice of ophthalmology these days revolves around maximizing efficiency because that's what it's all about in the private practice. Everything relates to providing the service as quickly and as efficiently as possible so reimbursement can be maximized financially. It's a far cry from the days when we would sit and talk with the patient for a half hour and not necessarily on the particular condition of their eyes. Those days are over, and now the patient is left in the room while the ophthalmologist goes to the next room where the patient has been prepared for him to see and there's little time to talk about anything other than a few words about their eye condition.

One other difference between the way we practice now and the way we used to practice is the subject of advertising. In the old days, you were not even allowed to put out the shingle in front of your office to specify whether you were involved in allergy or orthopedics or ophthalmology or retina or glaucoma or anything—simply a shingle that stated your name with MD afterward was all that was allowed. Now, doctors advertise in the newspaper, and they advertise on the radio and on TV. There's a full-page advertisement this month for a surgeon who does the lasik procedure on the corneas to change the refractive status of the eye, which is the rage in the late 1990s—keratorefractive surgery, lasik or PRK—and there are some full-page ads for the Laser Center of New York or the Laser Vision Center, and basketball players are seen endorsing it. And on the radio every day, the New Jersey Eye Center or the Laser Center of New York offers testimonials from those who have had laser surgery, and doctors advertise just like any other business would advertise. In the old days, if anything like that were done, the doctor would be ostracized by his community medical society and wouldn't be eligible for many different benefits from the society because he would be considered unprofessional. It's a totally different world where medicine is now considered a business as well as a service. In the old days, the business aspect of it was frowned upon and it was considered strictly a professional service. That's the way I grew up in medicine and that's the way I still practice, but that makes me a dinosaur, as we approach the millennium.

Besides all the journals I just mentioned are the so-called throw-away journals, which are more like newspapers in size. They come out every two weeks, and they're full of advertisements as well as articles. The articles are of interest mostly in relation to practicing ophthalmology and doing keratorefractive surgery or corneal work, although some articles in these journals relate to the subspecialties. They're filled with advertisements for instruments and different technical advantages commercially available. *Ophthalmology Times* is one of them. *Ocular Surgery Report* is another one. You peruse these journals quickly and throw them away— so they're called the throw-away journals. They have some useful information in them, and they are very well-written, but they're not what we call refereed journals and so they are not saved.

Those are the journals in ophthalmology I read every month. There are also journals I get that I hardly ever read, but I do still subscribe to them. *The Journal of the American College of Surgeons*, of which I am a Fellow, *The Journal of New York State Medicine, The Journal of Urban Medicine, The New England Journal of Medicine,* the so-called bible of medical journals in this country. I must admit I do not read very many of the articles in these journals.

The amount of reading that comes to me every month is overwhelming, as this list reflects. Of course, that leaves very little time for me to do any reading other than in medicine. I used to like to read novels as well as history and political commentary, and the number of books I've read in the past few years is virtually zero. I will start a book and read maybe half of it, then don't read any more of it because I'm too busy reading everything else I have to read, along with practicing medicine. Of course, I still have time to read *Corvette Fever,* the journal of my hobby of my antique Corvette, and I never fail to read *Golf Digest* and *Golf Magazine* as well. I also still subscribe to *Tennis Week* and *Tennis Magazine*. The waiting room is filled with other magazines, such as *People* and *The New Yorker* and *Time* and *Newsweek* and, of course, I never have a chance to read any of those.

Among books I've read in the past few years, the last book I completed was *Angela's Ashes* by Frank McCourt, and I can't remember the last book I completed before that. It might have been *The Bonfire of the Vanities* by Tom Wolfe. I started a bunch of other books, like *Death of Outrage* and *Primary Colors* and some other political books I'm interested in because I did major in American government, but I almost never get to finish any of these books I start.

There are physicians better at reading than I am, mostly because they don't play golf all day like I do, and also because they're faster readers. I'm a slow reader. I read like one reads medical material—every word and every sentence and every paragraph. I don't read in wholes gestalt—the way a good reader would because I have to know everything I'm reading. And, of course, I have to follow the New York Yankees for six months, and I have to follow the New York Football Giants for a little bit, and I have to follow the professional golf tour on weekends and tennis tournaments four or five times a year, at the slams and other big tournaments, and I do like to go fishing. And so my reading time is not what it used to be.

A reflection from 2021:

I have described some of the activities of a physician in the training and execution of the practice of medicine. Most lay people—those not in the medical world—have little idea what else an MD does. Certainly it is not reading, at least reading anything not connected to the profession. There is just no time. Here is a brief list of activities that sometimes occupied my time—evenings or weekends:

Professional journal reading (list of journals described above), evening meetings (hospital, societies), guest lectures, preparation of my own lectures, all related to medicine, and reading medical journals. That is why doctors are lousy cocktail party guests—we're boring. Lawyers are the most interesting for parties. They read everything.

Unfortunately, the medical profession requires a level of dedication, which precludes time for some activities others enjoy. That is our choice, and how much or how little we do outside the profession does vary. What does not vary, however, is the lifelong effort required to be a capable physician. I think back on my own and it seems like I have been taking an exam of one kind or another almost every June for 75 years. Here is an incomplete list:

- final exams in June starting in the 8th grade, and every year of high school until graduation, and SATs;
- final exams in June every year for four years in college;
- final exams in June every year for four years in medical school;

- National Board of Medicine exam after second year of medical school and after final year—in June, in order to get state license to practice medicine;
- final exam in the basic science course in ophthalmology in June 1961;
- two years active duty USNR—1963-65;
- written exam of the American Board of Ophthalmology in 1963, and oral exam in 1965;
- required courses from medical liability insurance carrier (malpractice insurance) almost yearly—with exam on completion;
- required courses by New York State education department, with exam on completion;
- OSHA course and exam on the disposal of hazardous material (blood contaminated from HIV); and
- continuing medical education courses, with exam on completion for CME credits necessary for hospital re-certification staff privileges appointment—to the present.

Not difficult to conceive of MDs as boring. What else do we have time for?

Of all the exams enumerated here, the most important were two—the first the two-part national boards of medical examiners that certify a doctor to practice medicine in several states. Florida and a few others had their own board exams in the old days. The second is the boards—short for the exam of the American Board of Ophthalmology—in order to be certified by the American Board. That is essential for any ophthalmologist desiring to practice, to become a member of a hospital staff, and to be accepted in the community as a true specialist in ophthalmology.

Some ophthalmologists never pass the boards—the oral exam that follows the passage of the written boards. Pass the written boards first, then pass the oral boards, and you become board-certified. You hang a plaque on the wall in your office that tells everyone you are certified by the American Board of Ophthalmology.

I was on active duty in the U.S. Navy, following my residency at MEETH, when I took the written boards. I passed. When I got close to taking the orals, my civilian consultant at the Navy Hospital—Dr. John McLean, chief and professor of ophthalmology at Cornell Medical School—simply said, "Well, you pass it or you don't." That doesn't fill you with much confidence, but he was a man of few words, and fewer compliments.

I went to Chicago and checked in to the Palmer House Hotel, frequently the site of the annual meeting of the Academy of Ophthalmology and the site of the board exam, the oral examination of candidates who had successfully passed the writtens. What I remember of the oral exam is the following, somewhat. I remember four of the several different exams—one in strabismus, one in pathology of the eye, one in medical conditions, one in neuro-ophthalmology. There might have been one or two more; I don't remember. The two examiners for each exam were a senior member of the board and a junior member, an old professor and a young one. This was in 1965, so my memory is imperfect, but the following is like it was yesterday, it was that critical.

I remember the neuro-ophthalmology exam. The junior examiner asked the questions; he was soon to be the chief and professor at the venerable Cleveland Clinic in Ohio. I knew him briefly from my time at Columbia as a Fellow.

He asked me, "What is the most common symptom of ophthalmic migraine?"

I said debilitating headaches, usually familial, usually one-sided, more often in women, sometimes with associated visual phenomena, rarely with neurologic signs. I knew my migraine.

"No," he said.

I racked my brain. I thought of all the others, and struck out. I looked at the senior examiner and he looked at me with an expression of "what is he looking for?" Finally, I gave up and the junior examiner said, "Photophobia." Okay, common in migraine but not exactly the most common symptom of all.

I left. I had struck out. But he knew I knew my neuro-ophthalmology and I knew he knew it. I was confident I passed. But my next exam was the most interesting—pathology. Who studies pathology except someone particularly interested in it? The senior examiner asked the questions. He was Gerard Devoe, dean of all ophthalmologists in NYC at the time, professor and chief at Columbia, and certainly no one to be trifled with. He beckoned me to a microscope on his desk, with four microscope slides next to it.

He said, "Look at these slides and I will be back." He left the room. Twenty minutes later he returned and asked me to tell him what they represented.

"Dr. Devoe, I am still on the first slide."

He went berserk. He said I was supposed to look at all of them. Well, the first slide I looked at was very interesting and complicated, a slide of an eye with a very unusual condition—

not even in existence today because cataract surgery has been modernized by my dear friend, Dr. Charles Kelman. The condition was phakoanaphylactic endophthalmitis, a rare allergic phenomenon resulting from retained cataract elements (fragmented pieces) left in the eye, causing an allergic reaction with devastation to the eye.

Dr. Devoe asked me to describe what I had seen. I described it in detail and diagnosed phakoanaphylactic endophthalmitis. He calmed down and thought a moment.

"Okay, tell me about the masson blue stain."

Microscopic materials are stained with different colors to highlight cells seen on slides under the microscope. For whatever reason, I have no idea why, the night before the exam, in going over my notes on pathology lectures from more than a few years ago, I thought to look up what I had on microscopic slide preparation. Don't ask me why. I told Dr. Devoe all I knew about the masson blue stain of microscope slides.

Exasperated, he said, "You are excused."

About an hour later I was traversing the lobby of the immense Parker House when I passed Dr. Devoe going the other way. He turned around, pointed his finger at me, and said, "What do you know about electron microscopy?

I smiled at him. "Nothing, sir, nothing."

It was too late—no exam there in the hallway. My exam had been finished an hour before. Besides, he knew what he needed to know anyway. The oral exam is not designed to find out how encyclopedic a candidate's knowledge of minutia in ophthalmology. It's designed to find out who should be let loose in the country to be responsible for the health of the eyes of the populace.

Apart from all that, I knew I was going to pass. I had a secret weapon. Another candidate at that exam was my dear friend Ed Dailey, ex-Princeton tennis star, ex-resident of the Wills Eye Hospital in Philadelphia. When two of the American Board examiners, the two chiefs of the board to be precise— Edward Maumenee from the Wilmer Eye Institute at Johns Hopkins Medical School, and Irving Leopold, professor and chief at Mt. Sinai Hospital in NYC—found out that these two ex-tennis champs were among those sitting for the board exam, they arranged a doubles tennis game one afternoon after the day's exams were complete. They were avid tennis players, and, by nature, very competitive. Ed Dailey and I joined them for the match. Ed took Dr. Leopold for his partner, and I took Dr. Maumenee. Ed and Dr. Leopold won the first set, Dr. Maumenee and I won the second. Wonder how that happened. And wonder why the sets took so long that it was too late to play a decider. Both professors left happy. And no wonder both Ed Dailey and Richard Raskind became certified by the American Board of Ophthalmology that spring in 1965.

A final curious note about the boards. Now, every ten years ophthalmologists have to retake the written exam to be recertified by the American Board of Ophthalmology. The curious and absurd part of this is that, if one was certified more than twenty years ago, one does not have to take the exam. He or she is "grandfathered in." The one group of ancient doctors who should have to brush up and study and retake the boards does not have to. They are grandfathered in. I was certified in 1965.

Charlie Kelman was a good friend. He was beginning his work on cryo, in which you put a freezing probe on the cataract before you take it out. This was before he invented phacoemulsification. He was not getting encouragement from Dr. Don Shafer, who was head of the surgeon directors at the time. He was also getting obstruction from Dr. Richard Troutman, who was envious of what Charlie was doing. They tried to block him, but he persevered. He did his research right there in the annex building.

Charlie and I had airplanes that we hangered at Teterboro Airport, across the Hudson River in New Jersey. At one point Charlie wanted me to go in with him on a plane that we would buy together, a more expensive one than either of us had. Charlie's was a real puddle jumper that had an engine in the front and engine in the back. It wasn't on each wing like most twin engine airplanes. He was smart; with one engine in the front and one in the back, you still have one if the other one fails, and you're not out of balance. Charlie wanted me to go in with him on this new plane. But one day his brakes didn't work and he skidded off the runway and ran into the rampart at the end of the runway. At which point I decided, ah ha, I don't think I want to go in on a new airplane with Charlie.

Charlie learned to fly a helicopter and used it to go to operate at St. Barnabas Hospital in New Jersey. I used my plane for personal pleasure. I didn't know instrument flight rules or anything very sophisticated about flying. I used visual flight rules. "There's the Long Island Expressway. We are on our way to East Hampton." Jack Dodick used to say I was the only one he ever knew who would fly to East Hampton by way of the Throggs Neck Bridge. We had a lot of fun flying around. We had fun flying with Charlie, too, but back at the hospital the board of surgeon directors gave him a hard time because he was ingenious and he was about to do something big.

It would be a revolution in cataract surgery. To be able to do phakoemulsification, you had to learn a whole new discipline. It's the way all cataracts are done today, and it's a savior. It saves the posterior capsule. It lets you put the new lens right up against the posterior capsule, and it only requires an incision the size of a pinpoint. It was remarkable, and it happened during the five years I was away. So many other things happened at that time too. Changes in retina detachment surgery, lasers, phakoemulsification, all of those things.

Very little changed surgically in strabismus. Techniques we were using were by and large the same as before I took my sabbatical from medicine, so I didn't have much in the way of new techniques to learn when I came back to practice.

Oh well, back to my diary...

Monday, October 18

It might have been a dull four weeks, with little of importance to discuss. Perhaps the tapes were misplaced and, twenty years later, can't be found. Maybe I just got tired. Anyway, almost a month later, I pick up my story.

We saw 12 patients this afternoon, starting with Debbie Weissman, who had a gold ball implanted in her left upper eyelid so the eyelid would close a little better. I've operated on her inferior rectus for hypotropia. She's doing pretty well.

But Martha Eichinger is not. Martha is 78 years old and has had three corneal transplants, two cataract extractions, an implant in one eye replaced, a retinal detachment operation in one eye, a vitrectomy in the same eye, and two eye muscle operations for a strabismus secondary to the retinal detachment operation. And she still has a gigantic residual right hypertropia, and she wants me to operate on her. She still has sutures from her corneal transplant in the right eye and sutures on the limbus from an emergency done on the right eye a couple of months ago. She wants me to operate on her for her right hyper because she says she sees double. She's one of the most difficult cases you could imagine to have to deal with. We went over and out and around and about on doing her surgery.

And then I saw Carol Weiner, who had lasik done by David Haight. She had a pineal tumor removed from her brain and she's got a residual esotropia and hypertropia and torsional diplopia. She's one person on whom it's a reasonable idea to do monovision so she has one eye for distance and one for near. That's what I suggested for her.

Lawrence Mooladi is a totally difficult patient to examine. He's already 10 years old and he's got tremendous developmental delay. You can't look at his eyes because every time you shine a light in his eye, he deviates it either way down or way up so you have absolutely no view of the inside of his eye. It took me almost an hour to try to look at his retina and to look at his refraction. Totally impossible to examine him.

Tuesday, October 19

We saw another 20 patients. Barbara's not here because she's got some medical problems.

David Haller has a residual head tilt following a superior oblique tuck out on Long Island, and it is a severe head tilt still. I'm going to have to do some more surgery on him.

Samuel Michel is 13. He had a traumatic cataract from a projectile shot at his eye when he was eight years old. We talked about eventually doing his cataract and putting in an implant, but we're going to wait until the implants are better designed so he has some ability to see up close with it, as well as far. We'll use a multifocal implant.

Everyone was rather routine except poor Victor Glenn, who is so hyperopic and so astigmatic he can't see very well even with full correcting. He's only seven years old. I gave him a new prescription, and I told the board of education to let him sit up front in class.

Catherine Bagwell wants me to operate on her. Catherine is 83 and has a pacemaker, and her cardiologist won't let her be done under general anesthesia. If she can't be done under general, she's probably not a good candidate for local, either. She might talk me into doing her under local and doing one eye.

But Martha Eichinger was something. She insists she wants me to operate on her, and she's got so many things wrong with her eyes. Add them all up: three retinal detachments, two corneal transplants, two cataracts, repositioning of lenses, vitrectomy, and two strabismus procedures secondary to diplopia following the retinal detachment procedure. She still has a cloudy cornea. She needs another corneal transplant on one eye, and she's got sutures all over her right eye from recent surgery, of which kind I know not. And she wants me to operate on the muscle of her right eye, after it's been done twice elsewhere.

Thursday, October 21

This was an interesting day in the office. We saw Linda Canheimer, who is very, very nervous about her eye muscles and about her eyes in general. She wanted to know how long it would take before the drops would wear off, and these drops were only for her pressure check. They don't dilate the pupil or make anybody blurry, and she knows that. She still came back into the room and asked me about the drops wearing off—topical anesthetic.

Sue Beinin is happy because we straightened her eye after five operations. She's very, very grateful.

We saw a four-month-old child for the first time because the mother thought the light reflex in the child's right eye was not as bright as the other eye in a picture. When we looked at the child, the eyes looked normal. It was a perfectly normal examination.

"Come back when he's a year old," I told the mother

Another new patient has a left eye drifting out. The parents had taken the child to Dr. Raab uptown, and he said it was a problem with the other eye. I think he's right. I think it's a problem with the right eye not being able to adduct, and that makes the left eye go out much farther in left gaze. I think we'll just keep an eye on that child.

The problem case for the day was little Taylor Flippin. I first saw her at the age of 13 months. An eye was turning in. I said, "Let's patch the other eye and bring the child back in a couple of months." They came back a year later, having gone to another doctor and having had surgery on the eye muscles by the other doctor. Now they're back with us and I said, "Okay, you went to another doctor for an operation and now you came back." We took care of her and gave her another recommendation for treatment and she went away. She came back today, at the age of four, having had another operation by the same doctor who did the first one, and now they're coming back for us to look at her again because the one eye is not seeing so well. I refused. I said, "No." I can't remember the last time I did that. I said, "No, I'm not going to examine her. We'll give you the names of three doctors you can take her to, or go back to the doctor who's taking care of her now who operated on her twice, but you don't bring a child to someone at 13 months, then go away, be operated on somewhere else, and then come back and get an opinion again from the first doctor, and then go away and then go back to the doctor who operated on her the first time and have her operated on the second time by that doctor, and then come back to the first doctor all over again. You just can't do that." So that was the story with her.

The next child was also someone who went to another doctor for a prescription for glasses after having come here originally. This child needed a different prescription than what he'd been prescribed. I'm hopeful the mother will get the new prescription filled and the child will be a lot happier.

Gerald Dent came in. He's straight after we operated on him. His mother wants to know why he still needs to wear glasses. Actually, he doesn't. He does have a big astigmatism, but he's using both eyes together, and he could take his glasses off part of the time now, and I'm going to let her do that.

Andrea Foster is going to need more surgery. She's the young woman who had so many operations that the wall of her eye was weakened and we were only able to do one muscle. She's going to have another crack at it in a couple of months when she's healed up enough from this operation.

We finished with Sam Millman. We operated on Dr. Millman a couple of weeks ago, and he's delighted his eyes are now straight at the age of 54. He should have done it a long time ago.

A reflection from 2021:

Besides the actual office visit descriptions of 1999, other activities should be mentioned. I saw patients in the office

Mondays, Tuesdays, and Thursdays—usually nine until two in the afternoon. A new patient consultation might take more than one-half hour. A yearly checkup might be fifteen or twenty minutes, but if the patient needed to be dilated it would be longer. Fifteen patients might be the average for a session.

A colleague once quipped, "Renée, you don't have an office, you have a boutique."

Maybe, but that is the way I practiced. Wednesdays I operated at MEETH on my private patients, and then assisted surgery by the post-graduate Fellow in pediatric ophthalmology or the resident assigned to the pediatric clinic at that time on the service cases (patients from the hospital clinic). My services on clinic patients were gratis. I attended the pediatric clinic once a week, where I supervised the resident and the Fellow on Wednesdays, also gratis. I was at first assistant attending surgeon, then attending, and finally surgeon director at the hospital. I was also director of the eye muscle (strabismus) department. Doctors on the staff at MEETH were not paid; they were the voluntary staff. The compensation for us was the use of the hospital operating rooms and staff for our private surgical cases. In the late 1990s, some clinic patients had insurance, and a fee for their surgery was collected—a small one compared to private practice cases—and the funds from those insurance cases went to Manhattan Eye Associates, a group formed by attending eye surgeons at the hospital. I only had one day of clinic a week during the 1990s and after. Before that, I was for a time on the staff at New York Hospital-Cornell, where I attended clinic once a week in addition to MEETH and supervised the residents there in clinic and in the OR, and was associate clinical professor. I had stayed at NY Hospital-Cornell until I took my sabbatical from medicine in 1976 and did not return there when I came back to practice in 1982.

Wednesdays after surgery and clinic, if I finished in the afternoon, I would often drive across the East River to Tennisport, the tennis club where I played for years after I returned to NYC. Many top players, including pros, played there, the elite of NYC in business as well—doubles with my friend, ex-Wimbledon and US Open champion Virginia Wade, and also old friends from tennis days when 'Dick' was a top eastern player. I never had to arrange a game, just showed up and it was taken care of for me.

Fridays, I saw patients up in Brewster at Northeast Eye Care—Hal Farquhar's gigantic practice. He had been one of my residents in the early '60s at MEETH when I was resident instructor; now he lived in Carmel (next to Brewster) and had the largest private practice of ophthalmology in Putnam County. Very different setting for me than in my boutique in NYC. Many (maybe ten) examining rooms; the doctors went from room to room to see each patient, each having been worked up (visual acuity, glasses check, intraocular pressure, dilation, this after taking history), and all the MD had to do mostly was counsel the patient. In my case, not quite so simple. I did have my orthoptic technician, Ricky Cohen, who would come with me Fridays to see the patients. Ricky would measure the degrees of misalignment of the eyes with prisms (two prisms for each degree of turn) and check visual acuity for progress of amblyopia (lazy eye therapy), but I would still do the rest of the exam myself. Usually fifteen patients, like in the NYC office, but mostly less complicated, although I did see some patients with severe and complicated problems. I would operate on them at Putnam Hospital, with my colleague and former pediatric and strabismus Fellow, Steven Greenberg, assisting. Steven helped me write my textbook, *Strabismus Surgery*—text and atlas—published by Chapman and Hall in the UK and Williams and Wilkins in the USA. He had his own practice in Westchester County, which he gave up when he joined a large conglomerate group, WESTMED, a few years ago. He likes that—all he does is see patients; the business end of the practice is done by the group.

Then the work week was over. I only saw some post-ops Saturdays, never office hours. Weekends were for tennis, golf, boating, fishing, swimming, pleasure. I have never worked on Saturdays, unless it is to see an emergency patient.

I have already described the journals an ophthalmologist reads. MDs only read professional literature; attorneys read everything else—I know from my dear friends who are lawyers. We MDs as such are a boring lot, I suppose. But besides the reading we have to do to keep up with advances in our specialty, some of us do some writing as well. In my *curriculum vitae* are listed the five book chapters I wrote, in addition to the strabismus textbook, but I have written numerous articles in our refereed journals (one of which I am on the staff—*Journal of Pediatric Ophthalmology*). My very first appeared in the *Archives of Ophthalmology* in 1965, a case report of an infant on whom I had to enucleate one eye with severe deformity and suspicion of cancer while I was in the Navy at St. Albans Naval Hospital. The second was published in *Documenta Ophthalmologica*—an international journal—about bilateral superior oblique muscle palsy (the same condition for which I operated on Tyrone Wagenhals' eyes in 1999).

In 1999, I published one paper, in the *Journal of Pediatric Ophthalmology*, which I co-authored with my post-graduate Fellow at that time, Dr. Mitchell Strominger—now professor and director of pediatric ophthalmology at Tufts Medical School in Boston. It was titled, "Adjustable Sutures."

In addition to weekly clinic duties and assisting residents and Fellows in the OR, other activities were connected to the hospital. One was weekly grand rounds, where the entire staff of ophthalmologists would meet, a presentation would be made by a resident or an attending surgeon, and discussion followed.

Not long after I first returned to practice medicine after my five-year sabbatical, I had occasion to present at grand rounds. There had been much skepticism amongst the staff about how capable I would be after all this time away from medicine and in my "new" incarnation. No one had ever done this before, as we know. I presented a case of Duane's retraction syndrome—a developmental abnormality of the eye muscles—and then discoursed at length on the condition for maybe twenty minutes, no notes, no slides. The staff just listened. RR was back.

Besides clinic and grand rounds, there were meetings throughout the year—once-a-year the three-day meeting (usually at a nice and warm resort) of the American Association of Pediatric Ophthalmology and Strabismus (AAPOS), once-a-year three-day meeting of the American Academy of Ophthalmology (AAO), frequently in Chicago or Dallas, for ophthalmologists of all specialties.

Participation at these meetings is quite necessary for clinicians to amass CME (continued medical education) credits in order to renew staff membership and operating privileges at the hospitals.

I was also a member of the august society—the NY Society of Ophthalmology—dinner club where the members—chosen without election, leaders of the ophthalmic medical community in NYC—would present unusual cases to each other and discuss them after dinner, usually at a private club or hotel in Manhattan.

We also had meetings every few months of the Greater New York Society of Pediatric Ophthalmology—same format, dinner and discussion of case presentation after a lecture given by a guest ophthalmologist.

There are other meetings every year that I have forgotten because I don't attend most of them anymore. But when I did, my evenings were frequently kept busy.

One meeting that should also be mentioned is the infrequent meeting of the board of surgeon directors at MEETH. These meetings were uncommon and usually boring, that is, until the conflict over the demise of the hospital in 1999 became imminent. Then there were combined meetings of the lay board and the board of surgeon directors—lies and deceit on the part of the lay board, protestation on our part—far different from the days when the lay board and the board of surgeon directors were one and the same. R. Townley Paton, MD, once was head of both the lay board and the surgeon directors' board. The same Townley Paton—who was my patron throughout my training, after first meeting me at the Meadow Club in Southampton, Long Island, at the tournament there—introduced by my dear friend Gene

Scott. Dr. Paton was instrumental in my being selected for the prestigious Heed Fellowship in 1966, which started my career in strabismus. He immediately took a liking to me way back when I was introduced to him. He had captained the Princeton tennis team in 1926. He started the first eye bank at Manhattan Eye and Ear and was the first to do a corneal transplant there in the 1940s.

He referred many patients to me for surgery as I became the strabismus expert at the hospital, including children of prominent families, the likes of which I would ordinarily have no connection. One time he sent the daughter of one of the U.S. president's in-laws, a family far more lofty than that president. Before I operated, I called Dr. Paton and asked him what I should charge them for the operation. He asked, "What is your usual fee?" I started to stammer out "a thou—" when he interrupted me and said, "Double it."

In those days, patients stayed overnight after surgery. This patient had a magnificent corner room on the ninth floor of the hospital with a view of the city beyond. When I walked into the room, the patient asked, "Dr. Raskind, why do you operate on Fridays? Then you have to come to the hospital on a Saturday to see the patient."

Her mother blurted, "Don't be silly, dear, that's the only day the young surgeons get to operate." She knew the ropes.

I was an expert on strabismus for some decades it is true, and in *New York* magazine—1999 among other years—I was listed among the best doctors in NYC. But, as much as I knew about pediatric ophthalmology and strabismus, that's as little as I knew about the business end of the practice of medicine. I knew we had a billing office a block from ours at 40 Park, but that's about it. What we charged and how it was paid for office visits and surgery—I have little knowledge. Most patients paid by cash or check; no credit cards back then. A few patients had private insurance. The managed care plans were just coming into existence.

A consultation fee was $300, an ordinary new patient fee was $150, a yearly revisit maybe $60. Surgery was frequently $1,000. Arleen would tell the billing office personnel, and they would do the rest. Our accountant came to the office periodically to check the books.

I operated on a number of celebrities; they were charged the usual fees. One time I remember Arleen asking for more when I operated on the son of the attaché from one of the countries in the United Arab Emirates. He asked, "How much is the surgery?"

Arleen said, "Four thousand dollars."

He reached into his inside pocket and pulled out $4,000 in $100 bills.

Sometimes we didn't get paid. One time, I straightened the eyes of a two-year-old girl. Her parents whisked her away from the hospital as soon as she woke up, never to be seen by us again. Her name—assumed—was Tina Chiron. They were gypsies.

Many events took place at the end of the century. I don't remember much. I was pretty involved with my own life and practice. I do remember the building next door to our office on Park Avenue was the Consulate of El Salvador. In the late 1990s there were always protests, sometimes armed policemen in front of the entrance, citizens marching back and forth shouting slogans—"no more war, no more war, we want peace in El Salvador." The protestors always let me through to get to my office. I often gave them samples of antibiotic eye drops I got from the drug salesmen to take back to El Salvador.

The All Union League Club took up the whole building on the corner of Park and 37th Street. Sometimes we would have trouble getting into the office if a notable showed up there for dinner—Vice President Dick Cheney, President George W. Bush, or some other Republican. I would get mad if the pizza man couldn't deliver to us in the apartment and I would come downstairs from there to suggest he be allowed to deliver. I took care of all the building staff—doorman, footmen, elevator men in 40 Park, so they all took care of me.

In 1999, private practice was changing. Some MDs joined larger private groups; for others, it was the start of managed care as we know it now—large conglomerates of physicians and hospitals. I was a dinosaur then, actually still am. I never joined a group. But I do now participate in several managed care plans, accepting the fees given by the particular plan for services rendered, like Oxford. Maybe not such a dinosaur after all. Even back in 1999, I participated in a few of the plans, like GHI, the Group Health Plan for NYC teachers, police, and firemen. Hey, not a dinosaur at all?

Oh well, back to my diary...

November and December

I did not dictate for my diary every day of November and December. Maybe I ran out of steam? Who knows? Not likely, as compulsive as I am. Whatever, I can say what happened those last two months in general terms, if not patient-by-patient detail. I do have some memories of the final two months. Arleen reminds me we moved from our house in the Sedgewood Club to our present home—one mile outside the club—in December, or rather she moved us—"You just took your pocketbook and moved across the road." Anyway, that gigantic undertaking might have resulted in losing the tapes for those two months.

Thanksgiving —always a big holiday for me, for many years at the old house in the club with Grandpa, Arleen's mother Heidi, and friends, and sometimes at the Pollack's in Bedford. Thanksgiving 1999, Arleen and I went to Kenny and Fran Piersa's home close by in Yorktown Heights. Not sure why we didn't have it at home.

Christmas—probably had moved to our present home by then. Arleen had help from our groundskeeper Bill and from my golf pro Clarence for the move. I did just drive down the road here as she says. Not much to report. Grandpa was in his house in Forest Hills with his helper Sharon, semi-invalided by the TIA he had had a few months before but determined to make it to January 14, to make it to 100. Nick and Oxana were living in Grandpa's house, still.

I continued to see patients in the city and operate right up to Christmas week, when I stopped until after the new year. Details?

I remember nothing stupendous. I was at that time looking for a new country office, my days at Northeast Eye Care maybe coming to an end.

New Year's Eve was special, the end of the millennium. Every New Year's Eve, my patient from the Park Avenue office, Linda, who was in charge of tickets for Lincoln Center, would arrange for me to have four seats at the gala performance at the Metropolitan Opera at Lincoln Center. One year we took Les and Yvonne Pollack, another year we took my close friend Burt Berson and his girlfriend as our guests. In 1999, we took our friends Kenny and Fran Piersa from up here. Kenny the Cookie Man is famous more recently for his role in "Last Ride for the 'Vette" in *Spy Night*.

Kenny had never been to an opera, his wife Fran maybe—she is a bigshot at ABC-TV. Kenny rented a tuxedo; everyone gets dressed up for the MET on New Year's Eve. He looked like a million bucks. We drove down from up here, Kenny always the chauffeur, his whole life driving, first for Coca Cola, then Brunckhorst's Boarshead Meats, and then for Pepperidge Farm cookies, hence his nickname, Cookie Man. We had a sumptuous dinner at the Szechuan restaurant on Broadway across from the opera house. The opera was one of my favorites, *Die Fledermaus* by Johann Strauss. Even Kenny loved it. And always on New Year's Eve cameo performances by celebrities, this time the mayor of the city, Rudy Giuliani, in drag. And then the countdown to the end of the year, the century, the millennium. And everyone kissing each other.

I don't recall much about specific surgery that month—I

probably did not do much—elective operations not favored by parents for their kids at Christmas time. Maybe a few adults were operated on.

The biggest events for me were the selling of the house and the move across the state road and around the reservoir to the new house where we still live. As I said, all I did was take my pocketbook and move across the road, Arleen did the rest.

The best memory I had of the end of the millennium, the century, and the year, of course, was the New Year's Eve celebration at the opera with Arleen and Kenny and Fran. For some, the millennium ended symbolically dramatically, sadly, on September 11, 2001, but for me the winding down of my practice in NYC and in Putnam County, and the changes in the hospital, were most notable Dec. 31, 1999. Private medical care like the way I practiced it was dwindling, big organizations were taking over practices and hospitals. I was a dinosaur then, but a stubborn one, because now, nearly 20 years later, I am still in private practice—an independent contractor—although not a proprietor of my own office.

In 2003, I sold my practice to Harvey Rosenblum—Rosenblum Eye Centers it is called, one block from my office at 40 Park Avenue—and moved over there to continue seeing my patients. He owns the patients' charts; his staff runs the office. Other ophthalmologists work there too, all independent contractors—a retina specialist, a glaucoma specialist, also two optometrists. He pays each of us a percentage of the fee he collects for the office visit, even for surgery. I no longer had to hire, and fire, and administer my own practice. It was fine with me; all my patients were just as happy to walk around the corner to my new location. The business end of things meant nothing to them. I stayed there for 18 years, and near the end of that time we no longer had the apartment above the office at 40 Park. We were living only up in the Putnam County house, and, when I went to the NYC office, I had to either drive or take the Metro North railroad train to Grand Central Station and walk to the office (five blocks, I never minded that). The early morning drive around the reservoir in the ice in winter to the train finally became too much for me, so I left Harvey's on November 30, 2018—simply said goodbye and took the train home. My practice in New York City had started in 1968 and, with a few interruptions quite well-known, lasted until 2018.

It was not the end of private practice for me, however. I still see patients in my office up here in the country, and yes, some of my NYC practice patients do come up here to see me from Long Island, New Jersey, Staten Island, and Manhattan. I don't operate anymore. I gave up surgery when I turned 80. I figured that was enough, although I am sure I could still operate on an eye muscle if I felt like it.

In 2003, I left Northeast Eye Care in Carmel, Putnam County, ten minutes from our home, and opened an office in the Barns, a medical office complex across from the Putnam County Hospital, where I continued to operate on the patients from the country office. Arleen was the office manager and everything else. After a few years, we rejoined Northeast Eye Care because it was too much office work for Arleen and me to run our own office, no matter how small the practice. We stayed at Northeast

Eye Care and left there in 2009 because Alan Farquhar, Hal's son, had taken charge of the practice and had sold it to one of the budding big conglomerate groups, Mt. Kisco Medical Group (now Caremount), which had started buying up several private practices in the community in all specialties. We left because Mt. Kisco Medical Group had a ruling policy—no physician over the age of 70 allowed.

I moved my practice to join Dawn Rush in her office in Yorktown Heights in northern Westchester County. She is a superb pediatric ophthalmologist. She sees mostly children. I am considered a pediatric ophthalmologist but also a strabismus specialist, and I do see some adults who have general ophthalmological problems. Dawn Rush does the surgery for our patients. As I said, I gave up surgery four years ago. Her office is one of the last of the type known as private practice, with no connection to a large group. Seems to me to run just fine, but I have nothing to do with the business end of things. She pays me a percentage of the fees collected on my patients, which is great.

How long will she be able to continue an independent private practice? Who knows? Caremount would take her in a minute. But not me. I am older than 70—Caremount's age limit—by just a little.

Grandpa made it to 100 just as he planned. We had a big party at the house in Forest Hills on January 14, 2000. He was born January 14, 1900, in Ekaterinoslav, Russia, now Dnipropetrovsk, Ukraine.

Nicky and Oxana stayed in the Forest Hills house until Grandpa died six months later. I was with him when he died.

Quietly, he just went to sleep.

Nicky was doing real estate by then. He sold the Forest Hills house to a rabbi—one of a sect of Bucharin Russian Jewish émigrés who were buying up all the houses in our beautiful neighborhood of Old Forest Hills. He promised Nicky he would keep it as is—a beautiful old colonial built in the early 1900s—instead of tearing it down and building a garish modern monstrosity. I don't know if he kept his promise.

Nicky moved into the Park Avenue apartment above the old office.

He and Oxana got engaged and then broke up. He moved to Florida a few years later.

Medicine in the past century and now in the new millennium? Like I always say, *"Tous ca change, tous c'est le meme chose."* Everything changes, nothing changes—mantra for my life?

Anyway, a little perspective, not just on 1999 and the present day—the subject of this book—but a little retrospective.

My father, a scholarship student at Yale and its medical school, took his internship at Harrisburg Hospital in Harrisburg, PA, where he met my mother, Sadie Muriel Baron, who had recently graduated from Women's Medical College in Philadelphia, after college in Bryn Mawr, where she by happenstance grew up. They married and moved to NYC, settling in Sunnyside, Queens, just across the east river from Manhattan. My father, his whole lifetime looking up to his colleagues there—"a Manhattan man," he would say, and of course especially me, whose medical career was mostly there. They lived in Sunnyside, that combination of second-generation immigrants from Germany, Poland, Eastern

Europe, Ireland, mostly on one side of Queens Boulevard, and a smattering of Jews and other intellectual liberal types. Yes, some of them were Fellow travelers (Commies actually, though they would rather have been called liberal socialists) on the other side of the boulevard.

My father's first office was his only one—5 Court Square, across from the courthouse in Long Island City, just across the river from Manhattan, where many factories were located—for more than 50 years. Like me, a lifetime in medicine, so to speak. He had had no formal training in orthopedics, but, because the area around his office was populated by factories—Adam Chicklet Gum factory, Block and Guggenheimer pickles, Wonder Bread, Breyer's Ice Cream, and more—he developed a practice from trauma injuries to bones and joints; hence, his first interest in orthopedics. He never took a residency in orthopedics because he yielded to my mother's further training—only one of them could pursue that with a young family to support during training. It cost him dearly in his chosen field—no residency, no board certification, no referral practice. He did the trauma work for all the factories, was self-taught in orthopedics, and was for years an assistant attending surgeon at the Hospital for Joint Disease, the first of the orthopedic hospitals in NYC.

My mother became the first woman resident in neurology and psychiatry (combined in those days) at Columbia–Presbyterian Hospital in NYC and then attended clinic there for her lifetime once a week while starting her own private practice in our apartment in Sunnyside and then later in our home in Forest Hills. She was her own secretary and biller and appointment-maker. She said she practiced psychoanalysis (she did have a training analysis with a famous analyst, Sandor Rado, but I don't think it had much effect on her own neuroses). She became an attending physician and assistant professor at Columbia Medical School, board-certified of course, with all the imprimatur my father abdicated from achieving in deference to her training. She had a busy private practice and made enough money to run the house and bring up the kids—Josephine and me—without asking my father for money.

His practice was busy; besides all the trauma work, he joined one of the first managed-care groups in the country in the 1950s, HIP (Hospital Insurance Plan), a model for what was to come in managed care. It was the plan for teachers and other NYC employees, police, and firemen. He received a stipend for taking care of the patients in the group. They had a clinic office where he would see the patients, I think, twice a week, in Flushing, Queens, not far from Sunnyside. He did get to do the orthopedic surgery on patients from that group, but rarely from private patients. He stayed in HIP until he stopped practicing at around 75 years old. My mother continued her private practice until she got sick with cancer of the colon and died at 61.

My father's office on the corner at 5 Court Square, Long Island City, Queens, had a sparse waiting room with no rug because of all the trauma cases coming in, with blood from the accidents common. I remember his secretary had a window in the wall of her office room to talk to the patients in the waiting room. I remember the ancient X-ray machine, the room where he would put on the plaster casts on the fractured legs and arms, the cubicles with a curtain between each one where he would have patients hooked up to electric diathermy machines for the stiff backs, and a small office of his own with a couch where I sometimes waited for him to finish work unless I was watching him put on a cast or sew up a laceration. In his mid-career, he became part-owner of a private hospital, Horace Harding Hospital on Queens Boulevard. I had a summer job there once in the X-ray department. Josephine worked in medical records. I quit my job in midsummer to go play junior tennis tournaments. Besides, I didn't like taking the X-ray machine on portable X-rays at patients' bedsides. I was afraid of getting sterile from all the exposure.

My father's office was so different from my mother's.

I can go back earlier than them, for my continuity, but theirs was the first I knew firsthand. My father told me stories of colleagues of his—general practitioners—in the early days (circa 1920) who would make house calls by horse and buggy in the farmlands of Astoria, only a mile from where his office was in Long Island City. Now I hear Amazon is building a giant center employing 30,000 people right there. So I have read.

As for my mother, private office psychiatry continues to this day but with many, many new therapists of all varieties of training and experience. True Freudian psychoanalysts? Not so many anymore except in NYC, maybe LA and San Francisco on the other coast.

My sister, of course, is a physician too. Interesting that my mother, as feminist as my sister, retained her maiden name in her medical practice. Socially, to her friends and family, she was

Mrs. Raskind or Sadie. But her professional name was S. Muriel Baron (her maiden name). My sister, Josephine Baron Raskind, the moment she married Peter Von Hippel (esteemed professor of microbiology and eventual Academy of Science member), became Dr. Josephine Von Hippel. There is a logical explanation for the difference, however. My mother was a physician before she was married. My sister became a physician after she married. Peter's great-uncle in Goettingen, Germany, was the famous ophthalmologist Eugen Von Hippel—famous for finding Von Hippel's disease, better known now as angiomatosis retinae (almost all eye diseases had German names before WWII because all academic ophthalmology stemmed from Germany).

Professor Von Hippel was maybe ahead of his time. Now doctors go from patient to patient, usually from one room to another, rather than staying in one room and having each patient come in and out (like I do still). He would have all the patients in the clinic in Goettingen lined up on a bench and would go down the line with his monocular ophthalmoscope looking at the retinas. A wonderful professor when I was studying in Iowa in 1966 had known him. He said he was a good ophthalmologist but he had central scotoma (blind spots) for residents—not much caring or interested in them. So much for the elder Von Hippel.

The one of more interest, of course, is my sister Josephine Baron Raskind Von Hippel, winner of the Westinghouse (now Intel) Science Talent Search Grand Prize in 1948 from Forest Hills High School—girls' tennis champion there too—who graduated from Bryn Mawr College like her mother, went to MIT for one additional year, then matriculated at Women's Medical College, like her mother, but transferred to Harvard Medical School so she could be with her husband, whom she had met when she took the post-grad year at MIT, where he was a student and his father a professor. After graduation from medical school, she interned at George Washington University Hospital and then had two years of residency in internal medicine at Dartmouth Medical School, Mary Hitchcock Hospital, and then two more in psychiatry. I am not positive, but I don't believe she ever became board-certified in either specialty, for what reason I have no idea—she was certainly smart enough to have done so.

She moved to Eugene, Oregon, when her husband became chairman of the microbiology department there, started private practice in psychiatry, not psychoanalysis, raised three children, retired at 75, rode and attended to her horses, played tennis at her swim and tennis club, and never ever mentioned that her brother had become her sister, Renée Richards, despite everyone in Eugene knowing the connection for years. Why did she did not pursue getting boarded I do not know. I am sure she was a first-rate psychiatrist. Like her father, she practiced without all the imprimatur of professional status. Like his/her mother, RR pursued it all and then some.

As I have written in the past, I have probably had the best education of anyone alive in the USA in the past century. Sunnyside Park School for nursery years, PS 150 in Sunnyside for kindergarten, three blocks from home. First three grades at PS 3 in Forest Hills, three blocks from home, the only public school in NYC with no fence around it (commentary on the community), PS 144 in Forest Hill in the IGC (Intellectually

Gifted Children) class until 8th grade, Horace Mann School, Yale College, University of Rochester Medical School, basic science year in ophthalmology at NYU Medical School (first in the class at the end of the year's course), Manhattan Eye, Ear and Throat Hospital ophthalmology residency, Heed Fellowship in strabismus, Columbia Medical School, University of Oregon Medical School, Iowa University Medical School,

My Fellowship was not in pediatric ophthalmology; it was in strabismus. Now, training in strabismus is part of the subspecialty known as pediatric ophthalmology and strabismus. Pediatric ophthalmology as we know it now only started to be called by the present title in the 1960s because the famous Dr. Marshall Parks—along with his chief, Dr. Frank Costenbader—coined that term. When I returned to the practice of medicine in 1981 after playing and coaching tennis for five years, I spent the winter months before my return in Dr. Parks's office on Massachusetts Avenue in Washington, D.C., and with him in the operating room at Children's Hospital, as he gently reintroduced me to what I had left behind five years before.

This all meant I had studied with the five most renowned strabismus experts in the country in that era—Harold Whalley Brown at MEETH, Phil Knapp at Columbia, Ken Swan in Oregon, Hermann Burian in Iowa, Marshall Parks in Washington, D.C. What I didn't learn in the world of strabismus from them I picked up on my own during the next 50 years. They gave me the start.

After 1999

Sunday, December 3, 2000

The best thing that happened in 1999 didn't come about that year—it was near the end of the following year. As 1999 faded out, the clinic at the hospital closed, and we all waited for the judge to decide the fate of Manhattan Eye and Ear. The glorious news came December 3, 2000—Judge Fried ruled the hospital must remain an eye hospital, as per its charter. Thanks to him and to State Attorney General Eliot Spitzer (another Horace Mann School graduate), there is no more clinic but still a hospital for eyes, ears, nose, and throat.

I happily read this article from the *New York Observer* of Monday, December 4, reprinted here in part:

Surely a measure of any great city is the quality of its healthcare, and since 1869 Manhattan Eye, Ear and Throat Hospital has been providing New Yorkers with a devoted medical team whose specialists are arguably the best at what they do anywhere in the country. That is why all city residents should applaud the decision on Dec. 3 by Justice Bernard Fried of State Supreme Court in Manhattan that prevented the hospital's board of directors from destroying this venerable East Side institution by selling off the real estate. Justice Fried acted in response to court papers filed by State Attorney General Eliot Spitzer, who stepped in when it looked like the hospital's board was going to get away with taking the easy way out: bury the hospital that their own mismanagement had badly damaged.

The hospital's superb ophthalmologists, cosmetic and reconstructive surgeons and other extraordinary medical professionals fought the idea of a sale. The problem with Manhattan Eye and Ear, after all, had nothing to do with how patients were being served. Excellence in the operating room was unfortunately matched by incompetence among the board and top management. ... While other private hospitals rushed to adapt to the changes brought by managed care, Manhattan Eye and Ear dozed. But the core of doctors remained deeply committed to keeping the place alive.

Now that Justice Fried and Spitzer have done the right thing, it's clear the hospital is ready for a new board and a new administration who have a vision and resources to back that vision. The doctors, patients and the hospital's proud history deserve no less.

Yes indeed, Monday, December 3, 2000, was a very happy day in my world.

Thursday, April 11, 2019, is and will always be the most wretched day of my life. On that awful day, I received the devastating news that my son Nick had taken his own life in Florida. He was 47. It is impossible for me to express my crushing sorrow, nor will I try in these pages. After all that had happened to me, all the dangers I survived, suddenly, the worst of anything possible in the world happened. I lost the most important being of my life, and I will suffer every day for the rest of it. The following weeks were miserable and hectic. The phone ringing all day every day, and friends coming from all over, even up from the city. I sat shiva for a week.

I spent one particular afternoon at home with Eric Drath, who had done the ESPN documentary about me years ago. He had helped me get Nick to rehab in Miami ten years ago and has been a close friend since. His opinion was that Nick wanted to leave on his own time. He did not want to grow old. He had some mental problems that we don't have labels for.

Billie Jean said something similar, "He had his own demons."

My friends have been so smart, so supportive, and so wonderful to me. I am fortunate to have them.

I arranged for a niche—like a vault—at the Chuang Yen Monastery, which happens to be only four miles up the road from the house, for Nick. Forty niches were to be enshrined there on the Thousand Lotus Wall. I am sure Nick would like this. He had some Buddhist leanings, although we never talked much about it. I have his two black belts from karate and, in my bedroom, a small wooden Buddha that was his.

His mother Barbara and his brother Philip wanted some of his ashes to be scattered in the ocean off their Southampton, Long Island, home. I was not happy about dividing them, but I reconsidered and arranged for that too.

The Chinese Hawaiian Kenpo Academy in NYC wants a permanent memorial for Nick there. They have never done this for anyone before, and they want his fifth-degree black belt. In due time, I will give it to them. Nick would want that, I know.

A reception at the house followed the memorial for Nick at the Chuang Yen Monastery. First, the ceremony to bless the urn—incense and prayers—was very intimate. Then the sermon was held in the Great Buddha Hall—it's the largest Buddha hall in North America, overflowing with a thousand or more—and translated into English after each paragraph. Lots of chanting. Repetitive, over and over. Everyone transfixed.

Oxana, Nick's fiancée years ago, stood next to me.

"Who is that?" I asked, pointing to a beautiful woman right behind her.

"It's Barbara." Oh my God.

Nick's aunts Patty and Peggy also attended.

After the sermon, some of us, the families of the 40 to be enshrined, hiked up to the Thousand Lotus Wall. After another sermon, each enshrinee was called to the wall. They said only one family member could bring the urn up. I asked Barbara if she wanted to do it, and she said I should do it. Oxana had been watching, and she said she saw a few instances where two people brought up the urn. So Barbara and I both brought it up to the wall and placed it in the niche with Nick's name inscribed on the door to it. About 30 Chinese and maybe 10 Americans were in the group.

The ceremony lasted about two hours, and we all came

back to the house—except Barbara and Peggy and Patty—for the reception. About fifty friends, including three of Nick's childhood friends, all said a few words. I remember one of them saying Nick was the most fearless guy he ever knew. I remember that. In attendance were several of my old friends and students from ophthalmology days, my eight close friends and their husbands from the golf club—who all helped out with the tents, the food, the liquor, etc.—my three surviving cousins, my friend and former tennis protégée Toni Moss from Austin, Texas, and a few old tennis friends of mine who came a long way to be here.

And then some of us sat outside on the lawn overlooking the reservoir until after dark.

A reflection from 2021:

As I have reported, the day-to-day diary of November and December 1999 was lost during the busy time then of selling the Sedgewood house and moving down the road to our present house on the reservoir. I did see patients those two months on the regular schedule, however, with a brief few days off for Thanksgiving, Christmas, and New Year's Eve. In order to recover some of the records from those last two months, Arleen took the train—the same route I did weekly after we left the NYC apartment not long into the first decade of the 21st century—to the city office at 220 Madison Avenue—Rosenblum Eye Centers. (I stopped going to the city office just over three years ago, the first week of December 2017.) She went to try to recover from the basement some charts of patients we saw in November-December 1999. She found some, brave soul, amidst the thousands down there among the mice and rats and other vermin.

Here is one summary of a patient I saw at the end of December: Lennie Bryant, 34, post-auto accident, with deep facial wound, scars from cheek to nose, orbital fracture, upper eyelid paralyzed (eye closed), palpable plastic plate on the orbital rim, pupil almost fixed—no reaction to light—for which reason I summarized his exam on a second page of my notes as follows.

1. Orbital floor fracture, 2. Orbital rim fracture, 3. LeFort 3 fracture (facial bones), 4. Fixed pupil, 5. Soft eye (consider ruptured globe), 6. Dislocated intraocular lens, 7. Vitreous hemorrhage, 8 Restrictive strabismus—esotropia and hypotropia (horizontal and vertical traumatic strabismus), 9. Ptosis, 10. Facial lacerations, 11. Tear duct obstruction.

I operated on his eye on August 12, 1999, performing recession of right inferior rectus, recession of right medial rectus, release of scar tissue and adherence of eye to eyelid (symblepharon). He was improved, but not enough to relieve his double vision. I saw him frequently in the office until the end of December. I re-operated in 2001 in collaboration with Dr. Richard Lisman, an oculoplastic surgeon, who repaired the upper eyelid. His chart in a manila folder, 8" x 10", is a half-inch thick and includes letters of consultation, letters from attorneys, insurance agents, etc.

The last time I saw him was in 2005. He actually was doing well—visual acuity in the right eye 20/40, left eye 20/20, and able to have binocular vision without seeing double with a small vertical prism incorporated into his glasses.

In 1999, patient records were on 8" x 11" pages inside a manila folder, handwritten by me except for dictated letters that were typewritten, and some of the non-medical notes were typed too. When I first arrived at 40 Park Avenue and took over John Herman's practice, the office notes were on 5" x 8" inch cards, handwritten by him, with non-medical details and letters folded and placed in an open envelop all together. Not long after I took over the practice, I started with the 8" x 11" format, and Dr. Herman's cards were pasted on the back folder of each patient's charts. Since I retained many of his patients during the subsequent years, many of my charts in 1999 still had his notes affixed to the back folder. As my practice grew, most of my referrals came from other ophthalmologists or patients, but I still have some patients who came to me who were Dr. Herman's when he died in 1982.

Arleen brought me a few charts from the city (New Yorkers call Manhattan "the city") office last week for me to see who might have been seen in the office those last two months of 1999. Reading and describing them could be a book in itself. I picked out a few for some comments, mainly to contrast what practice was like in 1982, 1999, and the present.

Tommy Lambright's office chart—in a manila folder, 8" x 11"—is 96 pages long; affixed to the back cover is John Herman's folder of 5" x 8" cards—only three cards. Tommy was 17 months old when I first saw him in September 1982, and my first notes were written on those 5" x 8" cards. I had not yet switched to the 8" x 11" charts. Tommy had undergone surgery for congenital glaucoma in August. On Sept. 22, 1982, I operated on both eyes for strabismus, and my note—written in red (operative notes were written in red ink)—were "resection RMR-8 mm, resection LMR-8 mm." I described, in red, the condition of the eye muscles I operated on and then the results of the EUA (exam under anesthesia), including IOP (intraocular pressure) and exam of the retina and optic nerves. Included is a letter describing hospitalization for further surgery for strabismus—with cancellation of the operation due to respiratory difficulty—September 1983—following intubation, to be rescheduled at a future time. On May 2, 1984, I did re-operate on each medial rectus and also did tenotomy of the right superior oblique.

My chart notes in the 8" x 11" format begin in January 1983. Congenital glaucoma strabismus, amblyopia—complicated subjects; my final notes are from June 3, 2003. On that visit, his visual acuity with glasses for high myopia was 20/20 in the right eye, 20/25 in the left eye. Eyes were straight on cover test, IOP was 13 in the right eye, 8 in the left eye; he was on lumigan and timoptic drops daily for each eye.

I had seen him on November 10, 1999. By then he was under the care of an HIP specialist for his glaucoma. I still saw him for strabismus. His eyes were straight on that visit. His best corrected visual acuity was 20/25 in each eye for pressure.

Here are some of the pages apart from my clinical notes of each visit. It is not even complete—to do so would take hours.

Cover sheet with family data—office information, several pages, bills for services rendered (family belonged to HIP), father was an NYC firefighter, HIP special services fund.

Bills, correspondence from insurance company and our office, multiple.

Correspondence—several between referring and consulting MDs and me.

Visual field examinations, several.

Examinations by my orthoptic technician, several, measuring misalignment (strabismus) in prisms and visual acuities.

A total of more than 90 pages—in the present day, such a chart would be scanned into the computer and recovered instantaneously to be printed out or sent to another office if indicated.

Madeleine Buchinski was first seen by me at the age of four months in March 1985. Her parents, sophisticated New Yorkers had taken her to Dr. Philip Knapp at Columbia, and they wanted a second opinion. By 1984, my reputation as one of the experts in strabismus had been reestablished— it was by then two years since my return to NYC. There were at that time five or six specialists in the city who were considered the tops. I was one of them. I was referred patients by other ophthalmologists, and a few pediatricians, no longer needing the patients I had inherited from John Herman. I did keep many of his patients in my practice. I don't know how many I lost to other doctors. That I was referred a patient who had already seen Phil Knapp was interesting, certainly. He had been my first professor during my Fellowship in strabismus at Columbia, and I respected him and admired him. But if a patient, or parent, sought me out for consultation after seeing Phil, nothing unethical about that. Madeleine had been referred by one of the top eye surgeons at MEETH—and one of the last of the WASP leaders of the hospital during my early years there. That he would send patients like Madeleine to Renée

Richards was a compliment. Ophthalmologists get referrals from patients, pediatricians, other ophthalmologists, and, if they are on staff at a general hospital, referrals from other specialties. I was only on the staff of the eye hospital. My referrals came only from patients, ophthalmologists, and pediatricians.

My second opinion was consistent with Dr. Knapp's: Madeleine had a large convergent strabismus, infantile since it occurred so early in life, and she would likely need glasses and surgery. Dr. Knapp had started some alternate patching to stimulate abduction (movement of each eye to the outer side). In those days, most eye surgeons operated on children with strabismus at 11 months of age, though some did so at six months. My preference was close to one year. I gave my opinion, and the parents decided to stay with me. If Dr. Knapp had sent me the patient for consultation, ethics would dictate I give the opinion and send the patient back for continued care. He had not sent Madeleine to me, so I was free to take care of her if her parents so wished.

Despite the patching, I could never elicit full abduction (looking to the side) of either eye. I operated on October 25, 1985—recession of each medial rectus for a large esotropia. When I saw her in the office at the beginning of January 1986, her alignment was improved but not perfectly straight. I started some patching of her preferred right eye and saw her frequently and prescribed glasses for her hyperopia, with prisms for a vertical deviation. I re-operated on Madeleine's eye muscles on September 3, 1986, performing a resection of each lateral rectus and a recession of each inferior oblique muscle.

Following surgery, she maintained good alignment of her

eyes with her glasses on, correcting her hyperopia, but without them the accommodative component of her strabismus was large (focusing caused esotropia without glasses). I prescribed bifocals to help with her focusing for years until 1995, when I operated again. I re-recessed each medial rectus muscle and further recessed the left inferior oblique with anteriorization (the whole operation is much too difficult to explain). Examination in the office the following week showed straight eyes.

The last time I saw her in 1999 was November 15. She was a freshman in high school. Her eyes were straight with no glasses, her vision 20/20 RE, 20 LE.

That was the last visit for 1999, but not the last event for Madeleine. In July 2007, I re-operated on her left eye, a recession of the left lateral rectus for a divergent deviation in left gaze. Her eyes were straight post-op and have continued in good alignment since. I see her yearly or nearly so. She is grown up and has an important job in the government in Washington, D.C. Her mother still lives in New York. It is not a long ride for Madeleine to my Westchester office.

She was one of the last patients I saw in the city in 1999. When I see her at present, the examination is similar to the way it has always been—strabismus tests with prisms, glasses checks for vision; she now gets a glaucoma test as well. Her chart from the city office has been scanned into the computer and forwarded to the office up here by fax. My examination here is handwritten by me during and after the exam and scanned into the computer. I don't think Madeleine experiences much difference in her visits now from previous years. Maybe the financial end—she has medical insurance; her office visits are covered. The fee goes to my partner who owns our practice. I get my percentage of the fee from her. I don't know much about the financial life of the office. I just see the patients and get sent a check at the end of the month.

If my partner joins a conglomerate group someday, I will be gone. Almost none of the large groups employs dinosaurs.

Glossary

Amblyopia—Lazy eye (dimness of vision of one eye) often related to misalignment, sometimes related to a great difference in refraction between two eyes. Amblyopia can be functional (developmental) or organic (at birth from pathologic state of macula or optic nerve).

American College of Surgeons—A surgeon may become a Fellow of the college and then be designated as a FACS (Fellow of the American College of Surgeons) after submission of a certain number of operative reports and recommendations of Fellows. Largely ceremonial.

Anisometropia—Different amount of refractive error for each eye.

Applanation tonometer—Device to measure intraocular pressure.

Board-certified—Certified after intense examination by specialty, e.g., certified by the American Board of Ophthalmology [ABO] as a specialist in ophthalmology.

Brown's syndrome—Restriction of the superior oblique tendon causing limited elevation of the eye.

Dissociated vertical deviations—Drifting up of one or both eyes when binocular fusion is interrupted.

Duane's syndrome—Restriction of horizontal rotations caused by miswiring of cranial nerves to the eye muscles.

Epikeratophakia—Out-of-date operation to change the shape of the cornea in extreme refractive error.

Esotropia—One eye turns in. May be alternating or monocular.

Eye muscle disorders—Esotropia, exotropia, hypertropia, torsional (eye misaligned in, eye misaligned out, eye misaligned up or down, eye misaligned on an axis not 90 degrees .

Exotropia—One eye turns out.

Group practice—More than one doctor works in an office (may be owned by one or more of the group).

Hypertropia—One eye turns up.

Hypotropia—One eye turns down.

Intermittent convergent strabismus—Sometimes the eyes are straight; sometimes one eye turns in toward the nose.

Intermittent divergent deviation—Sometimes the eyes are straight; sometimes one eye drifts out.

Internuclear ophthalmoplegia—A complicated eye muscle paralysis from brainstem disease common in multiple sclerosis.

Iritis—Inflammation of the iris, the colored tissue of the eye that dilates and constricts from light. Part of the uveal tract, that is, the vascular layer of the eye.

Maculopathy—Diseases of the macula, the critical part of the retina needed for sharp vision.

MEETH—Manhattan Eye Ear and Throat Hospital

Motor exam—Examination and measurement of position and movement of the eyes.

NY Eye and Ear—NY Eye and Ear Infirmary

OCT—Ocular computerized tomography; for studying the optic nerve and macula.

Ophthalmic technician—Certified technician who performs preliminary tests for an ophthalmologist's exam. Tests include history, visual acuity, glasses prescription check, refraction by objective machine, intraocular pressure, and also instillation of drops for dilation. Techs may also be trained to do specialized exams, including visual fields and OCT.

Ophthalmologist—A medical doctor specializing in the diagnosis and treatment of eye disorders. Once called oculist (from Latin). Ophthalmologists are MDs (e.g., Renée Richards, MD) who took a residency after medical school to study diseases of the eyes.

Optometrist—Doctor who specializes in the measurement of refractive errors: near sight, far sight, astigmatism. Graduate of a school of optometry; not an MD but called doctor.

Orthoptist (orthoptic technician)—A technician who helps an ophthalmologist evaluate eye muscle disorders.

Pediatric ophthalmologist—Takes care of the eyes of children.

Pediatric ophthalmology and strabismus—Subspecialty that combines the care of children's eyes and the care of strabismus both in children and adults.

Private practice—Doctor who takes care of patient for a fee paid by patient. Patient responsible for the fee (patient may have private insurance that pays part of the fee).

Pterygium—A growth of abnormal conjunctival tissue on the cornea.

Ptosis surgery—Surgery on the upper eyelid for drooping.

Radial keratotomy—First operation to change the shape of the cornea (before lasik).

Radioactive plaque—Local application of radioactive substance to kill focal eye cancer.

Residual lateral rectus palsy—Persistent weakness of the lateral rectus muscle.

Sensorimotor exam—Combines the sensory and motor parts of strabismus evaluation. Many of the tests are performed by an orthoptist.

Sensory exams—Tests that evaluate visual acuity, double vision, fusion, depth perception: the way the eyes work together as interpreted by the patient's brain.

Solo practice—One doctor owns and manages the office.

Spasmus nutans—A form of nystagmus, more common in infancy and associated with head nodding.

Specialist—Medical doctor who specializes in the care of a particular organ, system, or disease. (For instance, an ophthalmologist takes care of all eye conditions. A retinologist is an ophthalmologist who takes care of disorders of the retina.

A glaucoma specialist is an ophthalmologist who takes care of patients with glaucoma.)

Strabismus—Eye muscle disorders related to misalignment of the eyes.

Strabismologist—Specialist in eye-muscle disorders (strabismus).

Torsional—One eye exhibits torsion, tilting of the axis of the eye.

Uveal tract—Vascular part of the eye.

Acknowledgments

A heartfelt thank you to Alan B Scott MD of the Strabismus Research Foundation, whose wonderful generosity helped bring this memoir to the printed page. Dr. Scott and the Foundation have preserved the eyesight of thousands of men, women, and children.

I am also in gratitude to my colleagues for their comments on the practice of medicine in this century—my former students, now my mentors:

Jack Dodick MD—Professor and former chairman, Department of Ophthalmology, NYU School of Medicine former chairman, Department of Ophthalmology, Manhattan Eye, Ear and Throat Hospital

Richard Gibralter MD—Former surgeon director, Manhattan Eye, Ear and Throat Hospital; associate professor, Albert Einstein College of Medicine

Steven Greenberg—Former Fellow in pediatric ophthalmology, Manhattan Eye, Ear and Throat Hospital; ophthalmologist at West Med Medical Group

Lisa Hall MD—Associate clinical professor of ophthalmology, Icahn School of Medicine at Mt. Sinai Hospital; former director of pediatric ophthalmology, New York Eye and Ear Infirmary

David Haight MD—Clinical assistant professor of ophthalmology, Weill Cornell Medical College; attending surgeon, Lenox Hill Hospital; director of refractive surgery, Manhattan Eye, Ear and Throat Hospital

Lawrence Parsont MD—Attending surgeon, Manhattan Eye, Ear and Throat Hospital

David Robbins Tien MD—Clinical associate professor of surgery (ophthalmology), Warren Alpert Medical School at Brown University; director emeritus of ophthalmology, Hasbro Children's Hospital.

Alex Tien—Clinical assistant professor of family medicine, Brown University

Lawrence Turtell MD—Former Fellow in pediatric ophthalmology, Manhattan Eye, Ear and Throat Hospital.

Lawrence Yannuzzi MD—Professor of clinical ophthalmology, College of Physicians and Surgeons, Columbia University School of Medicine; founder and president of the Macula Foundation, Inc., LuEsther Mertz Retinal Research Center

Peter Weseley MD—Assistant professor of ophthalmology, NYU School of Medicine

I deeply appreciate the contributions from all of you.

Renéee Richards

About the Author

Born in 1934 as Richard Raskind, Dr. Renée Richards grew up in Forest Hills, New York, the son of first generation Jewish immigrant parents, both physicians. An outstanding student and athlete in tennis, swimming and baseball (he was scouted by the New York Yankees), he found his true calling in medicine.

A Yale graduate, he went to medical school at the University of Rochester and then spent a year at Lenox Hill Hospital on a rotating internship. Several well-known ophthalmologists were on staff at Lenox Hill, where students headed for ophthalmology liked to take their internships. In 1961, he was accepted as a resident at Manhattan Eye, Ear and Throat Hospital, one of the most prestigious eye hospitals in the United States.

He finished his residency in 1963 and was awarded a Heed Fellowship to do a year of study in his chosen sub-specialty—strabismus, a disorder that occurs when the eye muscles do not work as they should. Before Heed, however, the U.S. Navy beckoned, and he was off to a two-year duty. He became the chief ophthalmologist at the Navy hospital in St. Albans, New York. He also played a little tennis for the Navy during the two summers he was in the service. He was two-time All-Navy singles and doubles champion and captained the Navy team in the inter-service matches in 1963.

When he left the Navy in 1965, the Heed Fellowship was still open and could be taken anywhere within the continental United States. He studied at Columbia University, the University of Oregon and the University of Iowa under three of the most famous men in the country in the field of strabismus. When he completed those studies, he returned to MEETH with the title of resident instructor.

After his stint as resident instructor, he left medicine and took a six-month sabbatical from MEETH and his private practice. He went to Europe and had a trial run—trying to find his true self—living as a woman. He returned to New York City in 1968 and resumed his private practice.

In 1975, he underwent male-to-female sex reassignment surgery. Richard Raskind became Renée Richards. Following the operation, she was denied entry into the 1976 U.S. Open by the United States Tennis Association. Dr. Richards took her case to the New York State Supreme Court, which ruled in her favor. She played professional tennis from 1977 to 1981. After retiring, she coached Martina Navratilova to two Wimbledon tennis titles.

In 1982, Dr. Richards returned to private practice in ophthalmology, specializing in strabismus. In a career spanning nearly 60 years, she has trained generations of ophthalmology residents on operating techniques on the muscles of the eyes and the way the eyes work together. In 2001, she was honored by Helen Keller Services for the Blind for her dedication in training ophthalmologists, her tireless work as a mentor-consultant, and her innovations in surgical techniques. She is retired as the head of the strabismus department and surgeon director at Manhattan Eye, Ear and Throat Hospital.

Dr. Richards taught the residents at MEETH, first as the resident instructor (the only one—in 1967), then as attending in the clinic, then as director of the Eye Muscle Clinic, and taught the post-graduate Fellows in pediatric ophthalmology and strabismus. She did all this teaching gratis—no financial compensation. Clinic, lectures, assisting at surgery—these activities occupied probably one full day each work week. She gave a lecture course in strabismus at MEETH, where the residents from many hospitals in NYC attended.

"From a personal standpoint," Dr. Richards said, "there is no doubt the exceptional training I received at Manhattan Eye and Ear played a significant part in whatever special skill I had as a clinician diagnosing complicated eye muscle problems and whatever special ability I had as a surgeon operating on eye muscles. I was fortunate to be a part of a proud era of ophthalmology there."

Although Dr. Richards no longer performs surgery, she still maintains a private practice in upstate New York, where her patients are primarily children and adults with strabismus.

For more on Dr. Renée Richards' remarkable life, see her three autobiographies—*Second Serve, No Way, Renée,* and *Spy Night,* a collection of short stories about her experiences.

Adapted from *The History of Manhattan Eye, Ear and Throat Hospital... 150 Years of Visionary History* by Larry Armour, editors Paul N. Orloff, MD, Richard Gibralter, MD.

Made in the USA
Columbia, SC
02 October 2021